One Colonial Woman's World

man steams many for
in hollow pruning for much
o poy world of by
South one of his bavol
4 3 5 Cade want Chamberlin
hed

Whatubol Coit
Her Book 1714

September the 4 1712
Mr waters his

an account of ye
Mr Runatos
to ham walters
to James Rogers
to Thomas
to Mr Shut
to Din Holon

One Colonial Woman's World

The Life and Writings of
MEHETABEL CHANDLER COIT

Michelle Marchetti Coughlin

University of Massachusetts Press

Amherst & Boston

Copyright © 2012 by University of Massachusetts Press
All rights reserved
Printed in the United States of America
ISBN 978-1-55849-967-6 (paper); 966-9 (hardcover)

Designed by Jack Harrison
Set in Adobe Garamond Pro
Printed and bound by Thomson-Shore, Inc.

Library of Congress Cataloging-in-Publication Data

Coughlin, Michelle Marchetti, 1965–
One colonial woman's world : the life and writings of Mehetabel Chandler Coit /
Michelle Marchetti Coughlin.
p. cm.
Includes bibliographical references and index.
ISBN 978-1-55849-966-9 (library cloth : alk. paper) —
ISBN 978-1-55849-967-6 (pbk. : alk. paper)
1. Coit, Mehetabel Chandler, 1673–1758.
2. Connecticut—History—Colonial period, ca. 1600–1775.
3. Connecticut—Social life and customs—18th century.
4. Women—Connecticut—Biography.
5. Coit, Mehetabel Chandler, 1673–1758—Diaries.
6. New London (Conn.)—Social life and customs—18th century.
7. Women—United States—History—18th century—Biography.
I. Title. II. Title: Life and writings of Mehetabel Chandler Coit.
F101.3.C65C68 2012
974.6'02092—dc23
[B]
2012030818

British Library Cataloguing-in-Publication Data
A catalogue record for this book is available from the British Library.

Frontispiece: Inside front cover endpaper of Mehetabel's diary.
Photograph by Robert and Elizabeth Hughes.

For Mark

To study the flow of common life
is to discover the electricity of history.

Laurel Thatcher Ulrich

CONTENTS

ILLUSTRATIONS

PUBLICATION OF THIS BOOK

IS SUPPORTED BY A GRANT FROM

Jewish Federation of Greater Hartford

ACKNOWLEDGMENTS

To begin, I want to express my deep appreciation of the scholars who have enriched the field of early American women's history through their dedicated and innovative efforts. I have been particularly inspired by the work of Laurel Thatcher Ulrich and Mary Beth Norton. Ulrich's uncovering of so much meaning in what had been dismissed as "trivia" in Martha Ballard's diary stands as a model of the insights that can be gained through scholarly creativity. She has also done pioneering work on using material culture to help interpret colonial women's experiences. Mary Beth Norton set new standards with *Founding Mothers and Fathers,* her analysis of seventeenth-century notions about gender. By mining early court records, she was able to recover the speech and perspectives of a multitude of early American women. "Hearing" women tell their side of the story in their own words may, in some ways, be the closest one will ever get to knowing them.

I am indebted to the University of Massachusetts Press for bringing Mehetabel's story to a wider audience. In particular, I would like to acknowledge the efforts of managing editor extraordinaire Carol Betsch and talented and efficient production manager Jack Harrison. Senior editor Clark Dougan has been a pleasure to work with, and I am grateful for his dedication to this project. Historians Marla Miller and Mary Beth Norton provided invaluable insights on an early draft of the manuscript, and this book is a much stronger work as a result of their review.

I am also thankful for the assistance provided by the staff at numerous libraries, archives, and historical societies, particularly Manuscripts and Archives at Yale University, the Boston Public Library, the Connecticut Historical Society, the Connecticut State Library, the Massachusetts Archives, the Massachusetts Historical Society, the New England Historic Genealogical Society, the New London County Historical Society, and the Woodstock

Historical Society. Closer to home, the dedicated staff of the Old Colony Library Network kindly obtained numerous materials for me through inter-library loan.

Tracking down the whereabouts of Mehetabel's diary proved to be an adventure in itself, and my efforts were assisted along the way by many gracious people who ultimately directed me to Robert, Marion, and Elizabeth Hughes, the diary's current owners. The Hughes family has been more than kind in allowing me access to the diary. It has been my great good fortune to make their acquaintance.

My interest in the Puritans was first sparked by a course on Puritan literature taught by Harvard University's Sacvan Bercovitch, who forever transformed my views on this group with his enthusiasm and compelling insights.

John Brooke, my former adviser at Tufts University, who is now Humanities Distinguished Professor of History at Ohio State, continues to be unfailingly generous with his time. I am deeply grateful for his guidance and support.

During the years of researching and writing this book I have benefited from having a wonderful network of family and friends. I regret that my father, John Marchetti, did not live to see its publication. For the unwavering faith shown by my mother, Janice Marchetti, I cannot adequately express my gratitude.

Finally, I thank my husband, Mark, who has provided seemingly limitless encouragement. Always willing to listen to news of my latest discovery (and never asking if I had any idea as to when the book might be finished), he has been a paragon of support and generosity.

INTRODUCTION

Despite the great strides made in the field of early American women's history over the past few decades, only a small number of primary sources written by women have yet been made widely available. It is true that few women in the seventeenth and early eighteenth centuries left behind written records of any kind, and fewer still of these writings have survived; but it is also true that only a fraction of the surviving documents have been published. Many scholars are currently working to remedy this situation; however, it remains the case that what has often been missing from the story of early America are the voices of its women. This book, based on the writings of Mehetabel Chandler Coit, a New Englander who lived from 1673 to 1758, is intended to help fill this void.

The bare outlines of Mehetabel's life are as follows. She was born in Roxbury, Massachusetts, where she lived until 1688, when she and her family became some of the first settlers of Woodstock, Connecticut. In 1695 she married John Coit, a shipbuilder of New London, where she lived out the rest of her days. She and John had six children together and led a relatively comfortable existence until John's death in 1744 at the age of seventy-three. Mehetabel remained a widow for the final fourteen years of her life.

For over sixty years Mehetabel kept a diary: her first entry dates from May 1688, when she was fourteen, and her last from May 1749, when she was seventy-five. Since the prevailing view among historians is that no female-authored diary from the seventeenth century has survived, the dozen or so entries dating from before 1700 may qualify Mehetabel's as the earliest extant diary written by an American woman.[1] The work usually given this distinction is the 1704 travel journal of Madam Sarah Kemble Knight—who, ironically, was a neighbor of Mehetabel's in New London—however, Knight's original manuscript no longer exists, and recent scholarship indicates that the first published edition may have been altered by its nineteenth-century editor.[2]

It is unclear why historians have overlooked Mehetabel's diary, particularly given that extracts were published by her descendants in 1895 as *Mehetabel Chandler Coit: Her Book, 1714.* Over the years this volume of extracts has been listed in several bibliographies of American diaries, such as William Matthews's *American Diaries: An Annotated Bibliography of American Diaries Written Prior to the Year 1861,* Harriette Forbes's *New England Diaries, 1602–1800,* and Joyce Goodfriend's *Published Diaries and Letters of American Women.* The diary transcript was also cited by Lyle Koehler in his 1980 *Search for Power: The "Weaker Sex" in Seventeenth-Century New England;* by Estelle Jelinek (who dismissed it as an "undistinguished family history") in her *Tradition of Women's Autobiography* (1986); and more recently by Kirsten Phimister, in her 2008 essay on white women in colonial America in *British Colonial America: People and Perspectives.*[3] Despite this general familiarity with the extracts, it appears that no one had ever tried to locate the original manuscript.

I first came across the published extracts while researching early New England diary literature. The diary's age and the intriguing nature of the entries impelled me to search for the original, which I eventually located in private hands. Genealogical research showed that the diary had been passed down in Mehetabel's family to her son Joseph's great-grandchildren, Maria Perit Gilman, Emily Serena Gilman, and Louisa Gilman Lane, who had arranged for the 1895 publication. In the twentieth century the diary descended through the Gilman sisters' brother Edward's family to his great-granddaughter Elizabeth Lawrence Gilman Anderson. Elizabeth Anderson, a remarkable woman who lived to be 101, preserved the diary for decades before ultimately entrusting it to a favorite nephew, who retains possession of it today. He kindly shared its contents with me, revealing that the original manuscript contains material not included in the published extracts, such as poems, recipes, herbal and folk remedies, financial accounts, religious meditations, and even some humor. These elements help round out a portrait of Mehetabel's personality and interests and add immeasurable value to the diary.

The search for the manuscript also revealed the existence of approximately two dozen letters written by Mehetabel and her mother, mother-in-law, sister, and daughter between 1688 and 1743, as well as a sixty-four-page poem completed by her mother in 1681. The poem and letters had been passed down in the family along with the diary, and in the 1940s Elizabeth Anderson donated them to Yale University. (A selection of the letters had been included in a companion volume to *Mehetabel Chandler Coit: Her Book, 1714,* published by the Gilman sisters in 1895 as *Martha, Daughter of Mehetabel Chandler Coit, 1706–1784.*) Although these manuscripts provide additional insights into the nature of Mehetabel's experiences and offer an exceptional look at an early intergenerational female network, they, too, had been overlooked by scholars.

Both the diary and letters deal with a variety of subjects: travel, work and social activities, illness and death, and family and community news originating from Boston, Newport, Long Island, and various areas of Connecticut. The letters written by the women of the earliest generation focus mainly on spiritual matters; those written by Mehetabel and her daughter Martha, more conversational in tone, tend to reflect more worldly concerns. This variation reflects broad cultural influences and provides a framework for assessing the ways in which women's lives changed over the period. Mehetabel's long life covered a fascinating period in American history, and one of my goals here is to explore the ways in which her experiences were linked to social and political developments.

The personal perspectives provided by the letters are especially welcome since there are significant obstacles to getting to know the person behind the diary. In keeping with diary-writing conventions of the day, Mehetabel's entries are brief and chronicle external events rather than imparting private thoughts and feelings. Moreover, there are many years for which she recorded only a few entries, and several for which she recorded none at all; in total, the diary is only about fifty pages long. Given these limitations, a biography into which the full text of the diary and letters could be incorporated seemed to offer the best format for exploring both Mehetabel's life and her writings.

In this book, I have sought to delineate as far as possible the external and internal realities of Mehetabel's day-to-day existence: the nature and scope of her work and leisure-time activities; her religious and folk beliefs; her intellectual and emotional consciousness as reflected in her writings; and her interactions with those in her household and her community. I also explore the ways in which gender, race, and class played a part in her experiences.

It is clear from the diary and letters that Mehetabel regularly interacted with people of varying socioeconomic backgrounds; in fact, one letter her daughter wrote her in the 1720s even contains a cryptic reference to a meeting Mehetabel held with a local Mohegan sachem. Roxbury and Woodstock were each home to Native and African Americans, and the seaport town of

New London, with its large transient population, was particularly diverse. The cargo brought into New London often included slaves, and Mehetabel and her husband, like many of their neighbors, were slave owners. When possible, the stories of these members of Mehetabel's household have been interwoven with her own. Particular emphasis has been placed on Mehetabel's relationship with her servant, Nell, who lived with her for more than forty years.

Valuable background information was provided by additional primary sources, such as diaries, letters, and other contemporary accounts; the published 1711–1758 diary of Joshua Hempstead (1678–1758), Mehetabel's distant kinsman and near neighbor in New London, was particularly useful. Secondary sources concerned with early American women's lives and with such topics as colonial medicine, religion, politics, communications, travel, work, family life, social institutions, and race relations also proved helpful, as have newspapers and town, court, and church records. Because providing a sense of the material realities of Mehetabel's daily life is an integral part of reconstructing her story, I have tried to supplement the use of written sources with a material-based approach through the examination of wills, probate inventories, and family artifacts.

At the time they published the extracts from Mehetabel's diary, the family editors noted that there remained a "traditional remembrance" in New London of Mehetabel "as a person of unusual energy and power, physically and mentally." And, indeed, Mehetabel's writings show that she lived a rich and varied life, not only running a household and raising a family, but reading, writing, traveling, conducting business on both her own and her husband's behalf, and maintaining a widespread network of family, social, and commercial connections. While her lifestyle and activities were circumscribed by gender norms of the day, she took a lively interest in the world around her and played an active role in her community. A complex individual who proved equal to both the challenges and opportunities of her time, her twenty-first-century descendants have come to refer to her as "the incredible Mehetabel."

An analysis of Mehetabel's experiences and writings offers a rare opportunity to provide a multidimensional picture of one woman's life during the middle years of the colonial period. While the field of American women's history has benefited from several studies of individual lives of Revolutionary-era and nineteenth-century women, very few works have focused on individual women born in the seventeenth century. Collective works on seventeenth- and early eighteenth-century women offer welcome information about various aspects of their experiences but lack the cumulative detail that only a sustained examination of one woman's life can provide. Because Mehetabel Chandler Coit shared many of her contemporaries' personal experiences, beliefs, and points of view, this attempt to re-create her world also illuminates the lives of countless other women of her time and place who left behind no written record—or whose record we have yet to discover.

A NOTE ABOUT THE DIARY

The diary is one of America's oldest literary forms, and New England Puritans of the seventeenth and early eighteenth centuries qualify as some of the most avid diarists in history. Many New Englanders kept "spiritual journals" intended to help them monitor their religious commitment; the majority of colonial diarists, however, maintained what could be described as "life diaries"—although they were markedly different from the daily journal in common use today. Early life diarists were concerned with recording details pertaining to their day-to-day existence, but they were also motivated by the desire to document the ways in which God manifested himself and his messages in the world around them.[1]

Throughout the seventeenth and even well into the eighteenth century, diaries chronicled the wonders, signs, and portents the colonists commonly perceived in their environment. (A 1666 entry in the diary of Boston merchant John Hull, for example, enumerates such strange occurrences as a series of loud noises of unknown origin heard in New Haven, Connecticut; a man killed by lightning in Northampton, Massachusetts; and the birth of several "monsters" among a flock of sheep in Narragansett, Rhode Island.) Unusual happenings were generally understood to carry messages from God, but the Puritans also believed that even the most ordinary developments—changes in the weather, births and deaths in one's community—could be interpreted as being part of a divine plan. As a result, early diarists focused almost exclusively on external events.[2]

Because of their common purpose, early diaries often displayed striking similarities in both style and content, even though their authors varied in gender, social status, geography, and chronology. For example, most diarists—whether merchants or farmers, tradesmen or housewives—used a plain style of language, according to the Puritan tradition that it was the most effective in seeking spiritual truth. Their diary entries consequently tend to be brief and are often of a repetitive nature. A typical entry might begin with—and sometimes consist entirely of—a notation about the day's weather. (In fact, John Demos has estimated that meteorology comprised 50 percent of most seventeenth-century diaries.) The 1689 epigraph commencing the diary of the Braintree, Massachusetts, stonemason John Marshall could be said to describe the contents of the vast majority of colonial-era diaries: "Here is contained in this book some brief memorials of my own business—how I spend my time, what work I do and where, some remarkable providences recorded, and the weather remembered."[3]

In their focus on external matters and their fascination with the countless ways in which God revealed himself in the world around them, early New England diarists all but neglected any mention of their inner lives. Indeed, one of the most distinctive features of their diaries is the lack of expression of emotion or introspection other than that of a spiritual nature. With few exceptions, seventeenth- and eighteenth-century New Englanders avoided committing their innermost thoughts and feelings to their diaries.

Although the terms "diary" and "journal" have often been used interchangeably—both words derive from a Latin root meaning "daily"—some critics have distinguished between the two forms by the latter's emphasis on internal rather than external matters and on subjective rather than objective experience. The journal form could be said to have emerged in the late eighteenth century, as a result of the cultural, social, economic, and demographic changes precipitated by the American Revolution. As the arts developed in the new nation and the Puritan literary tradition of valuing content over style was replaced by an emphasis on creative expression, Americans increasingly began to explore the stylistic potential of diary writing. And as society became more secular and more appreciative of the qualities of the individual, writers began to take advantage of the medium's opportunities for self-exploration.[4]

The popularity of diary keeping in early New England was made possible by the colonists' extremely high level of literacy. Since education—in particular, the ability to familiarize oneself with the scriptures—was considered vital to the well-being of Puritan society, New England settlers early on passed legislation calling for the establishment of public schools. The ability to read was nearly universal among free whites in colonial New England; however, the skill of writing did not become widespread until the late eighteenth century. Women, in particular, lacked writing skills. Because of their limited free time, those women who could write tended to "take pen in hand only in order to communicate essential information to others," as Mary Beth Norton has observed. As a result, diaries kept by colonial-era women are rare.[5]

Mehetabel Chandler Coit's extant writings do not indicate why she became a lifelong diarist; however, she may have inherited both her facility with language and her desire to leave a written record of her experiences from her mother, Elizabeth Chandler. Elizabeth's "Meditation, or Poem, being an Ep[ic?] of the Experiences and Conflicts of a Poor Trembling Soul in ye First Fourty Years of Her Life" reflects a conviction that her personal life was of consequence and worth documenting. She evidently placed a high value on her manuscript, for she only reluctantly allowed another daughter to take it with her on a visit to Mehetabel, offering the caveat that "theres no such instance to let such a thing go out of sight while Living, but if you may have benifitt I am content to Deny my self."[6]

Mehetabel's diary is a leather-bound volume, approximately three and a half by five and a half inches, with a flap that allows it to close like an envelope. The front and back covers are made of wood, possibly mahogany. Adhering to the inside front cover, and obscuring some writing beneath, is a remnant of a floral-patterned endpaper. The diary's pages are discolored with age and stained in some places, and the diary itself shows signs of wear, but overall it has weathered the centuries quite well.

Although Mehetabel probably purchased her diary or received it as a gift, she may have crafted her own quill pen and made ink from materials available to her. She was clearly comfortable with the mechanics of writing—her penmanship is neat and usually legible—although she, like her contemporaries, varied her spelling, capitalization, and punctuation, which at the time were not standardized. Mehetabel wrote in a rounded script known as the italic style, commonly used by women of the period. In general, the handwriting style one adopted tended to be based on one's gender, class, and occupation. Tradesmen used one type of script, gentlemen another. Those few women who were taught to write learned scripts considered easy both to adapt and to implement and thus better suited to a woman's "limited" intellectual abilities.[7]

Mehetabel's diary reflects many conventions of her time, but one characteristic does differentiate it from most of its contemporaries: the entries do not appear chronologically, likely evidence that some of them were copied from an earlier notebook or collection of scraps of paper into the surviving volume. The specificity of the entry dates ("feb^{br} 6 1688/9 Hannah Gary born the first Child that was born in Woodstock"; "may 2 1696 Wait Mayhew came to live here") indicates that they were first recorded at or near the time of the actual event, since early Americans were not closely attuned to the calendar and would not have remembered the precise timing of events long after they occurred. (In the seventeenth and eighteenth centuries, in fact, many people did not know the exact day of their birth.) Although the inside cover page of the diary bears the inscription "Mehetabel Coit Her Book 1714," indicating that she began using this particular volume that year, both pre- and post-1714 entries appear out of sequence. Many of the entries seem to have been organized thematically; for example, some pages carry entries relating to journeys taken by Mehetabel or members of her family, while others pertain to the births of her children or the launchings of vessels built by her husband's shipyard.

Diary scholar Margo Culley once observed that "evidence abounds in all periods that women read and reread their diaries. . . . Some diarists record comments on previous entries, some emend them, some copy over entire diaries and edit them." Since early American women diarists often took on the role of family historian, recording marriages, births, deaths, and information about other events that might concern later generations, it may have been the case that Mehetabel revised her diary to group together information of interest to other family members. It is possible she hoped her daughters would one day take up the practice of diary keeping and reworked hers to serve as a model. This is not to suggest that Mehetabel's diary is simply a family chronicle, for it is primarily autobiographical, containing a variety of notations that would likely have been of interest only to her. The inscription, "Mehetabel Coit Her Book," in its pointed statement of ownership, confirms the individualistic nature of the diary.[8]

Scholars of the diary genre, as Judy Nolte Temple has noted, will increasingly face challenges of form "as we uncover new materials, especially those from nontraditional writers."[9] The idiosyncratic chronology of Mehetabel's diary must be acknowledged, yet it should not diminish the diary's value as a rare example of a colonial woman's personal account kept over a period of six decades. Its status as being possibly the earliest surviving diary by an American woman would alone make it a valuable document, but an analysis of the wide variety of subject matter Mehetabel chose to record can only lead to a deeper understanding of what was important to a woman of her time.

STATEMENT OF EDITORIAL METHOD

The text of the diary and letters included in this book reflects a near-literal transcription, maintaining as closely as possible the authors' original spelling, capitalization, and punctuation, none of which were standardized in colonial America. Common early American contractions and abbreviations using superscript letters, such as "w[th]" for "with" and "coz[n]" for "cousin," have been retained, as has the archaic thorn, or "y" for "th" ("y[e]" for "the," "y[t]" for "that").

Nontextual elements, such as dashes at the end of sentences, and random underscoring not meant for emphasis have been omitted. Crossed-out words have been silently deleted unless they add insight to the meaning of the text. Any additional punctuation necessary for clarity has been supplied in brackets, as have suggestions for words that are missing or illegible. The goal throughout has been to ensure readability while preserving both contemporary stylistic conventions and each writer's individuality of expression.

An Old Testament name, "Mehetabel" has been said to mean "God's favor" in Hebrew. A more common variation is "Mehitable"; however, our subject chose to spell her name in the former manner, and that is how it appears throughout this book.

Mehetabel's Family Tree

William Chandler (1595-1642)
m. Annis Bayford (1603-1683)
m. 2. John Dane
3. John Parmenter

Thomas Chandler
m. Hannah Brewer

Hannah Chandler
m. 1. George Abbott
2. Francis Dane

John Chandler (1634-1703)
m. Elizabeth Douglas

William Chandler
m. 1. Mary Dane
2. Bridget Henchman
Richardson

Sarah Chandler
m. 1. William Cleaves
2. _____ Stevens
3. John Parker
4. George Allen

Elizabeth Chandler (1661-1688)
m. Robert Mason

John Chandler (1665-1743)
m. 1. Mary Raymond
2. Esther Britman Alcock

Hannah Chandler (1669-1692)
m. Moses Draper

Sarah Chandler (1676-1711)
m. 1. William Coit
2. John Gardiner

Joseph Chandler (1683-1750)
m. Susannah Perrin

Mehetabel Chandler (1673-1758)
m. John Coit (1670-1744)

John Coit (1696-?)
m. 1. Grace Christophers
2. Hannah Gardiner
Potter

Joseph Coit (1698-1787)
m. 1. Mary Hunting
2. Lydia Lathrop

Samuel Coit (1700-1703)

Thomas Coit (1702-1725)
m. Mary Prentis

Elizabeth Coit (1704-1725)
m. Samuel Gardiner

Martha Coit (1706-1784)
m. 1. Daniel Hubbard
2. Thomas Greene

William Douglas (1610-1682)
m. Anne Mattle (1604?-1683?)

Anna Douglas
m. 1. Nathaniel Gary
2. Thomas Bishop

Robert Douglas
m. Mary Hempstead

Elizabeth Douglas (1641-1705)
m. John Chandler

Sarah Douglas
m. John Keeny

William Douglas
m. 1. Abiah Hough
2. Mary Seamer Bushnell

One Colonial Woman's World

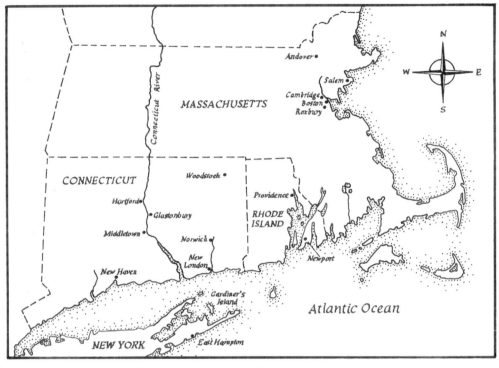

Map of Mehetabel's New England by Margaret McWethy.

CHAPTER ONE

The Years before the Diary,
1673–1688

To paraphrase John Milton, as morning shows the day, so childhood shows the woman. While few facts are available regarding Mehetabel Chandler Coit's early years, it is clear from her later writings that the events and circumstances of her childhood and adolescence played a major role in the formation of her identity. Her family life, social environment, physical location, and educational and religious grounding each contributed to the shaping of her personality in meaningful and lasting ways. Even though she spent the greater part of her life in surroundings far removed from her birthplace—and amid social and political conditions varying markedly from those of her youth—Mehetabel Chandler Coit remained, to some extent, a product of her early background. Any insight into her character, then, must begin with her own beginnings, and with an understanding of the factors that not only gave direction to her future but influenced the experiences of her entire generation.

The setting of Mehetabel's childhood and early adolescence was the town of Roxbury in the Massachusetts Bay Colony, where she was born on August 24, 1673. Situated approximately three miles south of Boston, Roxbury was considered a strategic outpost because it guarded the only road into Boston, a thin strip of land known as Boston Neck. Settled in 1630, Roxbury soon became known as a "fair and handsome country town," and one commentator could term its inhabitants "very rich" for possessing "fair houses, store of cattle, . . . and fruitful gardens." By the time of Mehetabel's birth, the town was considered one of the wealthiest in New England. The Chandlers and many of their neighbors supported themselves primarily by farming; members of some of the more elite families in town, such as the Dudleys (the poet Anne Bradstreet's family of birth), held positions of authority in the colonial government from the beginning.[1]

Since ancestry and family history were so important to Mehetabel—and to her society in general—her family's origins in New England provide a vital framework for her story. Mehetabel's parents, John and Elizabeth Douglas Chandler, were both children of English immigrants who had come to the New World during the Great Migration of 1630–1642, during which roughly twenty thousand religious nonconformists, known as Puritans for their desire to purify the Church of England, had settled in New England. John Chandler had been about three when his parents, William, a yeoman and "pointer of laces," and Annis Bayford Chandler, emigrated in 1637 with their other three children: nine-year-old Thomas, eight-year-old Hannah, and one-year-old William. A fifth child, Sarah, was born in Roxbury the year after their arrival. The Chandlers hailed from Bishop's Stortford, Hertfordshire, a market town northeast of London, and William and Annis most likely chose to settle in Roxbury because many of its residents had ties to their hometown. Another draw may have been Roxbury's minister, the Reverend John Eliot, who was originally from a neighboring parish in England.[2]

Roxbury was a largely Puritan settlement, founded by people who held to the Calvinist concept that some people were preordained for eternal salvation, while others were destined for hell. Central to their convictions was a belief in the importance of faith, of reading the Bible, of living an upright life, and of undergoing a personal conversion experience—the revelation of having received God's grace and thus salvation—which was required for official church membership. The Puritans, who were also known as Congregationalists because individual congregations held the power to select their leaders and determine how their churches would be run, regarded themselves as God's chosen people and America as a potential New Jerusalem.

William and Annis Chandler both became members of Roxbury's Puritan church, and by 1640 William had acquired twenty-two acres of land and was considered a "freeman," someone who held full political rights. He did not have a chance to prosper in Roxbury, however, for he soon became ill with a "consumption" that ultimately killed him at the age of forty-seven in early 1642. Despite having spent only a few years in town, William had apparently made a positive impression on the community, for Reverend Eliot remarked in the church records that he had "lived a very religious & Godly life," leaving "a sweet memory & savor behind him."[3]

William did not leave a will, and a probate inventory does not appear to have been taken following his death; however, his family was no doubt left with precious few resources: the house and land and perhaps some livestock, as an early town document lists William as the owner of a goat and a kid. In keeping with contemporary inheritance laws, Annis's widow's, or dower, rights would have entitled her to a third of William's real estate and personal property, with the balance to be held for the children until they came of age. These dower rights represented a life interest only; although Annis would have been able to derive profits from the property, she would not have been able to sell it, as the law dictated that it should pass into the hands of her children following her death. Dower rights were intended to provide a widow with some form of support, not with the means for her to become financially independent.[4]

Subsequent economic hardships faced by the Chandler family may have contributed to Annis's decision to remarry a little more than a year following William's death. Her second husband was John Dane, a widower and tailor who also had roots in Bishop's Stortford.[5] After they married, they moved with Annis's children to Ipswich on Boston's North Shore, where Dane owned some property. There they counted among their neighbors Nathaniel Ward, author of both the 1641 Massachusetts Body of Liberties—the basis for the colony's legal code—and *The Simple Cobbler of Agawam* (1647), a popular satire of English society; the Reverend William Hubbard, who would become one of colonial America's foremost historians; and the as-yet-unpublished Anne Bradstreet. Annis and John did not have any children together, and after a few years they returned to Roxbury, taking up residence in Annis and William's former home. In 1649 the General Court had passed ownership of the house and land to Dane at his request, because "ye said Dayne [had] . . . paid more debts of Chanlrs than ye house and land was worth, & also brought up ye children of Chandler w'ch have been chargeable to him."[6]

In 1658 John Dane died, leaving Annis a widow once again. Dane willed Annis the house and property that had formerly belonged to her and William, as well as most of his own "movable" goods. By this time the older Chandler children—Thomas, Hannah, and William—had married and were living in Andover, Massachusetts, a fledgling community approximately twenty-five miles northwest of Boston. (William had married John Dane's granddaughter, Mary Dane.) A few months after Dane's death, the twenty-four-year-old John Chandler married Elizabeth Douglas.

Elizabeth, who was about seventeen at the time of her marriage, was the daughter of William and Anne Mattle Douglas, who had emigrated to Boston in 1640 from Northamptonshire, England. One of five children, Elizabeth was born the year after her parents arrived in the colonies and was baptized at the First Church of Boston, where her parents were members. William, who worked as a cooper, owned property in Boston, and the Douglases also lived intermittently in Ipswich. Although there is no way of knowing for sure, it may have been in Ipswich that Elizabeth Douglas and John Chandler first met.[7]

In Roxbury, John Chandler made his living principally as a husbandman, or farmer. To supplement his income, he also occasionally filled various town offices. Starting out as a digger of graves in 1661, his positions eventually improved, as he later served as a constable (1677) and a surveyor (1680 and 1684). From 1659 to 1669 he also performed the duties of church sexton, receiving fifty shillings a year for ringing the bell and sweeping the meetinghouse and an additional three pounds for keeping "ye doore bowlted."[8]

John and Elizabeth made their home on property directly adjacent to Annis's lot. Their proximity was probably a comfort to Annis, but she was not long in need of companionship. In 1660 she married for a third time: she was fifty-seven; her new husband, a widower named John Parmenter, was seventy-two. In Parmenter's former residence of Sudbury, he had served as a church deacon and as one of the town's most prominent selectmen, but in Roxbury he took up the occupation of tavern keeper. At some point after his and Annis's marriage, he began running the tavern from their home. Annis apparently also played a role in the business; she is listed in a probate inventory taken following a local man's death as being owed a sum of money for wine and beer served after his funeral.[9]

At about the time Annis remarried, Elizabeth and John had their first child, a boy named John. The baby, however, lived for only nine months. For Elizabeth, coping with the loss of her son was possibly made even more difficult by her own family's recently becoming all but inaccessible. Her parents and siblings—with the exception of her sister Anna, who had married a Roxbury man and lived in town—had lately left the colony for the growing settlement of New London, Connecticut. Given the challenges of travel during the period, and the fact that Elizabeth was starting a family of her own, opportunities for visits between the Chandlers and Douglases would be limited for the foreseeable future.

In 1661, the year after baby John's death, Elizabeth gave birth to a daughter she and John named Elizabeth. In passing down their own names to their children, the Chandlers were following a local practice with roots in Puritan covenant theology: since it was believed that God would extend his grace to the families of church members, family lineage took on an added layer of importance. This child lived into adulthood, but the large gaps in time separating some of her later children's births seem to indicate that Elizabeth, like many of her contemporaries, experienced one or more miscarriages or stillbirths. She did not have another child until four years after Elizabeth was born, when she delivered a healthy baby boy. Following another seventeenth-century custom, Elizabeth and John named him John after his deceased sibling. This John survived, but a younger brother, Joseph, born two years later, died after eighteen months. A daughter named Hannah followed in 1669, and four years later Mehetabel was born. Two additional children—Sarah and another Joseph—came along in 1676 and 1683. Since Elizabeth's childbearing years covered more than two decades, there was almost a generation's difference between the oldest and youngest Chandler siblings.[10]

Mehetabel was born into a time of profound political, religious, and social change in New England. Since the restoration of the Stuart monarchy in 1660, the region had been beset by intensifying threats to its pseudo-independence from England. As King Charles II increasingly involved the British government in matters of colonial trade and taxation, he also made it clear that his ultimate goal was to revoke the royal charters, and thus many of the colonial governments' powers. This expanded presence of royal authority in New England, as well as the reestablishment of the Anglican church in the mother country, greatly alarmed the colonists, who feared for the future of the Puritan experiment. Their anxieties were only exacerbated by a crisis then taking place in the Puritan church.

Although Puritanism had been the target of various challenges over the years—from such dissenters as Anne Hutchinson, Roger Williams, and the Quakers—it had remained the dominant form of religious faith among New Englanders. After 1660, however, church membership began declining at a significant rate, particularly among males, as members of the younger generations became more interested in secular matters and in acquiring land and wealth. In response to this predicament, in 1662 some congregations began adopting the Half-Way Covenant, an innovation that provided right-living and pious adult children of church members who had not themselves undergone a conversion experience the opportunity to receive communion and have their children baptized. The Half-Way Covenant not only became instrumental in boosting church membership, but it also extended political rights to greater numbers of male residents, since at the time only church members were allowed to vote. Nevertheless, the move incited controversy that persisted for years, as well as a sense that later generations of Puritans had failed to live up to the expectations of the firstcomers.

To some degree the Chandler family's relationship with the church—and by extension with the state—manifested the complexities of the time. In many ways, the family could be considered devout in the traditional Puritan sense. By 1665 Elizabeth had been admitted to full communion within the Roxbury church (John became a full church member in 1679), and she and John eventually had all of their children baptized there. Mehetabel and her siblings were likely introduced to religious teachings at an early age, since this was widely held to be one of the foremost duties of Puritan parents. Ministers frequently emphasized that no opportunity for instructing one's children about the Almighty, no matter how mundane, was to be overlooked. As the Reverend Benjamin Wadsworth counseled in his *Well-Ordered Family,* "while you lay [your children] in your bosomes, and dandle them on your knees, try by little and little to infuse good things, holy truths into them. When you are *dressing* and *undressing* your Children morning and evening, you might very properly say something to them about religion, for the good of their Souls."[11]

As their children grew older, John and Elizabeth would have sent them to the local Sabbath school, where boys and girls were drilled each week on their knowledge of the catechism. The meetinghouse, located just a short walk from the Chandler home, was both a physical and spiritual focal point for the community; it was also a place of wider renown owing to the eminence of John Eliot, who served the church from 1632 until 1690. Eliot's numerous accomplishments included collaborating on the *Bay Psalm Book,* a 1640 translation of the Bible's psalms and the first book published in New England, but he was perhaps most widely known as the "Apostle to the Indians" for his decades-long efforts to christianize local tribes. To this end Eliot not only proselytized throughout the colony, but he also founded the first Indian church in Massachusetts, eventually established fourteen "praying Indian" villages, and even translated the Bible into the Algonquian language (published in 1663, this was the first edition of the Old and New Testaments to be printed in the colonies). Eliot also created schools for teaching English to the Indians, some of whom went on to study at Harvard College, and produced his own teaching tools by translating a grammar into Algonquian in 1666 and publishing the first American primer in 1669.

In addition to being esteemed for his achievements, Eliot was widely admired for his personal piety, charity, and humility. According to the Rever-

John Ritto Penniman, *Meetinghouse Hill, Roxbury, Massachusetts,* 1799,
oil on canvas, 29 in. x 37 in. Centennial Year Acquisition and Centennial Year
Major Acquisition funds, 1979.1461. *Courtesy Art Institute of Chicago.*

end Cotton Mather, Eliot was of such a spiritual nature that he frequently
found it difficult to concern himself with earthly matters: he so often distributed his salary among his needy neighbors, for example, that "his own family
was straitened for the comforts of life." (Fortunately for the family, Eliot's
wife Hanna (also known as Ann) was the primary manager of the Eliots'
farmlands, and through her efforts the Harvard education of the five Eliot
sons was paid for by "sides of beef, goat, mutton, apples, beans, [and] straw-
berries.") John Eliot's lack of regard for personal wealth and worldly goods
was a thing of legend—an image no doubt reinforced by his habit of going
about in a rustic costume featuring a leathern girdle like that worn by John
the Baptist. As the seventeenth century wore on and Eliot outlived most of
the first generation of ministers, his venerability increased to the point where
he personally became regarded as something of a biblical figure.[12]

While being associated with such a distinguished minister and place of
worship must have been a source of pride for most members of the Roxbury

congregation, it may also have translated into greater than average pressure to live life as a model Puritan. Church and court records make it clear, however, that Roxbury church members were not always successful in their efforts to live godly, productive, and well-ordered lives. Among those who experienced difficulties in attaining this ideal were several members of the Chandler family. In the early 1670s in particular, the Chandlers demonstrated that, despite their firm commitment to the Puritan faith, they were not above acting in ways that violated the norms of both church and society.

The Chandlers' period of troubles began in 1671, when Mehetabel's father was brought before the Suffolk County Court for "selling beere & Cidar (vpon publique fame) without Licence"; evidently, he had taken advantage of the holiday atmosphere and social drinking that often accompanied Boston's election and militia training days. Since the charge could not be fully proved, the case was dismissed and John was admonished and ordered to pay court fees. A little over a year later, however, he was back in court on charges of having allowed "disorder in his house at unseasonable times of night & suffering people to bee singing & fidling at midnight." This time John was convicted. He was ordered to pay a fine, reimburse both the court fees and charges of the witnesses, and post a bond for his good behavior.[13]

Although John Chandler's infractions may seem rather petty, and although alcohol was part of the everyday fare of early New Englanders, drink-related crimes were taken seriously in Puritan culture. Since drunkenness was considered both an offense against society and a sin against God that might provoke "woful Judgements," the sale and consumption of alcohol were closely monitored. Retailers were required by law to be licensed, and the quality and price of their product were subject to scrutiny. The colonial government placed restrictions not only on whom these retailers could serve (Indians, slaves, servants, and children were usually off-limits, for example), but on when and where they could be served. As drunkenness became a greater social problem over the course of the seventeenth century, liquor laws were increasingly tightened, and "informers" were sometimes employed by towns to ferret out violators.[14]

By choosing to sell alcohol on such public occasions as training and election days, John Chandler was obviously putting himself in jeopardy. That he placed himself at further risk by allowing a social gathering at his home to become disruptive so soon after he had been brought before the court certainly raises questions about his motives—or, at the very least, his judgment. Whatever his reasons, he managed to avoid any further run-ins with the law for the duration of his time in Roxbury. He succeeded in being released from his bond of good behavior a few months after his conviction, and by 1677, when he was appointed constable, any damage to his reputation had apparently been repaired. In 1682 John was, ironically, appointed a tithingman, a position whose responsibilities included informing on unruly households, on "Sabbath-breakers and disorderly Tiplers," and on those who sold liquor without a license.[15]

Before John Chandler's "rehabilitation" was complete, however, the Chandler family became the focus of investigation for an offense far more serious than selling liquor without a license or disturbing the peace. In 1674, the year after Mehetabel's birth, her thirteen-year-old sister Elizabeth and nine-year-old brother John were brought before the Suffolk County Court for "wanton uncivill & unseemely carriages." Although the charges were never explicitly defined, it appears that John and Elizabeth were suspected of having engaged in incestuous activity. The court, after having heard the case—"what was proved & what was Owned by themselves"—sentenced both children to be "severely whip't by theire Father & mother in theire own house in [the presence] of the Constable." The court also ordered that the children "bee put asunder & not suffered to dwell together till the Court take further Order."[16]

Given the lack of background to the case, there is no way of ascertaining what precisely constituted Elizabeth and John's behavior, how their actions were discovered, or what, exactly, "was proved & what was Owned by themselves." It is even difficult to come up with any satisfactory hypotheses, since so few incidents of this nature appear in the records; John and Elizabeth's youth make this case particularly unusual. What is clear is that the nature of their "crime" represented a grave breach of Puritan conduct. While the Puritans were, as Edmund Morgan has observed, "a much earthier lot than their modern critics have imagined," and while they considered a healthy sex life to be an integral part of marriage, sex outside of marriage was regarded with deep concern. Extramarital sex—not to mention "unnatural" sex—was believed to not only threaten the stability of Puritan society by undermining the institution of the family, but also to constitute a sin against God. All sexual offenses were considered a matter for the courts. Given this ideological framework, an instance of sexual contact involving close family members could only be regarded as a violation of divine, civil, and natural law.[17]

The immediate consequences for Elizabeth and John remain to a large extent unknown, but they almost certainly included the prescribed whippings, particularly since the constable had been ordered to be in attendance. There is no record of church censure of the pair; however, given both the institution's role in monitoring the conduct of its members and the nature of Elizabeth and John's transgression, it would be surprising if they were not admonished in some way—privately, it would be hoped, as opposed to from the pulpit. Although Reverend Eliot's style of preaching was generally a mild-mannered one, he would become passionate when warning his congregation about the evils of sin; as Cotton Mather tells it, "he would sound the trumpets of God against all vice, with a most penetrating liveliness, and make his pulpit another Mount Sinai for the flashes of lightning therein displayed against the breaches of the law given upon that burning mountain." Unfortunately for John and Elizabeth, "there was usually a special fervor in the rebukes which he bestowed upon *carnality*."[18]

Whether the court's recommendation that Elizabeth and John not be allowed to dwell in the same household was ever upheld is difficult to determine. In colonial times, the "putting out" of children to live with another family was a common practice for a variety of reasons. Most frequently, this step was taken for the purpose of allowing a child to learn an occupation, or when circumstances such as illness or death prevented a parent from caring for a child. It was also considered an option by both parents and the court when it was thought that an unruly child might benefit from the discipline of an impartial adult lacking a parent's deep emotional involvement. Although John or Elizabeth may have been sent to live with a neighbor or relative, it is possible that both remained at home, since no family or town records provide any evidence to the contrary. Punishments meted out by the court were sometimes mitigated because of an offender's youth or the intervention of an influential member of the community on his or her behalf.[19]

Although the whole affair must have taken a great toll on the Chandlers, it does not seem to have irreparably severed any family bonds, perhaps in large part because John and Elizabeth each managed to find redemption. Far from growing into troublesome adolescents, both were accepted for full church membership while they were still in their teens, the average age for this privilege being the mid- to late twenties. Elizabeth would go on to make a successful marriage, and John would eventually become a wealthy landowner and respected judge.

The reintegration of Elizabeth and John into the community clearly demonstrates an important, yet easily overlooked, aspect of Puritan culture: its openness to providing second chances. The church's forms of correction were aimed at helping a sinner to see the error of his or her ways and thus repent and reconcile with the church. And since there were no long-term prisons, the state likewise sought to discipline an offender in such a way as to deter further crime but then to allow that individual to resume his or her place in society.[20]

Elizabeth and John's ordeal may have been the most traumatic personal experience faced by the Chandler family during Mehetabel's early years, but the greatest external crisis of the period was undoubtedly King Philip's War. Beginning in 1675, the conflict, which pitted the colonists against Native tribes headed by the Wampanoag leader Metacom—or "King Philip," as he was known to the colonists—proved disastrous to both parties. Per capita, more lives were lost than in any subsequent American war. Although the fighting did not cross over into Roxbury's borders, it came uncomfortably close. As John Eliot noted, "We had many slaine in the warr, no towne for bigness lost more if any towne so many."[21]

So many frontier settlements were laid waste during the war that Metacom's threat to drive the colonists into the sea appeared a frightening possibility. The resulting widespread panic led to hostile treatment of even those Natives who were friendly to the colonists. John Eliot's Indian congregations, for example, were forced into internment on Boston Harbor's Deer Island, where scores perished from disease or starvation. Many of those who survived were sold into slavery or transported outside of the colony, some as far away as Africa. Eliot lamented in the Roxbury church records, "The profane [or unconverted] Indians p[ro]ve a sharp rod to the English, & the English p[ro]ve a very sharp rod to the praying Indians."[22]

Mehetabel's immediate family came through the hostilities relatively unscathed; however, John Chandler's sister Sarah, who lived in Roxbury, lost her husband, William Cleaves, in the April 1676 battle at Sudbury. Within the same week, John's sister Hannah and her husband, George Abbot, lost one of their sons. Twenty-four-year-old Joseph Abbot and his twelve-year-old brother Timothy had been at work in the fields when they were ambushed by a party of Indians; Joseph was killed immediately, while the younger boy was taken into captivity. Timothy was lucky: he was eventually returned to his home (although "almost pined to death with hunger") by a sympathetic Indian woman who had "always been tender of him whilst [he was] in captivity."[23]

Mehetabel probably retained few, if any, memories of the war—she was only three when it ended in 1676—but throughout her childhood she must certainly have heard stories about its great costs. In addition to having long-lasting economic and social effects on the colony, the war also took a great psychological toll. Indeed, many interpreted the war as a divine judgment for New Englanders' collective failure to live up to the ideals of the first Puritan settlers, for becoming too absorbed with worldly matters and not enough with spiritual ones. Ministers like Increase Mather lamented the extent to which the settlers had "foresaken Churches, and Ordinances, and all for land and elbow-room" and urged the "*Reformation* of those Evils which have provoked the Lord to bring the Sword upon us." Other writers, such as Benjamin Tompson, a schoolmaster, physician, and poet who spent his final days in Roxbury, pointed to the growth of specific vices—drunkenness, gluttony, love of fashion and gossip—as the provocation for God's wrath. (Interestingly, as subsequent historians have observed, the idea that God was punishing New England for its subjugation of the Indians never gained much currency in the colonies.) Not surprisingly, the war and its aftermath triggered a resurgence in piety and commitment to the Puritan way.[24]

When Mehetabel was about six she probably began both her religious education at the local Sabbath school and her secular education in earnest. In keeping with the custom, she would have been sent to a neighborhood "dame" school—so-called because such schools were typically conducted by women in their homes—to learn how to read. Dame schools used standardized methods and tools for teaching reading; instruction usually began with the hornbook, a single piece of paper or parchment typically inscribed with an alphabet and the Lord's Prayer and adhered to a wooden paddle. Once a child mastered the hornbook he or she would progress to a primer, which demonstrated how letters could be combined to form words. The final texts used were the Psalter, or book of psalms, and the Bible. It was customary for reading instruction to be conducted orally; writing and, to a lesser extent, arithmetic skills were considered the purview of the secondary, or grammar, school. Dame school teachers, in fact, were not required to know how to write, and many of them did not possess this ability.[25]

During Mehetabel's childhood Roxbury could boast of a well-established grammar school; in fact, the town was second only to Boston in the number of students it sent to Harvard College. The Roxbury school, and grammar schools in general, however, were intended for male students only. While the Puritans believed that both boys and girls should be taught to read so that they could learn the scriptures and would be equipped to wholeheartedly embrace their faith, they did not believe that the sexes should receive the same education. Advanced studies were considered integral to a boy's preparation to take his place in the world, but they were deemed irrelevant to the training that would help girls fulfill their duties as wives and mothers. Writing, in particular, was regarded as a specialized, job-related skill required by males to conduct business and so was considered an unnecessary attainment for girls, not to mention servants or slaves.[26]

Although it was left up to the individual towns to decide whether or not to admit girls to their grammar schools, few chose to do so. In turn, some parents contracted with private tutors to teach their daughters writing skills, but most had neither the funds nor the desire to pursue such an alternative. Those girls who did receive writing instruction usually were taught by their mother, as Mehetabel and her sisters likely were. The majority of New England women, however, were prevented by the constraints of gender, class, race, and sometimes location from ever becoming proficient at this skill.[27]

It is evident from Mehetabel's later diary keeping that she acquired mastery of both reading and writing, and that she remained interested in books long after her formal education had ended. The Chandlers themselves likely owned only a Bible and a few religious works, although several of their neighbors had respectable libraries and may have been amenable to loaning out books. Moreover, by the latter decades of the seventeenth century, a number of bookstores were operating in Boston and the surrounding area. Most of the literature available to Mehetabel would have been of a religious nature, such as sermons and devotional works. Some of these books were intended to be read in private, as part of an individual's "closet devotions"; others may have been shared within the context of a prayer group or read aloud at home for the benefit of the family.[28]

Mehetabel left a record of some of the works she read as an adult, but it is only possible to speculate on the nature of her reading during her childhood and adolescence. For example, she may have developed her love of poetry by reading the Puritan verse that was widely available. Other best-selling publications of the period included "ephemeral" literature, such as chapbooks and ballads, and captivity narratives—particularly Mary Rowlandson's account of her abduction by Indians during King Philip's War, which went through four printings in 1682 alone. Perhaps the literary work that most influenced Mehetabel's development as both a reader and writer, however, were her mother's own personal writings.[29]

It is unclear how long it took Elizabeth Chandler to compose her sixty-four-page "Meditation, or Poem, being an Ep[ic?] of the Experiences and Conflicts of a Poor Trembling Soul in ye First Fourty Years of Her Life," but it appears that she started it some time after her marriage and had completed it by 1681, when she was forty. Given the numerous constraints on women's time and the lack of encouragement of their literary efforts, that Elizabeth was able to produce such an extended piece of verse is astounding.

Elizabeth's poem focuses on her spiritual "Pilgrimage," describing various experiences in which she felt hope of receiving God's grace only to become overwhelmed by despair at her own unworthiness: "That god was Pleased sometimes to sustain / My wounded soul that oft was Full of Pain / But I no sooner Fix't my heart to Pray / On Christ but thousand fears would me Dismay." She wrote candidly of enjoying "vain company" in her youth, of being distressed by occasional, unnamed "domestic troubles," of suffering the loss of her "Darling first born son," and of the devastation she felt at the church elders' denial of her initial request for membership because they believed her professions "but pretense, and that of such things [she] had no real sense." (The latter incident must have occurred when Elizabeth was very young, as she had become a full member of the Roxbury congregation by the time she was twenty-four.) The process of writing about her trials and tribulations seems to have helped Elizabeth ultimately to come to terms with them, for by the time she ended her narrative she was able to express confidence in her future salvation: "Come then my Faith and Soar above the Sky / And Let thy Contemplation these [Joys] espie / That Blessed Region where thou shalt have Rest / And of Eternall Joy shall be Possest."[30]

Since Elizabeth Chandler evidently valued literacy, one hopes that Mehetabel was allowed sufficient time for reading and writing after her few years of formal education ended. At this point, she would have begun spending the majority of her time helping her mother with a continual round of domestic duties: the growing, preparing, and serving of food; the making and mending of clothing; the caring for younger children. Her list of chores would only have grown after her older sisters married and moved out of the house: in 1680, when Mehetabel was seven, her sister Elizabeth married a tailor named Robert Mason, and five years later her sister Hannah married Moses Draper, a local blacksmith. (Hannah was an exceptionally young bride, not yet sixteen; her husband was twenty-two.) Although Elizabeth Chandler may have hired some local girls to help out on occasion, the primary responsibility for assisting her mother with the work around the house and garden would have fallen on Mehetabel and, later, her younger sister Sarah.

Despite her level of household responsibility, Mehetabel also would have been permitted opportunities for recreation. Although children were held to

high standards with regard to learning their catechism, minding their studies, and performing their chores, their parents—and even Puritan ministers—made allowances for "lawful Recreation" that was just for fun.[31] In
addition to socializing with other girls her age, Mehetabel would have attended weddings, house-raisings, and get-togethers at neighbors' homes.
The presence in Roxbury of so many Chandler–Douglas relations—such as
Mehetabel's grandmother Annis and her aunts Sarah and Anna and their
families—may have ensured a steady stream of such gatherings. The little
evidence that remains suggests that these relationships were good ones, despite any strains caused by John Chandler's illegal activities and the John and
Elizabeth scandal. What is less clear is how they were affected by subsequent
turmoil involving John Chandler's sister Sarah.

According to the 1681 church records, Sarah had caused offense through
the "unseasonable entertaining & corrupting [of] other folks servants &
children." Sarah's error lay not only in allowing a social gathering at her
home to go on too late and become disruptive, as her brother John had done,
but in her choice of company. By serving alcohol to minors and servants—
including African slaves—she was breaking the law. These charges grew even
more serious in light of later actions taken by one of her guests. Upon leaving
the party, Maria, a slave owned by Joshua Lamb of Roxbury, "in a discontent
set her [master's] house on fire in the dead of the night & also Mr Swans."
A young girl was killed in the blaze and two families lost their homes. Sarah
was blamed for "corrupting" Maria, but whether by serving her too much
alcohol or by more direct means was never specified.[32]

Maria was sentenced to be publicly burned at the stake—the first such
punishment ever to be inflicted in Massachusetts. (Although this penalty was
never applied to the colony's accused witches, another female slave named
Phillis suffered the same fate in Cambridge several decades later after having been convicted of poisoning her master.) The rationale for the harsh
sentence was that, having caused a death by burning, Maria should meet
the same end; however, it may also have been designed as a warning to other
discontented slaves in response to a recent series of fires of unknown origin
set in the Boston area. Maria had two accomplices, "Mr. [Thomas] Walker's
Negro Man Chefelia by Name" and James Pemberton's "Negro Man Cofee,"
who were not tried for their part in the crime but were imprisoned until their
masters arranged to send them "out of the Country." A slave named Jack who
had set fire to a house in Northampton, however, was ordered to be hung by
the neck until dead and then burned to ashes in the fire with Maria.[33]

By the time of Maria's execution, Africans had been serving as slaves in Boston for more than four decades. The first Africans had been brought to the area by 1638, and in 1641 the colony's Body of Liberties officially authorized slavery. The number of black slaves in New England steadily increased as Native servants became rarer and less desirable after King Philip's War. Although slaves in Massachusetts were generally better treated and had more legal rights than their southern counterparts, their activities came under increased scrutiny as the seventeenth century wore on. Beginning in the 1680s, new regulations were passed that significantly restricted their behavior and freedom of movement.[34]

The institution of slavery was acceptable to the Puritans on religious, economic, and legal grounds. Mehetabel herself was a slaveholder later in life; however, she was not brought up in a slave-owning household, and it is highly unlikely that her aunt Sarah owned any slaves, given that she was a woman of modest means. Sarah's entertaining of servants and minors at her house indicates that she held a marginal place in society, and church records confirm that she had difficulty fitting in. Prior to being censured for her part in the Maria incident, she had been "solemnly admonished" in both 1670 and 1679 for unnamed offenses, and when she was admitted to full communion in 1675, she "penitently" confessed to some matter.[35]

The consequences Sarah faced as a result of her role in the 1681 affair pale in comparison to Maria's fate. Although she was excommunicated for a time, she "was accepted & reconciled to the church & released of her censure" less than three years later, after having confessed her sin. Her later life appears to have been led much more quietly. By the time of her readmission to the church in 1684, she was known as Sarah Parker, so she had evidently remarried (her second husband had died in 1678). She did not accompany the Chandler family when they relocated to Woodstock in the late 1680s, but after being widowed yet again moved to Sandwich on Cape Cod, where she married for a final time. (This gentleman, a Quaker named George Allen, may have regretted the union, as he attributed the source of some "disorderly practice[s]" he was accused of to "a wife which was one not Convinced of the truth & so no friend in truth.") After her fourth husband's death in about 1691, Sarah lived out her remaining years in Sandwich.[36]

It is tempting to imagine how Annis, the matriarch of the extended Chandler clan, might have reacted to her children's and grandchildren's crises during the decade between 1671 and 1681. By all accounts, Annis was a respected member of the community and of the church; in fact, an entry made in the Roxbury church records at the time of her death in March 1683 refers to her as "Old Mother Parmiter, a blessed Saint." John Parmenter had died in 1671, after having become "weake and Crazy in body," and Annis lived the remaining twelve years of her life as a widow.[37]

In her will, which she had written in 1670, Annis left Mehetabel's father the family's original home and land grant, provided he pay certain sums to his brothers and to John Dane Jr., whose father had specified in his own will that he receive ten pounds when ownership of the house was transferred. Annis left her movable estate—"as Cows Swine linnen woolen Clothes and other household goods"—to her daughters Hannah and Sarah. (In colonial America it was customary for sons to inherit land and real estate and daughters, household goods.) Since a probate inventory, if taken, has not survived, it is impossible to know specifically what material possessions Annis was left with at the end of her long life. One thing her will does make clear, however, is that she almost certainly did not know how to write, since the document is signed with her "mark."[38]

The same year Annis died, in an example of one of the many ways in which the colony had evolved since the arrival of the first settlers, the town of Roxbury received a positive response to its petition to the General Court to establish a settlement in former Native lands known as the "Nipmuc Country." (Although located in what is now northeastern Connecticut, the region remained under the control of Massachusetts until the mid-eighteenth century.) The diminishing land supply in established communities such as Roxbury was making expansion an increasingly attractive option, while the subjugation of area Natives as a result of King Philip's War had also made it a feasible one. Many Nipmucs, or "Fresh Water People," whose homelands had originally included parts of central Massachusetts, northeastern Connecticut, and northwestern Rhode Island, "provoked . . . to anger & wrath" by the usurpation of their land and threat to their way of life, had fought against the colonists during the war. They had subsequently been persuaded by the Massachusetts government to sell a tract of land approximately fifty miles long by twenty miles wide in exchange for the sum of fifty pounds and the privilege of living on a five-square-mile reservation. The settlement of New Roxbury, which was officially renamed Woodstock in 1690, became the first colonized outpost in the former Nipmuc territory.[39]

John Chandler, despite his recent inheritance from Annis, demonstrated early on a desire to participate in the New Roxbury enterprise. He had probably heard of the region's many natural resources from John Eliot, who before the war had ministered to about 150 Wabbaquassets, or "Mat-Producing People," New Roxbury's original inhabitants. The Wabbaquassets had formed a "praying" village in an area described by one visitor as "a very good inland country well watered with rivers and brooks," but had abandoned it during the war to join up with the more powerful Mohegans, allies of the colonists.[40] The Wabbaquassets' settlement was destroyed during the war, and they did not return to the area for several years thereafter.

Plans for the New Roxbury settlement progressed despite discouraging political developments. In 1684 Charles II finally made good on his long-standing threat to revoke the Massachusetts charter, which, among other implications, put the titles to all property into question. Charles died in early 1685, before having had an opportunity to implement any significant changes to the colony's government, but the following year his brother and successor, James II, announced his plans to replace Massachusetts's elected government with a royally appointed governor and council and to reorganize the New England colonies, together with New York and New Jersey, into the Dominion of New England. In May of that year Roxbury's Joseph Dudley began serving as interim "president" of the new government until the arrival of the king's appointee, Edmund Andros. Already widely considered opportunistic and egotistical, Dudley hardly endeared himself to his constituents by allowing the Anglican church to organize formally in Boston. Matters only worsened after Andros arrived in December and began introducing sweeping social, economic, and political reforms: new taxes were imposed, town meetings were restricted, and the judicial system was overhauled. As the Reverend John Higginson of Salem lamented to his son, "Y^e foundation of all our Good things ware destroyd."[41]

In spite of this upheaval, a contingent of about thirty families left to settle New Roxbury in the summer of 1686. John Chandler and John junior were among them; however, the remainder of the family—twelve-year-old Mehetabel, nine-year-old Sarah, three-year-old Joseph, and their mother—remained behind, perhaps to be spared the camplike conditions that prevailed while houses were being built. For the time being, they were also spared the arduous journey. As the nineteenth-century historian Francis Drake wrote of the Roxbury group's eighty-mile exodus, the "pioneers" had to "bivouac . . . by stream and grove," "toiling onward over the old 'Connecticut Path,' through . . . savage wilderness."[42]

On arriving in New Roxbury, John Chandler began service on a seven-man committee appointed to locate potential house lots. The settlers soon erected a common house near the site of the Wabbaquassets' former village and drew lots to determine the location of their new homes. Each adult male was entitled to up to thirty acres; because the land John Chandler selected was considered substandard, he was given an additional twenty-two acres, "to make up in Quantity what [his land] wanted in Quality." He ultimately settled by Saw Mill Brook on the "Eastward Vale" of the hilly township, near what would become the South Woodstock common and the main "highway." The New Roxbury acreage was not John Chandler's only holding in Connecticut, however: in May of 1686 he and eleven other Roxbury men had become shareholders in a grant of over fifteen thousand acres of what was then "wilderness and fforest" bordering Woodstock to the south. The group had been deeded the land by James Fitch, a major Connecticut landholder who had purchased the tract from Owaneco, son of the Mohegan chief Uncas. (The Mohegans, in turn, had acquired the land from their conquest of the Pequots.) Specific allotments would not be made until 1694, and John Chandler never settled there, but his purchase eventually proved to be a profitable investment.[43]

Almost two years passed before Mehetabel and her mother and siblings joined John senior and John junior in New Roxbury. It is likely that Mehetabel's father returned to Roxbury at least once during this period to check on the welfare of his family and property, but even so it must have been a trying two years for those who were left behind. Elizabeth, Mehetabel, and Sarah would have had their hands full tending to the needs of the farm, making preparations for their own eventual move, and caring for Joseph, the baby of the family. They may also have provided occasional child-care assistance to Mehetabel's older, married sisters, Elizabeth and Hannah. By the time the two John Chandlers left in July 1686, Elizabeth and Robert Mason were the parents of a two-year-old son named Robert, while Hannah and Moses Draper had an infant daughter, Hannah.

For Mehetabel, Sarah, and their mother, the emotional and practical difficulties created by the absence of the men were surely compounded by the knowledge that they too would soon be leaving the Mason and Draper families, both of whom endured a series of tragedies during this time. In June 1686 the Masons suffered the loss of their four-year-old daughter, Elizabeth, and the following year they experienced both the birth and the death of their final child, a boy named John. In 1687 and 1688 Hannah and Moses Draper lost two daughters (both named Elizabeth), each of whom died before reaching her first birthday. But the heaviest blow of all came in February 1688, when Elizabeth Chandler Mason died at the age of twenty-seven.

The cause of her death is unknown, but it is possible that she fell victim to a measles epidemic then afflicting the Boston area. In the church records a single line—which misidentifies her as her sister Hannah—merely records the fact of her burial. After Elizabeth's death Robert Mason and their young son moved to Boston, where Robert remarried within a few years and began a new family. (Robert junior remained in contact with the Chandlers and as an adult settled on Connecticut lands left to him by Mehetabel's father.)

The experiences of helping her mother head a household and of dealing with great personal loss certainly would have set in motion Mehetabel's transition from child to young adult. It can only be hoped that her ability to cope with these trials gave her the necessary strength to take leave of her friends, family, and childhood home and to face the anxieties and hardships of starting a new life in the "savage wilderness."

CHAPTER TWO

Coming of Age, 1688–1693

MEHETABEL'S MOVE to New Roxbury not only launched her on a new life course, but it also seems to have motivated her to begin keeping a diary. Such dislocations and major life changes have often impelled people to take up diary writing. Mehetabel's age at the time of the move may also have played a role; she was fourteen in the spring of 1688 and perhaps experiencing the physical and emotional transformations of adolescence. On some level, she may have viewed diary keeping as a way to maintain a sense of identity and exert a degree of control over her circumstances, which at the time she was largely powerless to determine.[1]

The first chronological entry in Mehetabel's diary, dated May 31, 1688, addresses the dramatic change in her situation with the simple statement, "My father with his family went to live att New Roxbury, afterwd called Wodstock." The "afterwd called Wodstock" signals that Mehetabel most likely copied this entry from an earlier notation she had made, since New Roxbury was renamed "Woodstock" in 1690. This line constitutes Mehetabel's only description of the move; it also represents her sole entry for the entire year. Mehetabel's economy of narration leaves a vexing number of unanswered questions—How was the journey? Did it take long to adjust to life in the new settlement? How did she feel about leaving Roxbury?—yet it is in keeping with the conventions of the time. Like other early New England diarists, Mehetabel provided few details about the events she recorded and little commentary with regard to how she felt about them. Although Mehetabel and her contemporaries were certainly not lacking in strong feelings about the occurrences in their lives, they did not view their diaries as the proper outlet for airing them.[2]

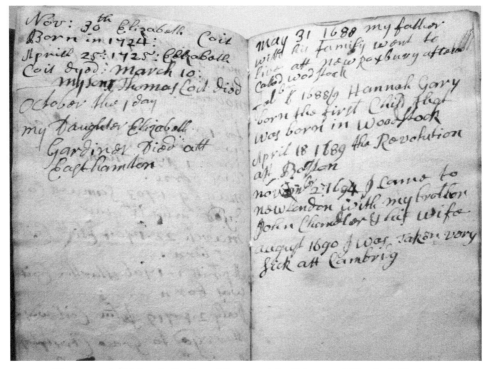

First entry in Mehetabel's diary. *Photograph by Robert and Elizabeth Hughes.*

Mehetabel's authorial reticence makes reconstructing a narrative of her experiences a challenging exercise; however, it is often possible to arrive at a more detailed picture by referring to external sources. For example, we can glean a sense of the difficulty of her journey from a 1694 letter by the Reverend Benjamin Wadsworth, who described the Connecticut Path—an old Indian trail that was the principal route between Boston and Hartford via New Roxbury—as "very rocky, bushy, [and] in many places miry." The trip may have taken the Chandlers several days to complete, depending on the weather and their mode of transportation. It is conceivable that Mehetabel walked much of this distance, as it is unlikely that the Chandlers owned many horses, and wagon space would have been largely taken up with household goods. Since there were no bridges or ferries, the party would have had to wade through any rivers or streams they encountered. The final thirty miles of the route following the last settled outpost would have been particularly rough; however, the Chandlers may not have been inclined to take any unnecessary breaks along the way, as the surrounding forest was home to bears, wolves, wildcats, and rattlesnakes. Despite the fact that any danger from human foes was relatively slight in this unsettled area, the group would have been armed and on the alert against such a possibility.[3]

Once Mehetabel and her family arrived in New Roxbury, they may well have found its frontier conditions daunting. Although the area was (and remains to this day) a bucolic place of rolling hills and fertile soil, it was also a lonely outpost that could offer few material comforts. The house where the family took up residence, like those of their New Roxbury neighbors, would at least at first have been rudely constructed and sparsely furnished. (In fact, at the time of Mehetabel's father's death in 1703, the family home still contained only basic furnishings; the probate inventory lists beds, a table and chairs, two chests of drawers, and six "Turkey Wrought" chairs with embroidered upholstery.) The Chandlers had never been wealthy people, but their home in Roxbury, described by John Chandler in a deed as a "mansion" house, had likely been comfortable by the standards of the day. Moreover, while living so close to an international port like Boston, the family would have had access to luxury items and been able to maintain a higher standard of living than was possible in a remote place such as New Roxbury. None of the village's few neighboring communities—the nearest, tiny Oxford, was miles away—could provide the level of social interaction or the types of goods and services the settlers had formerly had access to.[4]

Nonetheless, the change may also have offered the family welcome distraction from the stresses that had marked the beginning of 1688, particularly the loss of Mehetabel's sister Elizabeth. These months had been a time of significant political upheaval as well. New Englanders had grown increasingly dissatisfied with their government; as one later commentator described it, it was "a dark and threatning Season, . . . [when] the Administration of Sir Edmund Andross, Governor of New England, a Tool of the Court, [was] . . . grievously tyrannizing over the poor People here."[5] The month before the Chandlers left for New Roxbury, the Reverend Increase Mather, one of the most vocal critics of the new government, had sailed for London with the hope of airing the colonists' grievances before the king. Having earlier been put under surveillance by Andros, Mather had been forced to board the ship dressed in disguise and under cover of darkness. That it was necessary for a religious leader of Mather's standing to take such drastic action underscored for the colonists the desperate nature of their situation.

Because of its distance from Boston and its small number of inhabitants, New Roxbury was by and large beneath the notice of the new administration, so the settlers were able to concentrate their attention on the town's development, efforts in which the Chandler men played an integral part. When the first election of town officers took place in 1690, John junior—who was then twenty-five and himself a property owner—was named both the first town clerk and the community's first teacher. (The records are ambiguous on the matter of whether he taught girls as well as boys.) In 1686 John senior had been appointed to a committee responsible for laying out roads, finding a lot for a minister's home, and selecting a site for the meetinghouse. The following year he was chosen one of the town's first selectmen and was also asked to join a committee attempting to obtain government confirmation of the new settlement. (This petition received no recognition from Andros, nor did one presented by John Chandler and two other delegates in April 1688.) John senior's ascent to total respectability was completed in the early 1690s, when the local church formally organized and he was appointed a deacon. Given their rapid acquisition of both land and positions of respect and authority, the Chandler men seem to have found the greener pastures they had evidently come looking for.

The Chandler women, of course, were not offered the same opportunities for improving their fortunes; in fact, after moving to New Roxbury their quality of life in all likelihood declined, since they would have been faced with the prospect of having to accomplish much with far fewer resources. Their household would have had to be almost entirely self-sufficient: there were no shops one could turn to for food or clothing or tools. Since every other local family was essentially in the same situation, ensuring a shortage of labor for hire, Elizabeth Chandler would not have had the option of taking on local girls for temporary assistance, as had been a possibility in Roxbury. While John senior and John junior were out running the local government, building roads, and clearing and planting the fields and orchards, Elizabeth and her daughters would have attended to the countless chores and responsibilities of the family's day-to-day survival: looking after the livestock and the kitchen and medicinal gardens; foraging in the fields and forest for plants and fruit; making soap, candles, and cloth; tending fires; washing clothes; cooking meals; and cleaning house.

During the first years of settlement, few new immigrants arrived in New Roxbury, although the community's population gradually increased naturally. Mehetabel made note of one of the town's first births in her second chronological diary entry: "feb^br 6 1688/9[6] Hannah Gary born the first Child that was born in Woodstock."[7] (The use of "Woodstock" in place of "New Roxbury" denotes that this was another retrospective entry.) Hannah Gary was Mehetabel's first cousin once removed, the granddaughter of her mother's sister Anna Douglas Gary, who had remained in Roxbury. Hannah was actually the second child born in Woodstock—the first was her brother Nathaniel, born during the winter of 1686—but her birth was the first to occur after Mehetabel's arrival.

New Roxbury's inhabitants would have even more to celebrate than births in the coming months, after the Catholic king James II was deposed following the December 1688 invasion of England by the Protestant William of Orange, who was married to James's daughter Mary. Even before they had received official confirmation of William and Mary's taking of the throne, the citizens of Boston staged a coup of their own, arresting and imprisoning Andros, Dudley, and others associated with the *"Arbitrary Government* then imposed on them," in a move that would inspire another group of Boston patriots generations later. Mehetabel herself was sufficiently affected by the turn of events to record a third entry in her diary: "April 18 1689 the Revolution att Boston."[8]

Entries such as her notation about the Glorious Revolution are an important feature of Mehetabel's diary, demonstrating that her concerns ranged far beyond domestic issues. Mehetabel did not offer her opinion of the outcome of the "Revolution att Boston"; however, at some point she did transcribe a poem that indicates her thoughts on the subject of liberty:

> *for the few Hours of Life*
> *Alotted me*
> *Grant me great god*
> *but bread and liberty*
> *I'll ask no more*
> *if more thou'rt plees to give*
> *I'll thankfully*
> *that overplus Receive*
> *if beyond this*
> *no more be frely sent*
> *I'll thank for this*
> *and go away content*[9]

These lines are from a well-known essay by the poet Abraham Cowley (1618–1667), "Of Liberty," which opens with the proposition that "the liberty of a people consists in being governed by laws which they have made themselves, under whatsoever form it be of government: the liberty of a private man, in being master of his own time and actions, as far as may consist with the laws of God, and of his countrey." It is remarkable that, within the context of the patriarchal and restrictive society in which she lived, Mehetabel was not only engaging with Cowley's words about personal and political liberty, but that she went to the effort of writing them down. Although women of her time could certainly be mindful of political developments, despite being prohibited from taking part in politics and formal public life, very few women left behind documentation of any type indicating their views on such concepts as freedom.[10]

Massachusetts would not receive a new charter until 1692; however, most residents were content to restore their former governor, Simon Bradstreet, to head a temporary government consisting of an elected assembly and a council. (Bradstreet, then in his eighties, was the former husband of the late poet Anne Bradstreet, who, ironically, was also a half-sister of the deposed Dudley.) New Roxbury's response to the removal of Andros was to resume its pursuit of official recognition of its patent. At a town meeting in December of 1689, John Chandler senior and three others were asked to travel to Boston to appear before the General Court to request confirmation of the New Roxbury land grant. The delegates also sought to replace the New Roxbury name and asked for a five-year period of tax relief as well as "a committee to regulate as in the case of any differences that we cannot issue ourselves." The court granted the town's petition in March 1690, bestowing the name Woodstock on the community.[11]

Some months following John Chandler's trip to Boston, it appears that seventeen-year-old Mehetabel also traveled back to the area, for the next entry in her diary, dated simply "august 1690," makes the surprising announcement, "I was taken very sick att Cambridg." Unfortunately, Mehetabel provides no reason for her presence in Cambridge, and supplementary research offers no satisfactory explanation. Her sister Hannah and her family lived in Roxbury, not Cambridge, and the Chandlers had no close relatives there, although the town was home to some of their more distant relations, members of the Denison family. (Of course, Harvard College, the most significant local attraction, would have been off-limits to her.)[12]

Whatever took Mehetabel to Cambridge, the sickness she alludes to was very likely smallpox. The disease had broken out in Boston the previous fall, evidently carried on a ship arriving from the West Indies, as diseases frequently were. By the summer of 1690 the epidemic had spread throughout New England and as far south as New York. Precise figures are not available, but Boston's mortality rate was estimated at almost 5 percent, with about 320 deaths in a population of approximately 7,000. Mehetabel was truly fortunate to have survived the disease, which was one of the most communicable and deadly scourges of the colonial years.[13]

Smallpox was feared not only for its high mortality rate, but also for its appalling symptoms and its potential to permanently disfigure its victims.[14] One early American doctor, Boston's Zabdiel Boylston, left the following vivid description of its manifestations:

> Purple spots . . . Hemorahages of Blood at the Mouth, Nose, Fundament, and Privities; Ravings and Deliriums; Convulsions, and other Fits; violent inflamations and Swellings in the Eyes and Throat; so that [the afflicted] cannot see, or scarcely breathe, or swallow any thing, to keep them from starving. Some looking as black as the Stock, others as white as a Sheet; in some, the Pock runs into Blisters, and the Skin stripping off, leaves the Flesh raw. . . . Some have been fill'd with loathsome Ulcers; others have had deep, and fistulous Ulcers in their Bodies, or in their Limbs or Joints, with Rottenness of the Ligaments and Bones: Some who live are Cripples, others Idiots, and many blind all their Days.[15]

Mehetabel was not left crippled, blind, or an "Idiot" as a result of the illness, but she may have been left physically scarred by pockmarks.[16]

The medical attention Mehetabel received after she was diagnosed most likely came from a variety of sources. It is doubtful she was seen by a professionally trained doctor, as licensed physicians were rare. Professional medical training did not become available in the colonies until the mid-eighteenth century, and although some New England doctors were educated in Europe. their numbers were small. Most medical care in early America was provided by doctors trained through apprenticeship rather than university education and by an assortment of self-taught practitioners who included ministers, midwives, and folk healers.[17]

The field's lack of professionalization allowed women broad opportunities for medical practice, both in their homes and in their larger communities. The overseeing of a family's health and well-being was considered one of a housewife's responsibilities, and most women maintained kitchen gardens in which they grew medicinal as well as culinary herbs. Some women became so proficient at doctoring that they were called on for help by their neighbors in times of sickness. The Reverend John Eliot's wife Hanna, for example, gained great renown as a healer; having "attained to a considerable skill in Physic and Chirurgery," according to Cotton Mather, she was able "to dispense many safe, good and useful Medicines unto the *Poor* that had occasion for

them; and [so helped] some hundreds of sick & weak and maimed people."
Roxbury had had another successful female practitioner in Sarah Palsgrave
Alcock (d. 1665), the wife of one physician and daughter of another, whom
the Reverend Samuel Danforth described as having been "very skillful in
physick and chirurgery, exceedingly active, yea unwearied in ministering to
ye necessities of others." In an age when so much effort was expended on
mere survival, those with medical resources often combined their expertise,
regardless of sex or social class.[18]

Like most patients, Mehetabel would have received the bulk of her care
from family members, even if she were also being treated by an outside practitioner. Either Elizabeth Chandler, if she had accompanied Mehetabel back
to the area, or the female head of the Cambridge family with whom she was
staying would have acted as her primary caregiver: preparing and administer-
ing medicines, monitoring and responding to changes in her condition, and
coordinating outside help.[19]

Contemporary approaches to medical treatment were based in the widely
accepted Galenic theory that illness derived from an imbalance in the body's
four "humors": blood, phlegm, yellow bile, and black bile. Restoring health
generally required ridding the patient of humoral excess through such means
as bloodletting and purging through the use of enemas or agents that would
cause vomiting. A growing belief in the Paracelsian theory of medicine,
which argued that illness was caused by specific diseases rather than humoral
imbalances, meant that chemical drugs were increasingly prescribed along
with herbal remedies. Unfortunately, these drugs often produced the same
results: nausea, vomiting, and intestinal distress.[20]

Some of the treatments for smallpox must have been almost as dreadful as
the disease itself. In addition to being purged, patients who failed to exhibit
the sores commonly brought on by smallpox were often plied with blistering
poultices so that the body would break out in a rash and rid itself of offend-
ing humors. The crisis point of the illness, according to Cotton Mather (who
would eventually introduce a smallpox vaccine based on advice given to him
by his African slave Onesimus), would "often be attended with frightful circumstances; Grievous Oppression, Fainting, Vomiting, Purging and the Va-
pours, which is to say in one word, All that is terrible." Were one fortunate
enough to survive the crisis, he or she might be subjected to a final round of
purging to ensure that all evil humors had been driven away.[21]

Until medical knowledge became specialized late in the colonial period,
information pertaining to the healing of illness was widely disseminated

through both published sources and oral tradition. Medical advice books printed in England, such as Nicholas Culpeper's *The English Physician* (1652) and *London Dispensatory* (1688), remained highly popular throughout the period and were sold in significant quantities by Boston booksellers. Almanacs containing folk remedies—of English, Native American, and African American origin—were also widely read. Women often obtained medical knowledge through household advice books such as Gervase Markham's *The English Housewife* (first published in 1615), adapting the English herbal remedies when necessary to incorporate plants found in the New World. (Here they frequently benefited from the knowledge of Native healers.) Folk healers who were illiterate were not necessarily at a disadvantage, since much of the existing body of medical knowledge relied on English tradition that had been orally transmitted for centuries.[22]

While much of what early American women knew about treating illness was verbally passed down from generation to generation, some women also kept a written record of this information, although very few of these records have survived. One valuable attribute of Mehetabel's diary is its almost two dozen medical remedies. Toward the back of the manuscript, interspersed among recipes, household hints, and assorted literary material, are treatments for headaches, coughs, cankers, fluxes, pimples, sleeplessness, toothaches, and sore eyes, among other disorders. Most of the forty or so ingredients involved in Mehetabel's medicinals could be found in the pantry or kitchen garden: cinnamon, columbine, eggs, peppercorns, sage, honey, St. John's wort, yarrow. A few, however, rely on an object's mystical properties ("the tooth of a dead man Carried about you presently easeth pain"; "powder of earthworms will make an Akeing tooth fall . . . out of itt selfe"). This was not unusual for the time, since all types of healers found it necessary on occasion to turn to what we would consider the paranormal. Certain magical beliefs brought over from England in the seventeenth century continued to circulate in New England throughout the colonial period. When ordinary means of healing did not produce results, lay people sometimes turned to folk traditions with roots in the supernatural.[23]

Many of the botanicals Mehetabel relied on had been in medical use for centuries. For example, her claim for the healthful properties of balm water—"Restores the memory when lost, quickens the sences, strengthens the brain, heart, and stomake, Causeth a merry mind and a sweet breath"—echoes the recommendation of an early Roman whom Nicholas Culpeper quoted in his *English Physician:* "[balm] causeth the Mind and Heart to becom merry." Like the author Gervase Markham, Mehetabel recognized the effectiveness of using fennel to treat eye ailments, rose water for headaches, and wormwood to stop vomiting. Her prescription for oral health matches, nearly word for word, one found in *The Queen's Closet Opened: Incomparable Secrets in Physick, Chyrurgery, Preserving, Candying, and Cookery,* an English book reprinted several times throughout the seventeenth century. (Mehetabel's recipe: "to keep your teeth from Rotting or akeing, wash your mouth every morning with the juce of lemmons, and Rub . . . your teeth with a sage leef, and wash your teeth after meals with fair water." *The Queen's* recipe: "If you will keep your teeth from rotting, or aching, wash the mouth continually every morning with juyce of Lemons, and afterward rub your teeth with a Sage leaf, and wash your teeth after meat with fair water.") Many of the herbs Mehetabel used medicinally continued to be relied on for generations (and a number of them are still in use today). The Maine midwife Martha Ballard, for example, according to her late eighteenth- early nineteenth-century diary, found botanicals such as anise seed, chamomile, mullein, and sorrel helpful in her practice.[24]

It is likely that at the time of her illness, Mehetabel was familiar with many of the cures she recorded in her diary, but that she did not actually write them down until after she was married and had her own family's health to oversee. One can only speculate as to how her experience with smallpox shaped her attitudes toward medicine and healing. The diary includes no treatments for smallpox; however, an undated entry near the end does contain what may be a clue to Mehetabel's philosophy of medical care. A play on words seems to suggest that one should use the means at one's disposal to prevent unnecessary suffering: "Take physack early[;] medicians [medicines] come to late when the doseag is groan inveterals [intervals]."[25]

One positive result of Mehetabel's illness was that it served to temporarily keep her away from Woodstock, which had recently come under threat of Indian attack. In the summer of 1688 Indians from French Canada had begun wreaking havoc on frontier settlements, and although the Maine and New Hampshire territories were hardest hit, other outposts were also vulnerable. In the Woodstock area, the Nipmucs and Wabbaquassets were becoming a more visible presence, to the discomfort of many of the town's inhabitants.[26]

Since the end of King Philip's War, many Nipmucs had been living on a reservation to the east of Woodstock, while others stayed with various tribes or traveled far afield to "seeke new habitations far remote in the wildernesse."

Most Wabbaquassets had spent the previous several years with their Mohegan allies. Disruptions caused by the new war, however, had driven members of both groups to return to their former homelands.[27]

The Wabbaquassets in particular had been friendly to the white settlers—tradition has it that a group carried corn on their backs all the way to Boston to relieve a food shortage during the colony's first year of settlement—however, they were disinclined to accept the jurisdiction of Massachusetts, which antagonized the colonists. Relations between the two groups soon deteriorated. In February 1692 John Chandler and the other Woodstock selectman requested that the General Court ban liquor sales to local Indians, reporting "many outrages" on the part of the Wabbaquassets. The following year local tribe members were ordered to take up residence within the bounds of Woodstock so the authorities would be able to monitor their movements; they were also told that they would thenceforth need permission if they wished to travel.[28]

Mehetabel's diary contains no entries for 1690 other than the one concerning her illness "at Cambridg" and no entries at all for 1691, 1692, or 1693. Although it is impossible to determine exactly when she returned to Woodstock, it is clear that she did rejoin her family at some time between 1690 and 1693, since in a letter her sister Sarah wrote her some years later, Sarah pointedly asked Mehetabel if she remembered living under "Garrison fears." Mehetabel does not provide a description of how she was personally affected by living in a potential war zone; however, the experience could not have been pleasant. In fact, the great apprehension felt throughout New England during this period contributed directly to a new source of trouble for the region: the witchcraft hysteria of 1692–1693. In a society in which belief in the supernatural was almost universal, the experiences of being besieged by Indians and by witches became linked; both were perceived as manifestations of Satan's plot against New England.[29]

The general facts of the witchcraft trials are well known: by the fall of 1692 nineteen people had been hanged and one man pressed to death. Hundreds of men, women, and children were accused, and scores were imprisoned. The crisis ran its course by the following spring after public opinion turned against the trials, and William Phips, the first governor to be appointed under the new charter, issued a general pardon for all those who had been accused.

Mehetabel's diary is silent on the subject; however, the episode had great ramifications for the Chandler family, as Mehetabel's aunt Hannah and uncles Thomas and William—John Chandler's siblings who had settled in Andover, Massachusetts—found themselves at the center of the crisis. Andover's role in the affair has long been overshadowed by Salem's, yet it actually had a higher rate of accusations and confessions, stemming from anxiety surrounding the town's frontier position and its involvement in the two Indian wars.[30]

The Andover and Woodstock branches of the Chandler family were separated by many miles, and no letters between John Chandler and his siblings appear to have survived, but they evidently maintained ties that were in turn preserved by successive generations. William Chandler's son Philemon, for example, moved to Woodstock in the late 1690s, and several of Thomas's and Hannah's grandchildren also relocated to the area. It was common in early New England for distant relations to maintain family connections; in fact, as the general population gradually dispersed over a wider region, these relationships often gained rather than lessened in importance as they came to represent meaningful "links to a wider world."[31]

By 1692 Mehetabel's aunt Hannah and uncles Thomas and William had established deep roots in Andover. Thomas, the eldest, was in his mid-sixties; he and his wife Hannah had had eight children together. Known as "Captain" for his long involvement with the Andover militia, Thomas was a man of means and influence, running a substantial ironworks and serving as a representative to the General Court in Boston.

William Chandler was also active in town affairs. For many years he operated a tavern in Andover, although at one point his license was almost revoked owing to allegations that he allowed gambling and encouraged people to spend too much time in his establishment, "till they know not their way to their habitations." (Perhaps William, like his brother John and sister Sarah, found it difficult to break up a party.) William had married Mary Dane, the granddaughter of his mother Annis's former husband John Dane, and they had had ten children together before Mary died in 1679. William remarried within the year and eventually had three children with his second wife, Bridget.[32]

Hannah Chandler Abbot Dane was in her early sixties in 1692; she had lost her first husband, George Abbot, in 1681 after they had had thirteen children together. In 1690 Hannah had married the Reverend Francis Dane of Andover, the son of her mother's husband John Dane by his first marriage. (She was Reverend Dane's third wife.) Francis Dane must have considered Hannah an exceptional woman, for his standards regarding female conduct were apparently very high. After having lost his first wife, Dane had written a poem about his difficulty in finding a suitable replacement, whom he described as one who would be "sober, chaste, and sage / That's Loving, meeke, no Tatler, not unruly / . . . That loveth goodness but hath a mind / To Conjugal subjection inclined." Hannah's solid character ultimately stood her in good stead, since it seems to have protected her from allegations of witchcraft even as many of those around her found themselves accused. Although her own children were never officially implicated, Francis Dane's two daughters, as well as his daughter-in-law and several of his grandchildren, were indicted and imprisoned. (One of his daughters and a granddaughter were condemned to death but were later reprieved.) Reverend Dane himself even became the target of some accusations but was never formally charged.[33]

As fears spread over the perceived level of satanic activity in Andover, several of Mehetabel's cousins became key actors in subsequent events. Hannah's son Benjamin and William's twelve-year-old daughter Phoebe, for example, were instrumental in bringing witchcraft charges against Martha Carrier, who was ultimately executed.[34] Another of Mehetabel's cousins, Sarah Phelps, the ten-year-old granddaughter of Thomas Chandler, played a significant part in the indictments of several local witches, one of whom, a widow named Mary Parker, was sent to the gallows. (Thomas's daughter Hannah Chandler Bixby also figured in an indictment against Mary Parker, although her deposition has not survived.) It is unclear how often Sarah provided formal legal testimony, but she never denied having been afflicted by those self-confessed witches who included her in their list of victims. Among those whom Sarah ultimately helped make cases against were Francis Dane's daughters Abigail Faulkner and Elizabeth Johnson and his granddaughter Betty Johnson.[35]

Ironically, Abigail, Elizabeth, and Betty were among those confessed witches who claimed to have attended witch meetings at "Chandler's Garrison," the home of Hannah Chandler Abbot Dane's daughter Hannah and her husband, Captain John Chandler (the son of Thomas and, thus, Hannah junior's first cousin). These meetings were reportedly large gatherings at which upwards of two hundred witches would drink wine and participate in satanic rituals. It is not known why the Chandlers' property was singled out as a center of malefic activity; the first allegations to this effect seem to have been made by Martha Carrier's children and were perhaps intended as an indirect challenge to local authority—John Chandler being a prominent member of the community—as retaliation for their mother's incarceration and impending execution. Given the repeated assertions that their home had been the site of mass devil worship, Hannah and John could ultimately count themselves extremely fortunate that they personally never became the focus of witchcraft accusations.

Amid the profusion of accusations and counteraccusations, many Andover residents came to realize that something had gone terribly wrong in their community. In October 1692 a group of twenty-six townsmen—including Mehetabel's uncles Thomas and William, some of her cousins, and Reverend Dane—forwarded a petition to the governor and his council on behalf of "persons of good creditt" whom they believed had been wrongly accused by "some distempered persons in the[se] parts." Despite the danger involved in criticizing the proceedings and those who claimed to be afflicted, the petitioners openly acknowledged that their "troubles[,] which hitherto have been great, . . . are like to continue and increase, . . . if the Accusations of children and others {who are} under a Diabolicall influence shall be received against persons of good fame." A second petition on behalf of some accused Andover witches, sent to the Court of Assizes at Salem in January, noted that many of the accused had "own[ed] what they were charged with" only after having been pressured to do so, and that "they did soon privately retract what they had said." This petition was signed by more than fifty residents, both men and women, who included Thomas and his wife Hannah, William and his wife Bridget, Hannah and her husband Francis, and several of Mehetabel's cousins. It is interesting to note that Mehetabel's uncles and aunts signed even though some of their family members were among the accusers; moreover, her uncle Thomas himself had testified against Samuel Wardwell, who had been executed in September. (Thomas's testimony consisted of a single statement: "I haue often hard Samuell wardle of Andour till yung person thire fortine and he was much adicted to that and mayd sport of it." The record states that Thomas "farther said not.")[36]

By the time the Andover residents filed their first petition, the crisis was already in the process of being checked. In October of 1692 Governor Phips brought a halt to the trials and disbanded the Court of Oyer and Terminer, which had relied upon spectral evidence, the claims that the afflicted were being visited by apparitions of the accused. Although the new Court of Assizes, which convened in early 1693, convicted three of the remaining witches—all of whom were from Andover, and one of whom was Francis Dane's granddaughter Betty Johnson—Phips subsequently issued reprieves for the three women. The proceedings had effectively been brought to an end.[37]

Mehetabel, like the rest of her immediate family, probably witnessed the witchcraft drama from afar; however, one tantalizing piece of evidence has the potential to place her at a much closer vantage point. In the records of the Second Church of Boston—also known as the "Church of the Mathers" because of its long association with Increase and son Cotton Mather (their combined leadership covered the years 1673–1728)—an entry notes that on May 14, 1693, Mehetabel Chandler was admitted as a member. Cotton Mather's registry of church members provides no additional information about this individual, other than that she was not buried through the church—suggesting that she left it at some point—but that she was never officially dismissed. These few details, combined with the fact that Mehetabel never became a full member of either the Woodstock or the New London congregations, increase the possibility of this being "our" Mehetabel, since if she had not been dismissed from the Second Church, she would not have been able to join another congregation. Given the significance that faith played in her life and the fact that church membership was extremely important to both her family of birth and the family she would have with John Coit (he and almost all the children they had together became members), it is unlikely that she never became a full church member at some time in her life.[38]

It is unclear why Mehetabel would have sought—and later maintained—membership in a church so far from her family, but the answer may lie in the church's prestige and in the special regard she held for Cotton Mather. In the popular imagination, Mather's achievements have long been overshadowed by his role in the witch trials; however, he was actually one of colonial New England's foremost intellectuals. Skilled in several languages and the recipient of two degrees from Harvard College—which he entered at the age of eleven—he eventually established the largest private library in the colonies and published more than 380 books, essays, and sermons. He also became the leading medical figure of the day and wrote the single most comprehensive medical work of the colonial period. Although Mehetabel's diary does not provide a specific indication of when her interest in Mather began, she may have received her first exposure to him when he lectured at the Roxbury church in the spring and summer of 1687. It is evident from the collection of family writings that her regard for Mather was of long standing and recognized by those around her. In later years a friend sent her a copy of his portrait, which was the first of a local "celebrity" to be reproduced in mass quantities, and in 1726, when her daughter Martha wrote to her while on a visit to Boston, she noted that she had made a special point of attending services at the Second Church, despite its distance, and that she had "Like't [Cotton Mather's] preaching very well, & I b'leave the better because you so much admire him."[39]

It is apparent from her later writings that Mehetabel had many acquaintances in Boston (some of whom were also members of the Second Church); however, family circumstances—in particular, the death of her twenty-two-year-old sister Hannah in the summer of 1692—may have been the determining factor in bringing her back to the area. (Hannah's cause of death is unknown, and no clues are given on her gravestone in Roxbury's Eliot Burying Ground, situated next to those of her two infant brothers.) Had the Chandlers learned of Hannah's illness ahead of time, they may have sent Mehetabel to Roxbury to help nurse her sister; on the other hand, if the family received news of Hannah's death after the fact, Mehetabel may have gone to help care for her motherless niece, six-year-old Hannah. It is possible that Mehetabel remained with the Drapers even after her brother-in-law remarried at the end of 1692, for, in what could be more than a passing coincidence, Moses Draper's first and only child with his new wife was baptized at the Second Church in 1693.[40]

It is tempting to imagine Mehetabel in the Boston area during the turbulent period of 1692–1693 and being that much closer to the unfolding of such a significant historical episode as the witchcraft trials. Although this prospect merits some consideration, it is ultimately impossible to prove. Given the sporadic and reticent nature of her writings and, in some cases, the lack of supporting contemporary sources, certain aspects of Mehetabel's life will remain forever lost to time. The early period, in particular, presents a number of mysteries. Mehetabel's diary does make it evident that, by the fall of 1694, she had moved to New London, Connecticut, with her brother John and his wife, Mary Raymond, whom he had married in 1692. Once again Mehetabel was taking leave of familiar surroundings to start a new life; this time, however, she was also parting from her parents and younger siblings. Mehetabel's move to New London would not serve to establish her independence—for although she was twenty-one, she was a resident of her brother's household and thus subject to his rules—but it would usher in a new stage in her personal development. In New London she would be exposed to a host of experiences that would figure prominently in the formation of her identity and complete her transition to adulthood.

CHAPTER THREE

Marriage and Motherhood,
1694–1696

MEHETABEL NOTED the exact date of her arrival in New London in her fifth chronological diary entry: "novem^br 2: 1694 I came to new london with my brother John Chandler & his wife." She did not disclose why she accompanied John, his wife Mary, and their one-year-old son, John, to New London, or whether she had ever been there before. John himself had previously spent time in the area; in fact, he had met Mary, a New London native, while doing some local surveying for Major James Fitch, an agent for the Mohegans and substantial landowner who in 1686 had deeded a fifteen-thousand-acre parcel to John Chandler senior and eleven other Roxbury shareholders.[1]

Mehetabel had family roots in New London, as her mother's parents, William and Anne Douglas, and three of her siblings—Robert, Sarah, and William junior—had moved there decades earlier. William Douglas had been one of the town's original grantees and had subsequently held a number of public offices, including that of deputy to the colony's General Court. He had also acted as church deacon for several years. Both he and Anne had died by the time Mehetabel was twelve, however, and in 1689 her mother's sister Sarah also passed away, a likely victim of the "distemper of sore throat and fever" that had spread throughout New London in the extreme heat of that summer.[2]

Little is known about Sarah other than that she left behind a husband named John Keeny and a grown daughter, Susannah. She had also attained the status of a member of New London's church, as had her mother. Sarah and Anne left behind no personal documents that have survived, and there is evidence that Anne, at least, may not have been able to write, since she signed a deposition she gave when making a claim on her father's estate in England with her mark. Unlike the male members of the Douglas family, who all achieved public recognition through roles they played in local affairs, Anne's and Sarah's names are conspicuously absent from town records.

Although her aunt and grandparents were no longer alive, the presence of so many other Douglas relatives, who by now extended into the fourth generation, likely helped ease Mehetabel's transition to life in the seaport town. In many ways, New London could not have been more different from Woodstock. Located on the Connecticut coast, at the convergence of Long Island Sound, the Thames River, and the Atlantic, the town was surrounded by water. The area had originally been part of the homelands of the Pequot tribe, whose numbers had greatly diminished as a result of a 1636–1637 war with the colonists. After the conclusion of the war, John Winthrop Jr., son of the Massachusetts governor and himself a later governor of Connecticut, set about establishing a permanent settlement, with the goal of capitalizing on the potential for trade with the New York Dutch and local tribes. Considered the "founder" of New London, the enterprising Winthrop recruited settlers, planned the town's layout, and organized the local government. His reputation as one of the colonies' foremost alchemical healers—using what he believed were divinely sanctioned medicines that were developed from metals and minerals rather than plants—ultimately turned New London into a hospital town, attracting prospective patients from across New England. Those unable to make the journey were often treated by Winthrop's widespread network of female healers, on whom he depended to dispense his pharmaceuticals and advice.[3]

Early settlers quickly established maritime trade networks, and by 1680 New London had become one of Connecticut's major harbors; New London merchants eventually conducted business with ports around the world. Much of the early trade was coastal; commodities such as wood, grain, livestock, and animal pelts were shipped down the Thames River and on to Boston, New York, Rhode Island, and other destinations, where they were in turn traded for clothing, tools, military supplies, and other goods. The seventeenth century also witnessed the development of a triangular trade: fish obtained in Newfoundland by New London vessels were transported together with provisions, horses, and locally produced goods to the West Indies, where they were exchanged for sugar, molasses, rum, salt, and cotton. These products were then either brought directly back to New London or carried to Boston or New York to be bartered for manufactured goods for the New London market. The town's trade with the West Indies eventually became a central part of its economy—and it also came to include the trafficking of slaves. Local ships not only transported slaves from Africa to the West Indies, where the harsh plantation system created a constant demand, but they also brought them back to New England in significant numbers for local sale.[4]

Many of the first slaves in New London had been Indian prisoners of war. Although Native servants continued to be a visible presence in New London through the eighteenth century, their numbers declined as the numbers of black slaves grew and ultimately reached a high of almost 10 percent of the population before the American Revolution. Blacks and Indians commonly worked alongside each other as household servants, farm hands, washerwomen, laborers, and shipyard workers; they were also employed in more specialized fields as blacksmiths, bakers, seamstresses, tailors, carpenters, and coopers.[5]

The frequent contact between New London blacks and Natives, as well as their shared low status, led to the forming of bonds between the two groups, and many intermarried. Rachel, a young Native captured in King Philip's War, for example, married York, a black slave belonging to another master. Likewise, in 1685 William Wright, a Native servant of James Rogers's, married Rogers's black slave Hagar. For a time, intermarriage between whites and blacks was also tolerated, although it was not common. In 1702, for instance, Adam Rogers, a "mulatto" who had formerly been an indentured servant, wed a white woman named Catharine Jones. No social stigma appears to have been attached to their children, most of whom married whites. As black slavery became more entrenched in New London, however, such unions grew increasingly unlikely.[6]

Although the black slave population was low at the time Mehetabel first came to live in New London—most likely under 5 percent of the town's total population of fewer than a thousand residents—many local families owned a slave or two. Mehetabel's diary provides no information on the subject of New London slavery; however, the diary of Joshua Hempstead, who was Mehetabel's near neighbor and who was actually a distant relative (her mother's brother Robert had married his father's sister Mary), provides a variety of details about the lives of local slaves. Himself a slave owner who also employed an indentured Indian servant for a time, Hempstead frequently recorded information concerning the work exchanges he arranged with neighbors: "I hired Madm Winthrops Cesar 40s[hillings] p[er] Mo[nth]"; "Adam [Hempstead's slave] & 3 hands gathering Corn[:] Tom[ha]s Sambo

& Pompey L."; "Josh[u]a adam & 2 mingos & Hurlbuts men weeding at Keeneys Lot." He also documented slave births, deaths, and marriages, as well as other events of note: "Scipio & Hannah [published]"; "at Jennings's House. a Negro Woman Died there. Come Lately from ye West Indies"; "Mr Pickets Man & Woman was whipt for Stealing £9 mony & Rum." The sheer number of such entries in Hempstead's diary attests to the extent to which individuals of African descent had become enmeshed within the social fabric of the community.[7]

To Mehetabel, New London must have seemed a world apart from isolated, rural Woodstock. The noise and bustle of the waterfront, the centrality of commerce to town affairs, and the diverse population of blacks, Natives, sailors, merchants, soldiers, traders, and transients would have offered a sharp contrast to Puritan village life. Early in its history New London had acquired a reputation for being a maverick community; as the nineteenth-century local historian Frances Manwaring Caulkins wrote, the town "was not, perhaps, a favorite in the colony: it frequently voted wrong; harbored foreigners; was often boisterous and contentious; manners were too free; actions too impulsive; in short, it had less of the Puritan stamp than any other place in Connecticut." In an effort to curb the level of "boisterousness," the town nightly rang a nine o'clock curfew bell; however, this attempt at controlling social behavior was not always successful. In September of 1693, for example, four young men were presented before the New London court for "nightwalking" on the Sabbath and for engaging in such mischief as knocking down fences, severing the tails and manes of horses, and barring people's doors with logs. Likewise, traders bringing stores from the inland were known to "parade the streets in noisy bands" after having taken part in "merry carousals" at waterfront taverns.[8]

Visiting mariners were also a source of disturbances. In general, the "roving unsettled life" of the sea had its own rules of conduct, which were frequently at odds with those of the rest of society. As one colonial writer complained, "Sailors, one would think, should be the best of men, there being, as we say, but a Step between them & death; & yet experience shows that they are commonly the worst." Although Mehetabel's personal contact with these transient and less respectable elements of society was no doubt limited, her move to New London did expose her to a broader, and more exotic, cross section of humanity than she ever would have encountered in Woodstock.[9]

Very little can be verified about Mehetabel's first months in New London, since she made no record of them. It is also impossible to determine how she felt about leaving behind her family and starting a new life—again; whether she liked living with her brother and sister-in-law; or what her hopes and plans were for the future. One thing that *is* possible to establish, however, is that not long after arriving in New London she became engaged to John Coit, whom she married early in the summer of the following year.

Just how Mehetabel and John Coit, who was three years her senior, became acquainted is unknown, although they may well have been introduced by one of Mehetabel's New London relatives. Like the Douglases, the Coits were a prominent New London family. John Coit's paternal grandparents, John and Mary Jennes (or Jenners) Coit, had settled in town by 1650, after which time John established the town's first shipyard. The shipyard was later taken over by his son Joseph, the younger John's father. Joseph had helped fill the role of deacon after Mehetabel's grandfather William died; he and his wife, Martha Harris Coit, a native of Middletown, Connecticut, were both church members. They had four other sons in addition to John, who was the eldest and the first to marry.

Martha Coit had actually given birth a total of ten times, but four of her babies had been stillborn and one child had died young. In a remarkable surviving document from 1689, Martha described how she was repeatedly sustained by her faith during the fearful and physically trying experience of childbirth. At the time she wrote this manuscript, Martha was in her late forties and unlikely to become pregnant again. She was well aware, however, that the "swift and sudden messenger of death" could appear at any moment, as one of her contemporaries put it, and evidently wanted to create such a record for the "edefiecation and incoragement of [her] offspring to trust in the lord att all times." Other women left behind similar counsel for their children. Sarah Whipple Goodhue of Ipswich, Massachusetts, for example, while on her deathbed in 1681, drafted a letter advising her children "to get a part and portion in the Lord Jesus Christ, that will hold, when all . . . [other] things will fail."[10] Such parting words were often treasured by a woman's descendants; indeed, Martha's manuscript was treated as an heirloom and passed down through succeeding generations of Mehetabel and John's family.

March 15. 1688   Martha Coite

    A few words for memory unto my own Speritual Comfort and for edefiecation and incoragement of my offspring to trust in the lord att all times: of gods gracious dealings with me in the times of sharp travil in Childe bareing: when as I was brought even unto death in my own apprehention and in the apprehention of all such as did be hold me in my weak estate of bodey —

As firs[t]: which was a great soport unto me: 66.psalm.14: I will pay thee
my vows which my lips have uttered and my mouth hath spoken when I was
in troubel. 20.ver⁵. blessed be god which hath not turned away my prayer.
nor his mercy from me. 31psalm.10 but he that trusteth in the Lord mercy
shall Compass him about. 18 psal.2. the Lord is my Rock and my foretress
and my deliver in whom I trust 63 psal.7 because as thou hast been my helper
therefore in the shadow of thy wings I will Rejoyce 81 psal.7 becaus as thou
Callest in troubel and I delivered thee 38 psalm15 for in thee lord did I hope
thou wilt hear o lord my god 36 psal.7 how excellent is thy loveingkindness
o lord therefore the Children of men put there trust under the shadow of
thy wings 77 psal.10. and I said thiss is my hope 45.isa: 8[?] in a littel wrath
I hid my face from thee for a moment but with everlasting kindness will I
have mercy on thee saith the lord thy Redeemer And declarring of such portions scripture as the Lord brought to my mind when I was in travil with my
son Daniel:[11] which was my soport in my greatist extrematy: 77psal.10: in yᵉ
singing psalms in the old translation att last I said my weakness is the Cause
of thiss misstrust god allmighty aloan can help all thiss and Chang it when
he list [?]

    my sixth Child when as I being in fear travil to misstrust and forget gods
mercy and help manifest to me in former travils. being castdown with fear
and disscouragements I was Redy for to faint under my pains and was under
soar temptations as if god dealt hardly with me which then my sins looking
me in the face I was ready to disspair of mercy but in my [. . .?] god Remembered me [and comforted me?] out of his holy word. As 7 micha.18. who is a
god like unto thee that pardoneth Iniquity and passeth by the transgression
of the remnant of his heritage he Retain not his anger for ever because he
delighteth in mercy: also the Lord in abeled me by faith to lay hold on that
promiss as Christ made unto peter: altho satan hath desiared to sift thee as
wheat yet I have prayed for thee that thy faith fail not: immediately I found
Comfort in my Spirit: my faintness was removed I found like unto a Cordial
thiss promiss boath soul and bodey after wards I was quickly delivered and
my Childe was still born I found Comfort in these words 99psal.33. never the
less My loveing kindness I will not utterly take from him nor suffer my faith-
fullness to fail. through gods mercy. so my Spirit submiting unto the hand of
god for the present: but soon after wards I meeting with som other afflicktion
I found my faith failing me which made me me cry out with the decipels o
lord increace our faith 73 psalm26. my flesh and my hart faileth but god is
the strength of my hart and my portion for ever: 103 psal.13. Like as a father
pittyeth his Children so the lord pittieth them that fear him—

    when I was in travil with my seventh Childe. being near unto death⁵ door
and all hope seemingly failed the lord being pleased to vouchsafe unto me
thiss promiss to lay hold on he brought this promiss unto my minde: 45 isa-
ia.19. I have not spoken in secret in a dark place of the earth. I said not unto
the seed of Jacob seek ye me in vain. I the lord speak Righteousness I declare
things that are Right. 44isaia.22: Remember this o Jacob and Israel for thou
art my servant. o israel thou shalt not be forgotten of me: these two gracious
promisses soporting me which made me say with Jacob I have enough. which

quickly after I being delivered which was beyond all expectation of humain Cretuars. my Child being still born thiss schripture came to my minde 32 psalm:6. for the incoriagement of others: for thiss shall every one that is godly pray unto thee in a time when as thou mayest be found so verily in the floods of great water shall not com nigh unto him: (turn over)

7 vears. thou art my hideing place. thou shalt preserve me from troubel thou shalt compass me about with songs of deliverance. selah. 34 psalm.6. thiss pooar man Cryed and the lord heard him and saved him out of all his troubels: 7 vears: the angel of the lord encampeth round them that fear him and delivereth them. 8 vears. o taste and see that the lord is good. o blessed is that man that trusteth in him. 9 vears. o fear the lord oye his saints for for there is no want to them that fear him. 41isaia.14. fear not thou worm Jacob and ye men of israel. I thy Redeemer. I will help thee saith the lord— being under great bodily weakness and my Spirits ready for to fail me these words I found soporting of me 6 hosea:1: Com and let us Return unto the Lord for he hath toaren and he will heal you he hath smitten you and he will binde you up:

my eighth Childe drawing near my time being under fears and troubels I beged of the lord for to send me som soporting promiss. takeing my bible wher in I had always found comfort the lord by his good providence brought thiss schripture unto me 56 isaiah.14: for thou shalt not fear for terrour for it shall not com near thee. now the lord by thiss promiss so strengthened my faith and gave me Curriage so that I Could so that I could full ly rely upon him for strength: 43 isaiah 25 I even I am he that bloteth out thy transgressions for my own name sake and will not remember thy sins 6.psalm.7. that I may worship with the voice of thanks giveing and tell of all his wonderous works. 8. lord I have loved the habitation of thy house. the place where thy honour dwells: I have had large experiance of the lords goodness towards me[.] after several months Confinement unto my house the lord hath carried me to his house for the first house after my long confinement was the house of god as I went unto: the lord had so strengthened me that I found[?] my body never the a whit the wors but my Spirits mutch quickened and I hope I can say in truth that I pass[?] one day spent in the house of god better to me than a thousand elswhere

my ninth Childe. I being in a dangerous Condition my Childe came wrong. the lord of his great goodness manifest unto me a pooar and unworthy Creture more then my deserts. gave me faith in my extremity for to lay hold on that promiss: 50 psalm.15 call upon me in the day of troubel and I will deliver thee. thiss schripture came unto me with such soporting Confidence as if the lord had Spoaken unto me in pertickeler: I will answer[?] thee, which promises he soon made good unto me for I was soon delivered beyond all expectation. also my Childe was still born—

my tenth Childe: my serious Consideration of my unthankfullness unto god for former great deliverances unto me in my former nesesaties when as he had delivered me nine times in Childe bareing: my former experiancis of gods assistance manyfest unto me in my weakness: and that I had not improved former mercyes unto gods glory was my duety to have don. yet the lord hath not taken advantage of my unworthyness: but hath still manyfestly answered me with thiss promiss 106 psalm.1. 43 psalm.44-48[?]. many times did he deliver them but they provoaked them him with there counsels: and were brought low for there Iniquityes[?]: nevertheless he Regreatded there affliction when he heard there Crys and he Remembered for them his covenant and Repented according to the multitude[?] of his mercyes the lord did soport my Spirit in thiss his gracious promiss given unto me and quick delivery & he gave me a liveing Childe which through his grace assisting of me will give me yet cause and grounds to hope in his mercy so as that he will never leave me nor forsake me—

    These experiancis of gods marcyes to me I do desiar for to leave with my Children when as I Shall leave them that they may trust in thiss god and not for get his marcyes—these are Such things as fall short far of what god hath don for me—[12]

Martha's childbirth testimonial is the only piece of writing in her hand that has survived, but it reveals a great deal about her. The document makes it clear, for example, that in addition to being an intensely religious woman, she was also highly literate. She successfully conveyed her experiences and emotions through the written word, and also made skillful use of a popular literary device of the time centered around the notion of providential salvation. The style and approach of Martha's testimonial, in fact, closely resemble those of Mary Rowlandson's famous captivity narrative, *The Sovereignty and Goodness of God* (1682), one well-known example employing this device. Rowlandson, a minister's wife living in Lancaster, Massachusetts, had been captured by Indians during King Philip's War but was eventually ransomed and reunited with her family. Where Martha set out to demonstrate the "marcyes" God dispensed to her when she was "castdown with fear and disscouragements," Mary Rowlandson's aim was to reveal God's providence in "preserving, supporting, and carrying [her] through so many such extream hazards, unspeakable difficulties and disconsolateness." Both women presented their experiences as a series of perils relieved by divine intervention: Rowlandson related these experiences within the context of the twenty "removes," or travels, she went on with her Indian captors, while Martha structured her account around her last five episodes of "sharp travil in Childe bareing." Martha and Rowlandson each interlaced their narratives with relevant biblical passages apparently intended to provide them with a framework for comprehending their experiences of suffering and redemption, and both seem to have taken comfort from the fact, in Neal Salisbury's words, that "such afflictions struck God's chosen people in ancient times and that he never forgets his promise to redeem those saints who do not forsake him." As Martha herself wrote, when she was "near unto death' door" while delivering her seventh child, she was greatly reassured when God "vouchsafe[d] unto [her]" his promise to the Israelites that they would "not be forgotten of me."[13]

Martha's testimonial also shares similarities with Elizabeth Chandler's poem, not only in that both women focused on instances in which their faith failed and then supported them, but also in that each seems to have written about her trials as a means of deriving her own personal meaning from them. Although both used the conventional concept of providential salvation to structure their narratives, they utilized it for their own particular ends, and in telling their stories they succeeded in expressing their creativity and individuality. While each woman presented God as the primary character in her account, it is actually she herself who is the main actor and who effects the change in herself necessary to improving her circumstances.

At the time Mehetabel met John Coit, he was working in the family shipyard, which he would eventually inherit. Although the Coit shipyard was no longer the only one in New London, it was the largest and the most profitable. The Coits constructed a variety of vessels throughout the colonial period, ranging from small ketches and single-masted sloops built for coastal trade to larger, multimasted brigs and ships intended for transatlantic voyages. At least one of their seventeenth-century ships weighed a hundred tons. Coit vessels were involved in the West Indies trade early on, and throughout the years many were used to transport slaves along with their other cargo.[14]

Several entries in Mehetabel's diary suggest that over the years various shipyard workers temporarily boarded with her and John. The first such notation—and the first entry to follow her declaration about moving to New London—actually predates her and John's marriage by several months: "feb 1694/5 thomas Avery came to live with my husband." (This is clearly a retrospective entry, but one that was probably copied from an earlier book, as it is highly unlikely that Mehetabel would have remembered—or been moved to record—the date of such an event years after the fact.) The Thomas Avery Mehetabel refers to was a local youth who was likely serving an apprenticeship with John Coit. In exchange for a boy's labor, the shipbuilder was expected to instruct him in the "art and mystery of a shipwright" and to teach him "to Read, write & cipher so far as to keep a tradesman Book" of accounts.[15]

Between 1695 and 1705 Mehetabel noted the names of five young men who came to live in her household, ostensibly in conjunction with apprenticeships. It is not known whether the boys arrived in succession, or whether there was some overlap in their residence in the household. That Mehetabel kept a record of these dates suggests that she was assisting her husband in keeping track of the apprentices' terms of service.

The next chronological entry in Mehetabel's diary concerns an event that would have been of much greater significance to her than the beginning of an apprenticeship, yet it is recorded with the same characteristic terseness: "june 25. 1695 we ware maried." Mehetabel and John's courtship had evidently been a brief one, as only seven months elapsed between the date of Mehetabel's move to New London and their wedding day. Although courtship customs of the time bear little resemblance to modern-day dating rituals, young men and women did have the opportunity to socialize—albeit in situations that were, for the most part, supervised by their elders. Visits to each other's homes and attendance at community events would have brought Mehetabel and John together; however, they likely shared few private moments before they were married. Since neither one left behind a written description of their relationship, and none of their letters have survived, it is impossible to know the extent to which romantic love played a part in their decision to marry. In general, however, the Puritans believed that love was essential to a marriage and would naturally precede a union. Deep affection and passion are evident in the letters exchanged by Puritan spouses such as John and Margaret Winthrop, in the poems Anne Bradstreet wrote to her husband, and even in the way minister Peter Thacher referred to his wife throughout his diary as "my dear."[16]

In addition to love, other factors influenced a colonial New Englander's choice of a mate, perhaps the most important being social rank. Individuals from families of similar economic and social backgrounds were believed to be best suited to each other. Mehetabel and John seem to have satisfied this requirement; both were from families highly regarded in their communities for their religious commitment, material success, and civic leadership. Both the Chandlers and the Coits would have taken an active interest in Mehetabel and John's courtship; in fact, before asking Mehetabel to marry him, John Coit almost certainly would have sought the consent of her parents, as well as the approval of his own mother and father. Puritan parents did not commonly arrange the marriages of their children, but their sanction was widely recognized as being integral to the proceedings. Parental opinion became less important as the eighteenth century progressed, however, particularly in the years following the Revolution.[17]

In the process of judging John Coit's ability to take care of their daughter, Elizabeth and John Chandler may well have sought information concerning his character, prospects, and background from both their son John—who, as the local stand-in for Mehetabel's father, would have closely monitored the relationship—and from Elizabeth's New London relatives. Once the match had been accepted by the Chandlers and the Coits, Mehetabel's and John's fathers most likely discussed, in person or by letter, the financial contributions each could make to the marriage. No record of their specific arrangements has survived, but it was common for the bride's family to provide money or household goods worth half of what the groom's family was willing to offer. A woman's parents considered it their duty to do their best to ensure that their daughter would be well provided for, particularly in the event something should happen to her husband.[18]

Mehetabel and John journeyed to Woodstock for their wedding; local church records state that they were married by the newly ordained Reverend Josiah Dwight on the date Mehetabel noted in her diary. By this time construction on Woodstock's meetinghouse had progressed to the point that it could be used for services (it had been delayed by lack of funds promised by Roxbury), and Mehetabel's father was serving as deacon of the church. In the Puritan faith, weddings were conducted as civil rather than religious ceremonies, and during the course of the seventeenth century most were presided over by a magistrate rather than a minister. Mehetabel and John's decision to travel to have their wedding performed by Reverend Dwight may have been motivated in part by their desire to celebrate Woodstock's finally having a minister of its own.

Mehetabel and John would have arrived in Woodstock a few weeks before the wedding, allowing enough time for the traditional banns—a declaration of a couple's intention to marry—to be publicized. This process usually involved an announcement made at successive church meetings and often entailed the posting of a notice on the meetinghouse door. The period preceding Mehetabel and John's wedding could also have included an espousal ceremony, which customarily took place in the bride's parents' home eight days before the wedding and featured a sermon given by her minister on how the couple should properly prepare for marriage. The espousal, like the wedding itself, would have been followed with a celebration. Although these gatherings would not have been marked by "dancing and riotous merrymaking," they would have been joyful feasts attended by both family and friends.[19]

Back in New London, the couple made their home on land John had purchased the previous year. The house in which they took up residence appears
to have been an aged structure, as its prior owner had died in 1665. Although
the home itself may not have been ideal, the rest of the property had much
to recommend it, including meadows, an orchard, and a stream. It was also
centrally located, bordering both the town's main road and the common.

At twenty-two, Mehetabel was of an age that New England women typically married; most brides were in their early twenties, while husbands
tended to be a few years older. The vast majority of early New England
women did marry; however, it was not a state into which they entered
lightly. Although the Puritans viewed marriage as a partnership, based on
mutual affection and with both spouses working toward the common goal
of the well-being of the household, it was far from an equal relationship.
The husband was considered the ultimate authority in a family, and it was
believed to be a wife's duty to bow to his will. Upon marrying, a woman
accepted *feme coverte* status, in which her identity literally became sub-
sumed under that of her husband. Her property and earnings became his to
control, and her labor, her movements, and even her body were regarded as
his possessions. Since the Puritans viewed marriage as a civil contract that
could be dissolved if necessary, early New England law did allow a woman
to obtain a divorce if she had what were considered the proper grounds—
extreme cruelty, bigamy, adultery, or desertion; however, few women pursued this option.[20]

Mehetabel's new role as John's wife would have required not only that
she act as his helpmeet, but that she assume the responsibility of running
their household. In Puritan culture there was great pressure on married
women to become "notable" housewives capable of accomplishing a wide
range of tasks proficiently and economically. Even though Mehetabel had
in all likelihood been performing many traditionally "female" tasks—cooking, cleaning, washing, gardening, dairying, sewing—since she was a child,
her new position as mistress of her own household entailed an additional
layer of duties and accountability. The nature and demands of her daily
work would have been varied and wide ranging. As Carol Berkin has written, a married woman "presided over a productive universe that ran from
kitchen, pantries, cellars, brewhouses, milk houses, and butteries to the garden, well, pigpen, henhouse, and orchard. . . . She was expected to man-
age resources, time, and the available labor to best advantage, balancing
production against maintenance, the needs of daily consumption against

long-term supply." For an early American housewife, managing a household was a constant juggling act that required a continual weighing of needs and setting of priorities.[21]

Of necessity, much of Mehetabel's time would have been taken up with the preparation of meals. At the back of her diary are some fifteen undated recipes, which she likely recorded at some point following her marriage. The foods represented generally fall into three categories: breads and cakes (biscuits, French bread, gingerbread, rusk [a sweet bread], plum cake, and sugar cakes); seafood (boiled fish, boiled trout, and roasted eels); and beverages (balsam, currant, and elderberry wines; "a Swe[e]tt Dram"; and "a fine Drink"). While these few recipes do not furnish anything approaching a complete picture of Mehetabel's diet or culinary skills, they do provide a glimpse into her kitchen, her personal tastes, and contemporary eating habits.

Mehetabel's recipes draw on a wide variety of ingredients that she either produced herself or purchased locally. Included are herbs such as angelica, balsam, catnip, fennel, feverfew, horseradish, hyssop, marigold, marjoram, parsley, rosemary, saffron, sage, savory, snake root, sweet flag, and tansy; dairy items such as milk and butter; and pantry basics such as flour and eggs. The recipes also call for more expensive, imported ingredients—allspice, cloves, currants, ginger, lemons, limes, rum, salt, and sugar—items that would have been available to Mehetabel via New London's involvement in the Atlantic trade (and because she and John could afford them). Oranges, limes, lemons, sugar, and spices were common exports from the West Indies and became increasingly available over time, although they continued to be regarded as specialty items.

In general, urban-dwelling colonists of some means enjoyed a varied diet that included both local and imported foods. For example, in the excavated privy of the seventeenth-century Bostonian Katherine Nanny Naylor (the wife of a merchant whom she eventually divorced for infidelity), were found olive, cherry, peach, and plum pits; strawberry, raisin, and pepper seeds; the bones of cows, pigs, and sheep—and parasite eggs, indicating that Naylor and her family likely suffered from gastrointestinal illnesses. Urban and rural eating habits alike, however, were greatly influenced by the seasons. The New England winter diet usually consisted largely of salted and smoked meat and fish, as well as fruits and vegetables that could be stored over long periods of time, such as apples, potatoes, squash, onions, and pumpkins. The colonists would continue to depend on these dwindling stores in the spring, as they planted their gardens. In the summer, daily fare could be supplemented with

fresh fruits and vegetables, eggs, fish, and wild game. The fall, which brought
the harvest and the slaughtering of animals, marked the "annual period of
abundance."[22]

Cheese and dried peas and beans were staples of the New England diet
throughout the year, as were a variety of baked goods. The breads and cakes
described in Mehetabel's recipes, which were commonly consumed, all draw
on the same basic ingredients: milk, flour, butter, and, with the exception of
the biscuits and French bread, sugar. The colonists were fond of sweets, and
this predilection likely contributed to their generally poor dental health. (It
is worth noting that among Mehetabel's medical remedies are four aimed at
preventing or alleviating toothaches.)

From Mehetabel's seafood recipes—and the proximity of both the ocean
and the Thames River—we can surmise that fish constituted a significant
part of her diet. These recipes rely on a broad cross section of flavoring elements: salt, beer vinegar, sage, fennel, parsley, sweet herbs, horseradish, ginger, and butter. Many call for fish to be boiled, a common method for cooking seafood, and one, for roasted eel, may have been derived from a Native
technique of splitting the eel and turning it on a spit.[23]

The beverage recipes included in Mehetabel's diary—all but one of which
feature wine or spirits as a main ingredient—are also reflective of contemporary dietary habits. Early Americans typically began drinking at a young
age; the common belief was that alcohol was safer to drink than water and
that it had healthful and medicinal properties. A wide variety of alcoholic
beverages were consumed by colonial New Englanders, including wine;
mead; metheglin (a mixture of honey, herbs, and spirits); punch; sack (a
sweet wine); sack-posset (sack mixed with ale, cream, eggs, and spices); and
syllabub (a combination of white wine, lemon, cream, and sugar). Beer and
ale were a fundamental part of daily fare, as they had been in old England,
and cider was also consumed regularly. Since John Coit began operating a
cider mill at some point after his and Mehetabel's marriage, it is likely that
the beverage was a staple in their home.[24]

Rum was also readily available, not only because of its high rate of importation from the West Indies, but also as a result of the proliferation of New
England distilleries (in turn, owing from the importation of West Indian
molasses). Although by the late seventeenth century many ministers had
begun decrying the widespread drinking of rum, claiming a direct link between "rum and ruin," it maintained its popularity. The "fine Drink" recipe
included in Mehetabel's diary is for a rum punch. Combining "4 pounds of

whitte Suger, one quartt of lime Guice; four Gallons of watter . . . one Gallon of Rum, [and] . . . 2 Cloves,"—typical ingredients for a rum punch—the finished product was probably intended for a large gathering and would have been served in a special bowl. (The household inventory taken years later following John Coit's death lists a "Large punch bowl," as well as several "Sillabub pots.")[25]

Mehetabel apparently had a particular liking for fruit wines, as three are included among her recipes. Although a quantity of the wine available in New England was imported from Europe and from the Canary and Azores Islands, the colonists also began producing their own at an early date. Many of these home vintners, like Mehetabel, drew on fruits such as currants, elderberries, blackberries, and cherries. Balsam, often known as balm, which Mehetabel also used, was a medicinal herb believed to produce a wine that would comfort the heart and drive away melancholy. Mehetabel seems to have used other spirits medicinally (a recipe for cough syrup included in the diary calls for brandy), as well as in cooking (wine is included in her recipe for plum cake).[26]

The actual work of cooking presented many challenges for early American homemakers. In the absence of thermometers—and in many cases clocks—housewives had to gauge not only the level of heat required to cook a particular dish but also the amount of time it would take. Most cooking was done over an open hearth, which was not only dangerous—the most frequent cause of death of colonial women was fire—but also labor intensive, and it required a great degree of skill. Housewives had to ensure that the kitchen fire was always kept alight, as restarting it was a time-consuming process that involved flint, steel, and tinder. They also had to maintain a sufficient supply of water and see that food was properly preserved, given the lack of true refrigeration. Most colonial cooks had a limited range of utensils at their disposal—some kettles, skillets, pots, and pans—and many kitchen tools had to serve double duty. A paddle used for stirring stews, for example, might also be used to stir lye to make soap. In general, with the exception of the introduction of the swinging crane and the relocation of the wall oven from the rear to the side of the fireplace, few advances in kitchen technology were made until well into the eighteenth century.[27]

The physical constraints of the colonial kitchen, as well as English tradition, influenced the types of meals that were produced in early America, a substantial number of which were boiled, stewed, or fried. Dishes became more elaborate in the eighteenth century, primarily owing to the proliferation of cookbooks. Although the first American cookbook would not appear until the last quarter of the eighteenth century, the colonists had some access to English cookbooks and housewifery manuals, such as Gervase Markham's *The English Housewife* (1615); William Rabisha's *The Whole Boddy of Cookery Dissected* (1661); and Hannah Wolley's *The Queen-Like Closet, or Rich Cabinet Stored with All Manner of Rare Receipts for Preserving, Candying and Cookery* (1670). A large part of the colonial American woman's knowledge of cookery, however, was, like her medical wisdom, passed down orally or in manuscript form from female relatives. Many surviving early American manuscript cookbooks, in fact, contain recipes authored by several generations of a single family. (A number of these volumes also catalog medical remedies alongside the recipes or in a separate section; Doro Petre's 1705 manuscript cookbook, for example, lists remedies from front to back and recipes from back to front.) Although the recipes included in Mehetabel's diary appear to have been written in her hand, the one for a "Swe[e]tt Dram" looks to have been recorded by someone else, perhaps one of her daughters or a later descendant.[28]

Women often personalized published cookbooks by adding their own recipes and notations on a book's blank pages; these volumes, like the manuscript cookbooks, were frequently passed down in families as heirlooms. Women also commonly copied printed recipes into their manuscript books. Mehetabel, for example, seems to have adopted a trout recipe from Izaak Walton's *Compleat Angler,* first published in 1653. Her recipe reads: "to boile Trouts wash them very Clean & Dry them with a Cloath then take out his guts and wipe itt very well within but wash itt not, and give it 3 gashes with a knife on one side only to ye bone. boile it in beer viniger & water & Sweet Herbs and . . . Horse-Radish Roots and the Rind of a lemmon, garnish your dish with slices of lemmon, and with your butter putt shaved horse-Radish & genger." Walton's directs: "Wash and dry your Trout with a clean Napkin; then open him, and having taken out his Guts, and all the Blood, wipe him very clean within, but wash him not, and give him three Scotches with a Knife, to the Bone, on one Side." Walton goes on to recommend that the fish be boiled with beer, vinegar, water, wine, horseradish root, and sweet herbs and then served with butter, horseradish, ginger, and lemon.[29]

Along with the recipes, Mehetabel also transcribed a few household hints in her diary. They include instructions for concocting a purple dye ("to make a good purple you must first Dye itt blue and then boile itt in bran & Allom-water & itt will be a speciall purple"); for preventing the rusting of iron ("take Lead filed very small and put so much oyl olive upon it as will cover it in a pot, then make your Iron very clean first, and anoint the Iaron with the oyl after it hath stood nine days"); and for preserving quinces ("take your quinces and put them in to a little vessel of small beer when it hath Done working").[30]

It is likely that Mehetabel's recipes were derived from a combination of oral, manuscript, and printed sources. She may well have obtained a basic repertoire from her mother that she later expanded as she became a more experienced cook with access to a wider range of ingredients, printed cookbooks, and the knowledge of other women. Mehetabel's recipes not only reflect the varied resources at her disposal, but they also speak to a continuity of tradition.

Given the female custom of sharing domestic knowledge, Mehetabel's transition to household manager may have been eased by the realization that she could always turn to a local female relative or neighbor for assistance or advice. Her extensive Douglas and Coit kinship ties, the proximity of other households, and the fact that activities such as washing and spinning often brought women together would have ensured that Mehetabel would not have lacked for female companionship. This contact may have helped fill the void left by her separation from her mother and sister, as well as helped lighten the weight of her many new responsibilities.[31]

Mehetabel's first diary entry following her marriage concerned the arrival of a new resident in her household; she writes that on "may 2 1696 Wait Mayhew came to live here." Wait Mayhew was the fifteen-year-old son of the lately deceased New London mariner John Mayhew and his wife, Joanne, and like Thomas Avery, he probably came to live with Mehetabel and John in conjunction with a shipbuilding apprenticeship. Wait's presence would have translated into extra help around the shipyard for John, but it also would have created additional work for Mehetabel, since the mistress of a household was expected to provide any servants or apprentices residing under her roof with food, clothing, and "moral guidance." These added responsibilities may have been particularly taxing for Mehetabel at the time, given that in May of 1696 she was in the final stages of her first pregnancy.[32]

Mehetabel marked the birth of her baby, likely named in honor of both her husband and her father, in her diary: "may 25 1696 John Coit was born." Although she provides no details, it is likely that her delivery was attended by a midwife, perhaps Sarah Latham Mayhew, who, according to Joshua

Hempstead, was "a very Sober Quiet & usefull woman" who served as "ye chief midwife in the Town for many years." A number of other women were probably also in attendance, since childbirth, like many other rites of passage in early America, was a community event. Although men and children were excluded from the delivery room, female relatives, friends, and neighbors turned out both to lend their support and to socialize.[33]

In the earliest stages of labor, Mehetabel would have acted as hostess, serving refreshments such as "groaning beer" and "groaning cake" to her guests. She likely would have prepared for the event by making up her bed with special "childbed" linen she had embroidered specifically for the occasion. (Mehetabel's late sister Hannah's childbed linen had been of sufficient value to be included in the household inventory taken after her husband Moses's death.) Until Mehetabel's labor became difficult, the mood was probably celebratory, as her attendants exchanged news, stories of past deliveries, and even bawdy tales. Once her labor advanced, the women would have acted as the midwife's assistants, fetching her apparatus and helping to position Mehetabel. The presence of women who themselves had survived childbirth, in many cases numerous times, must have been reassuring to Mehetabel as a first-time mother-to-be.[34]

Although Mehetabel was likely excited about becoming a mother, she may also have approached the time of her delivery with a feeling of dread, since childbirth could be life-threatening for both mother and baby. Throughout the colonial era, significant numbers of women lost their lives as a result of prolonged labor, hemorrhages, convulsions, and abnormal deliveries such as breech births. They also faced potentially serious postpartum complications; in fact, more women died as a result of an infection known as "childbed fever" than in childbirth itself. The birthing experience and first few weeks of life were equally dangerous for babies; colonial New England's infant death rate has been estimated at one in ten and as high as three in ten in congested areas where infections could more easily spread. To encourage Mehetabel to place her trust in God no matter the outcome of her experience, Martha Coit may well have given her daughter-in-law a copy of her childbirth testimonial at this time, a document that probably would have done little to allay Mehetabel's fears.[35]

Even those women who had easy births and whose babies thrived might still suffer physical discomfort in connection with motherhood. A considerable number of women experienced soreness when breastfeeding, and some developed inflammation, abscesses, and infection. Mehetabel evidently encountered such problems, for included in her diary is a remedy for easing "sore nipples" through the application of "the marrow of a Deers foot." Most women breastfed their children for at least ten months; however, following that time many took "weaning journeys"—extended visits to family or friends—intended to break the child's pattern of nursing.[36]

It is uncertain when Mehetabel's family first had an opportunity to see her new baby. Given New London's distance from Woodstock, it is unlikely that her mother and sister Sarah were present at the birth. Further delay may have been caused by the increased risk involved in travel between the two towns the summer after John was born in the wake of an Indian attack on Oxford, Woodstock's closest neighbor. In August of 1696 some "hostiles" believed to be Mohawks killed an Oxford man and his three children, as well as a male neighbor. The children's mother and uncle were able to escape to Woodstock, where the townspeople sent out an alarm to both Massachusetts and Connecticut military leaders. Their summons was answered by Major James Fitch, then stationed at Norwich, Connecticut, who arrived with a company largely made up of Mohegan and Pequot soldiers. Although the party thoroughly searched the surrounding countryside, the perpetrators were never found.

In the aftermath of the Oxford attack, a number of families left the Woodstock area; however, when the Massachusetts government declared Woodstock a "frontier town" the following October, residents were prohibited from abandoning the settlement and leaving it unprotected. Woodstock was expected to provide for its own defense without outside assistance, a situation that left its inhabitants feeling isolated and abandoned. These sentiments are reflected in a letter Mehetabel received during this period from her nineteen-year-old sister Sarah—the only letter the sisters exchanged that has survived. Sarah's letter may have reached Mehetabel via their brother John, who had been appointed superintendent of the "friendly" Wabbaquassets and Mohegans by the Massachusetts government following the Oxford attack. Although still officially residing in New London, John likely traveled frequently between the two areas to carry out his duties, which included directing members of these tribes "where to hunt and what sign to wear" to avoid being mistaken as hostiles.[37]

Dated October 19, 1696, Sarah's letter expresses an understandable anxiety over Woodstock's imperiled position, but it also has a reproachful tone; some of her fear seems to have been channeled into resentment of Mehetabel's good fortune of being "in prosperity."

Dear Sister

   you knowing my curcumstances will bear with my long silence, & I being Confident of y^t, may possibly suffer something of a neglect in me, yet the Respects, Love, & Dear affection y^t I bear towards you will not suffer a totall neglect. accept these lines I send as ye product of y^t Dear affection y^t longs to vent it self into y^{or} boosom; if I think it so long & tedious a thing y^t I should not hear from you y^t are in prosperity, how do you think I can take it y^t you are so Little concerned for me in so great adversaty, & suffering? Me thinks I want to feel ye poundings of y^{or} bowels,[38] & not to have a word all this while is very tedious. Let these mourning lines then Rowze up y^{or} affections. have you forgot Garrison fears? if not then Deign to bear a Sympathy, & let ye expressions of y^{or} pitty, & Compassion be sound Refreshm^t, & let y^{or} fervant prayers be allwayse on ye wing on my behalf who Live at ye mouth of the grave, & know not but it may be my portion to be forc^t in by ye butcherly hands of barberous Miscreants. but I hope better, & have cause to be thank-full for past, & present experience of Divine protection, thus with my thank-full acknowlegem^t for all y^{or} former Love, & kindnesses & my Dear Love to y^{or} self & my Dear brother[39] I Rest y^{or} only, & affectionate sister till Death
   woodstock octob 19 1696   S : C[40]

Whatever their basis in reality, Sarah's criticisms evidently brought forth results, as it appears Mehetabel asked Sarah to pay her a visit not long afterward. At least so we can surmise, given the circumstantial evidence that less than eight months after writing the letter, Sarah married John Coit's brother William. Mehetabel was likely delighted to have her sister near her again, for despite the nagging tone of Sarah's letter, it does speak of strong ties between the two sisters. This happiness, however, may have been tempered for both women by the fact that their parents were still so distant and living in such uncertain circumstances.[41]

CHAPTER FOUR
Establishing Roots, 1697–1706

MEHETABEL HAD married into one large and established New London family and was related through her mother to another. Nonetheless, it may have taken her some years to set down her own roots in the community. Her involvement with the Puritan church, which she seems to have attended regularly even though she did not become a full member, likely facilitated the process. During Mehetabel's first years in New London, the congregation was engaged in building a new meetinghouse, as the previous structure had burned down. Arson was the suspected cause, and although the charges were never proved, several members of a local religious sect known as the Rogerenes, followers of the dissenter John Rogers, were prosecuted for the crime.[1]

The Rogerenes had become notorious for their rejection of infant baptism, of the sanctity of the Sabbath, and of an established ministry, among other heresies. New London was a more tolerant community than many of its neighbors, but the Rogerenes actively sought confrontation with those who disagreed with them, lecturing passersby on the street and occasionally interrupting services at the meetinghouse. In March 1694, for example, John Rogers's sister Bathsheba barged into a church meeting to proclaim that she had worked on the Sabbath—an offense for which she was subsequently put into the stocks. Later that day, John Rogers disrupted the same service by attempting to auction off a wheelbarrow full of merchandise he had carted into the meetinghouse. (He had earlier managed to break out of jail, where he had been incarcerated himself for working on the Sabbath.)[2]

The Reverend Gurdon Saltonstall, a Harvard graduate who in 1691, at the age of twenty-five, had begun leading the New London congregation, did, despite his traditional views on obedience to authority, attempt to compromise with the Rogerenes. According to John Rogers Jr., at one point after Saltonstall became governor of Connecticut in 1708, he even promised them that if they would only "be quiet and worship God in [their] own way according to [their] Consciences, he would punish any . . . that should disturb [them] in [their] Worship." (The Rogerenes, however, declined to be "quiet.") Mehetabel, unfortunately, left no firsthand account of the Rogerene controversy, and she was equally silent on the topic of her minister. One admirer of Saltonstall's, however, was the travel diarist and later New London resident Sarah Kemble Knight. After passing an evening with Saltonstall and his family in 1704 on a journey to New Haven, Knight commented that she had been "very handsomely and plentifully treated and Lodg'd; and made good the Great Character I had before heard concerning him: viz. that hee was the most affable, courteous, Genero's and best of men."[3]

By the time Mehetabel began attending the New London church, she had undoubtedly spent innumerable hours in prayer, private meditation, and religious reading. Her diary does not provide specific information regarding her personal spiritual beliefs, but it does contain a variety of biblical excerpts, religious musings, and quotations from contemporary theological works that help shed some light on them. (All of these entries are undated.) The first such example lists the ten plagues visited upon the Egyptians for not releasing the Israelites, as related in the Old Testament's Book of Exodus:

> the ten plagues of Egypt
> 1 All waters turnd to blood
> 2 frogs numberless do sworm
> 3 lice loathsom thick as Dust
> 4 flys numberless do sworm
> 5 a murrin bests Disstroys
> 6 blains vex boath man & beast
> 7 Hail & fire spoil somthings
> 8 strang locust spoil the Rest
> 9 thick Darkness palpable
> 10 the Egytians first born Die
> these ten plagues [of] Egypt felt
> Rewards of Cruelty[4]

The Egyptians' oppression of the Israelites and Pharoah's obstinacy in failing to heed God's many "signs and wonders" result in terrible punishments: starvation, pestilence, festering boils. In its most basic form, this story's lesson—that disobeying God's will can only lead to destruction—was one that every Puritan would have learned at a young age. Mehetabel's inclusion of this passage in her diary can also be considered in light of the Puritans' consciousness of themselves as God's chosen people, like the Israelites. As the Puritan minister John Cotton once wrote, "The same covenant which God made with the national church of Israel and their seed . . . is the very same (for substance) and none other which the Lord maketh with any Congregational Church and our seed." The New World as the new Promised Land was a concept that had great force among the Puritans; it was also one with great staying power, since it has persisted, albeit in a more secular form, to the present day.[5]

Another entry in Mehetabel's diary based on biblical content concerns the story of John the Baptist as told in the New Testament:

> *Herod might have kept*
> *his oath, and not have*
> *cut of[f] the baptist*
> *head, he only promist to*
> *grant what she ask't*
> *to the half of his*
> *kingdom, wheras the*
> *prophets head was worth*
> *more then the whole*[6]

Mehetabel's interpretation of the circumstances surrounding John the Baptist's death—that Herod could have kept his promise to grant Herodias's daughter anything she asked for that was worth half of his kingdom without having John the Baptist executed, since his "head was worth more then the whole"—reveals an imaginative engagement with the stories of the Bible. To Mehetabel and her contemporaries, biblical narratives possessed entertainment value as well as instructive value. In a society without novels, plays, or a wide range of culturally sanctioned amusements, reading the dramatic sagas related in the Bible, alone or aloud with others, was a popular pastime, and some families read their favorite stories aloud so often that they were learned by heart.[7]

Evidence of Mehetabel's extrabiblical reading is found in an entry in which she copied a passage from the British author Matthew Henry's *Commentary on the Bible* (Henry was widely read in the colonies, and his works would not have been difficult for Mehetabel to obtain):

> *the patience of god to*
> *towards sinners is the*
> *greatest miracle in*
> *the world*[8]

Mehetabel seems to have been moved by the notion of God's powers of forgiveness and empathy, which diverged from the emphasis in Puritan discourse on his wrathful and vengeful qualities. Although Mehetabel would have considered herself a sinner, she, like her contemporaries, would also have hoped that God would reward the faithful with absolution and grace. The Puritans were familiar with the mercy God showed the repentant prodigal son, and many shared the expectation, as articulated by Mehetabel's mother in her poem, that there would come a time when "Sin and Sorrow now are past away / No Night of Darkness but Eternall Day," when true believers would "triumph in those Joys above / And [be] . . . Posest with Christs most Sweetest Love."[9]

Mehetabel's recording of these religious writings in her diary implies that she took her faith seriously; however, she also seems to have been wary of the hypocrisy with which some Puritans practiced their religion. Her transcription of an unattributed poem, variations of which were printed throughout the colonial period (Benjamin Franklin copied a version into his own commonplace book), could be taken as an ironic commentary on the observance of fast days.

> *the sick man fasts*
> *because he cannot eat*
> *the poor man fasts*
> *because he hath no meat*
> *the myser fasteth*
> *to augment his store*
> *the glutton fasts*
> *cause he can eate no more*
> *the just man fasts*
> *because he hath offended*
> *the Hypocrite*
> *because he[']d be Commended*[10]

Likewise, Mehetabel's inclusion of the following lines suggests that she had no patience for those who took pleasure in the personal failings of their neighbors:

> *a phylosopher seeing two*
> *vicious persons together*
> *cryed out see how the*
> *viper is borrowing*
> *p[o]ison from the asp.*
>
> *twas the wish of one*
> *that there was a law*
> *for hanging tale barers*
> *by the toung, and tale*
> *hearers by the ears.*[11]

The first of these excerpts is taken from a passage in *The Christian Man's Calling* (1662–1665), a three-volume work by the Puritan divine George Swinnock, that refers to people's ability to bring out either the best or the worst in one another. The second is a quote from the Roman playwright Plautus that was included in Arthur Warwick's popular *Spare Minutes; or Resolved Meditations and Premeditated Resolutions* (1632). Mehetabel's combination of these two references can be read as a direct expression of her aversion to gossip, which could do so much damage to one's reputation in a community.

Mehetabel was not without a sense of humor about her religion. A bit of witty verse taken from a volume of poems by Henry Needler, which first appeared in print in 1724, suggests that she was well aware of the sometimes woefully inadequate abilities of clergymen to inspire their congregations.

> *Deliverd in a Dull*
> *and lifeles strain,*
> *the best Discorses, no*
> *attention gain,*
> *for if the orater be*
> *half a sleep,*
> *he[']ll scarce his auditors*
> *from snoring keep.*[12]

Mehetabel's transcription of this rhyme is significant not only because it constitutes a rare extant display of a colonial woman's sense of humor, but in that it represents an almost subversive critique of some of the most esteemed and powerful members of her society.

Approximately two years after their marriage, Mehetabel and John became the owners of a new house; Mehetabel notes in her diary that on "June 4–1697

our house was Raised[;] ye 23 of Septem^br following we cam to live in itt."
House-raisings, during which neighbors gathered to help hoist a home's
framework into place, were festive occasions at which food and drink were
served and the community came out to celebrate with the property owners.[13]
Mehetabel and John's new home was undoubtedly similar to those in which
Mehetabel had lived in both Roxbury and Woodstock. Most seventeenth-
century New England houses were built according to a basic floor plan that
encompassed a central chimney and allowed for two main rooms on the first
floor—a "hall" where most of the day-to-day living occurred and a more
formal parlor—and corresponding bed and storage chambers above. Many
dwellings also included, or later acquired, a lean-to addition at the rear that
functioned as a kitchen. The resulting sloping roofline at the back of the
house gave it the appearance of a saltbox, providing the name for this architectural style.

Although Mehetabel and John's house has not survived, it is highly likely
that it resembled Joshua Hempstead's home, which is still standing. Hempstead's house was constructed by his father in 1678; its gabled, asymmetrical
facade reflects qualities of English medieval architectural forms that remained
popular in New England for many years after the first settlement. Building methods changed little over the course of the seventeenth century; most
New England homes were of timber-framed construction and insulated with
wattle and daub, a mixture of clay and straw. (Like Hempstead's house, Mehetabel and John's home's insulation may also have included seaweed.) Later
in the colonial period, with the wider availability of English architectural
pattern books, the growing number of skilled builders, and increased affluence among certain segments of society, buildings adopted more classical,
symmetrical, and formal detail. As John Coit became more successful, and as
New London grew more urban and sophisticated, Mehetabel and John may
have remodeled their home to reflect some of these newer design concepts.[14]

In the beginning, the interior of Mehetabel and John's home would also
have looked much like Hempstead's. The walls would have been plastered
or covered in wood paneling, and structural elements such as beams and
corner posts would have been left visible. It is also likely that, at least at
first, their house was left unpainted both inside and outside, and that it
featured small, irregularly placed windows. Although the probate inventory
taken after John Coit's death in 1744 indicates that he and Mehetabel eventually acquired a goodly amount of furniture, as well as high-quality table
and bed linens and a variety of dining and serving pieces, they would have

Joshua Hempstead house, New London, owned and operated by
Connecticut Landmarks. *Photograph by Nick Lacey.*

had only a modest number of belongings early in their married life. Their
rooms would have been minimally furnished and would have been used for
multiple functions—cooking, eating, visiting, sleeping—thus providing the
occupants with limited privacy.[15]

It is evident from John Coit's will that their property had a cellar and a
well—in her 1895 history of New London, Frances Caulkins observed that
there had been a "gushing spring" on the lot in colonial times—and that
it also eventually included a barn and other outbuildings, such as a blacksmith's shop and ropewalk. Attached to the kitchen there may have been a
buttery, a room built deeper into the ground to provide a cool place in which
to store food, as well as a stillroom, where Mehetabel would have operated
what one writer has termed "a combination brewery, dairy and apothecary's
shop." Here Mehetabel would have "made her cheeses, started her wines and
sugar-fermented drinks, brewed beers, set dyes . . . and made all her plasters,
salves, oils and waters." She would have grown much of what she needed for
these concoctions in her own garden.[16]

Mehetabel and John's house-raising took place five days before Sarah and
William were to be married in Woodstock by Reverend Dwight, so it is
uncertain whether they would have been able to attend the wedding. Giv-
en their dual relationship to the bride and groom, however, they may have

decided to make the journey despite their numerous obligations at home and the persistence of "Garrison fears" in the aftermath of the Oxford ambush. Woodstock remained in a crisis: several false alarms over the ensuing months had sustained a level of panic, and the perceived need to concentrate on the town's defense had brought other areas of its development to a virtual standstill. Attendance at town meetings had become sporadic, the meetinghouse was left unfinished, and the roads were suffering for lack of maintenance. (One local historian noted that, during this period, "few town acts were recorded, although on one occasion eight pence worth of drink was ordered to keep up spirits.")[17]

Woodstock was not the only New England community that continued to be in danger of attack as the French and Indian wars, which raged intermittently between 1689 and 1763, continued. Although the likelihood of an Indian assault on New London during this period was not great, the town did fear a possible attack from French warships. In the summer of 1697 the Reverend Gurdon Saltonstall wrote to his parents, who themselves had at one time lodged as many as sixty neighbors (and the family cow) in their Haverhill garrison house, that New London had recently been "alarm'd by the French. . . . A Ship of 16 Guns & . . . 110 Men," he wrote, "hath been Seen from our Town; She is still . . . hereabout, and we are ready to think may waite for More." Additional soldiers were shortly thereafter dispatched to the fort at New London, but the anticipated confrontation did not take place.[18]

Occasional sightings of French ships off the New London coast and Mehetabel's concern for her parents may have cast a shadow over the many positive developments in her life: her new home, growing family, and the proximity of her sister Sarah. It is uncertain how often Mehetabel received news of her parents; only three letters from her mother—along with an undated and mostly illegible fragment—have survived, and Mehetabel's responses have been lost. Mehetabel received the first of these letters, evidently intended to thank her for some small gifts she had sent her parents via Sarah, in the summer of 1698. Although Elizabeth Chandler did not refer directly to Woodstock's problems, her tone was clearly melancholy. Writing that she desired to be at her "jorneys end," she indicated that she was "in a poor condition." Unfortunately, the paper is torn and bears some discoloration, so in several places there are gaps or only parts of words are legible.[19]

> Lovi[n]g Daughter with much Difficulty next to an impossibill[ity] I am scrabling a Line or two as an expresion of gratitude for all y^{or} kindness manifested in y^r tokens by Sarah, w^c I cannot Recompence at present, but I Do

not forgit y^r Love, I am in a poor condition to write as Sarah can inform you, I long to see you but cannot expect it I hope you are hastening towards ye new Jerusalem where let god please to let us meet w^n [we pass in Death?], I long to be at my jorneys end, oh! I long for night y^t I may go to rest, y^t night y^t shall tern to an everlasting Day, where I shall have time enough or rather eternity enough [. . .] may a Done with this [weary?] world Dear child minde ye one thing needfull & let not ye world [retard?] you but eye y^t [Release?] of reward. We had a [. . .] Sacrament last Sabath Day about christs glory as ye reward of his passion. from heb 2:9.[20] christs glo[ry] compensates all his sufferings, & so it shall be with all his members y^t we may get a reall interest in christ, y^t so we may share in his [. . .]. Sarah has got my poor book [. . .] a hard case, but shee will have [. . .] all. pray let me charge [you?] not to expose it to veiw, theres no such instance to let such a thing go out of sight while Living, but if you may have benifitt I am content to Deny my self. I ad not but [hearty?] prayer & Love I am y^r Loving mother

Woodstock June 1 1698

Here, as in her "poor book"—her "Meditation, or Poem" she let Sarah borrow—Elizabeth Chandler was relying on her faith to see her through a difficult time.

That fall Sarah delivered a son whom she and William named Daniel; a few weeks later Mehetabel had her second child, a boy she and John named Joseph. (Mehetabel marked the date of her son's birth in her diary: "november. 15 Joseph Coit was born. 1698.") Although two and a half years separated John's and Joseph's births, such a gap was not unusual for the time. Since the practice of breastfeeding served as a natural contraceptive, "suppress[ing] the terms," periods of twenty to thirty months frequently separated births within a family.[21]

Both sets of mothers and sons fared well; however, the Coit family's pleasure at the arrival of two new babies was not long afterward dimmed by the death of John Coit's brother Daniel, after whom Sarah and William's baby had likely been named. The circumstances surrounding the twenty-one-year-old Daniel's death are unclear; Mehetabel writes only that "feb 3. 1698/9 Daniell Coit dyed att longiland." Daniel, who was unmarried, had probably worked at the family shipyard, as his brothers William and Solomon seem to have done. (John Coit's brother Joseph had graduated from Harvard in 1697 and become a minister; a few years later he joined the first graduating class at Yale.) Daniel's passing must certainly have been a heavy blow for Martha Coit, who had already lost so many children.[22]

In the fall of 1699, Mehetabel received another letter from her mother, only a portion of which has survived. Elizabeth addressed it to "her very

Loving Daughter Mehetabel Coite att New London I hope." Elizabeth's "I hope" reflected the harsh reality of a seventeenth-century existence, particularly on the frontier: lives could change—and end—in an instant. This letter, like Elizabeth's earlier one, expresses a deep sadness over her distance from Mehetabel, but also confidence that they will be reunited after death. Although the letter is as pious in tone as her previous one, it is also successful in conveying her "Dear Love" and affection for her daughter.

> I long to see you all & my poor Little grandchildren, & other Dear friends, I Little thought w^n I parted with you y^t it would be so hard a thing to get to gather as I finde it now on both sides either for you or me. but why should we complaine when tis by ye all wise Dispose of a gracious god y^t [sets & layes?] out all ye bounds of o^r habitations & besides 'tis but a Little while & we must part by Death, & we knowing this should endeavour to have weaned affections y^t so we may not be surprized when we come to ye knowledge of such bereavments, ye Lord grant y^t we may all of us so Live in this world by being interested in christ & ye covenant of grace, y^t thô we must part by Death, yet we may obtaine such a Joyfull meeting at ye resurrection y^t we may never part more but enjoy eternall fellowship & society.
>
> I give you hearty thanks for yor by, & yor Love to yor Father, I am heartily sorry I have nothing in all y^e [world?] I can send you at present I give my Dear Love to yor self & to all ye rest of o^r friends & am yor most Dear & affectionate Mother till Death
>
> Woodstock october 7 1699 Elizabeth Chandler[23]

Shortly after Elizabeth Chandler wrote her letter, Mehetabel noted in her diary the arrival of a local boy in his late teens who was likely another shipyard apprentice: "October 21. 1699 Joseph Shaply came to live here." By this time, John Coit had become the owner of the family business, and in December 1699 the town of New London granted him a more favorable site for the shipyard, where the water's depth would allow for the building of larger vessels. It was a busy spot, near a landing place used by both private boats and the town ferry. (Many years later, after John Coit built a wharf in this location, he retained rights to the ferry.) The shipyard's expansion was timely, as the need for locally built vessels would increase after New London was named one of Connecticut's eight legal ports in 1702. Although New London was already one of the colony's major market towns, its official designation as a legal port boosted trading activity and ushered in a period of prosperity that lasted, for the most part, until the years before the Revolution.[24]

Not long after John received the land grant, Mehetabel gave birth to their third child; she writes that "feb 18. 1700 Samuell Coit was born." Mehetabel was safely delivered, and the baby was healthy. In contrast, Sarah's baby, born several months later, did not survive her first year. The child had been named Elizabeth, perhaps in honor of both Sarah and Mehetabel's mother and their deceased sister.[25]

Mehetabel's diary provides scant details concerning her life over the next couple of years. In 1701 she noted that another young man came to board with the family—"Septem^r 1701 Samuell Loomes came to live here"—and the following year she recorded the birth of her fourth child: "june. 1 1702. Thomas Coite was born." (In January 1702 her sister Sarah had delivered a healthy boy named William.) Mehetabel's next entry, dated almost a year later, briefly related the fact of her father's death: "Aprill. 15 father Chandler dyed. 1703. in his 69^t year." The cause of John Chandler's death is unknown, but it may have been simply old age. His contemporaries would have agreed that, at sixty-nine, he had lived a long life. His gravestone, which still stands in the Woodstock burial ground, identifies him as "Deacon," a position connoting the dignity and authority he had acquired despite his earlier indiscretions.[26]

By the time of his death, John Chandler had amassed an estate valued at more than five hundred pounds, which included over four hundred acres of land, as well as additional undivided acreage in Woodstock and neighboring Mashamoquet (which would later become the town of Pomfret). He had also retained fifty acres in Roxbury. In his will, he specified that Elizabeth Chandler was to have the Woodstock house "to dwell in; the use of one milks cow; a bed and furniture, necessary utensils for the same, and Eight pounds per Annum." He also willed her "What more of my Estate her necessity may require," to be paid by their children according to the proportion they received of the estate. John junior was named executor and was deeded a double portion of the land, as well as the house. (Although Elizabeth Chandler had been given the right to remain in her home, she, like most widows of the time, was not made its actual owner.) The rest of the estate was divided equally among John, Mehetabel, Sarah, and Joseph, with Joseph receiving three hundred acres of Mashamoquet property and an extra ten pounds. The will also included bequests to the children of John Chandler's deceased offspring: ten pounds was granted to Hannah Draper, and Woodstock land valued at ten pounds was allotted to Robert Mason. John Chandler also willed five shillings to his former son-in-law, Robert Mason senior, indicating that they had remained on good terms after Mason's remarriage following Elizabeth Chandler Mason's death.[27]

After John Chandler's passing, Mehetabel's brother John and his family left New London to settle permanently in Woodstock. Although he now owned his parents' home, John also retained ownership of the property he had bought when he first moved to Woodstock, and he and his family may have moved back into his former residence. Elizabeth Chandler likely welcomed the opportunity of having more family around; by this time John and Mary had five children, including a baby daughter named in Elizabeth's honor. Mehetabel's brother Joseph, who was almost twenty at the time of their father's death, continued to reside with his mother for a time, but eventually married and settled on the Pomfret lands he had inherited. The Chandlers had relatives already living in Pomfret, including Nathaniel and Samuel Gary, sons of Elizabeth Chandler's sister Anna, and Philemon Chandler, son of John Chandler's brother William.

Even though her father had been a man of advanced years, his passing may have deeply grieved Mehetabel; yet she was to experience an even greater loss soon after his death. Within the space of two days in May, Mehetabel's son Samuel and Sarah's husband William passed away. Mehetabel registered these painful events in her diary—"may 7. 1703 William Coit dyed"; "may. 9. 1703 Samuell Coit dyed in his 4th year"—but provided no additional details. That Samuel and William died within days of each other, however, suggests that New London may have been experiencing some type of epidemic. The previous year outbreaks of smallpox and scarlet fever had occurred in Boston, and it is possible that a strain of one or both diseases had made its way to the New London area.[28]

The death of children was a fact of life in colonial New England. Owing to their susceptibility to infection, rates of mortality among young children surpassed those of any other age group. Fatal childhood accidents were also common. Mehetabel's sister Sarah had almost lost her young son William when he nearly drowned at the age of seven, an incident that Mehetabel recorded in her diary: "june 14. 1706 billy Coit fell into the cove, & was allmost drowned." In the precarious world of early America, many parents must ultimately have felt powerless to protect their children.[29]

The realization that children might not survive to adulthood did not make the loss of a child any less agonizing. As the Puritan poet Edward Taylor wrote in "Upon Wedlock and the Death of Children," although he eventually resigned himself after God "crop[ped]" the "sweet breathd . . . flowre" of his baby daughter, it was yet an "unlookt for, dolesome, darksome houre." Mehetabel's grief may have been intensified by the knowledge that her mother and sister were also suffering. While she and Sarah could give each other support during this period, their distance from Woodstock would have prevented them from providing their mother with the same type of solace.

For her part, Elizabeth Chandler attempted to console her daughters in the only way available to her at the time: she sent them a letter. Dated June 12, 1703, it is addressed to "Hon^d Mehetabel & Sarah Coite at New London" and was later labeled by Mehetabel as "a letter from Mother Chandler." Elizabeth included an apology for not having contacted her daughters sooner; inscribed vertically on the left-hand side of the page is the line: "I have had no opportunity to write before now." As in her previous correspondence, she expressed her "yearn[ing]" and "long[ing]" for her daughters, but also emphasized the need to "patiently & quietly submit to ye will of god in every thing." Although she acknowledged the "sharp & cutting" nature of Mehetabel and Sarah's late afflictions, and noted that she "heartily mourn[ed]" for them, she urged them not to "repine at [God's] Dispensations."

Dear Children,

I am very sencible of yor sorrowful condition by yor late bereavments, & Do heartily mourn for you, & condole with you, tho, [. . .] am Distant from you. y^t yor affliction has been sharp & cutting mu[st?] be acknowledged, but it must also be acknowledged y^t it is ordered by [a?] wise, holy, & heavenly hand, by a good & gracious god, a god whose path[s?] are all mercy & truth to such as Love him & keep his covenant. when we consider y^t we & all y^t we have is at gods Dispossing, it should not seem strange to us if he takes any Comfort from us, when, how, or which he pleaseth, it is o^r Duty at all times to be at gods Dispose & not repine at his Dispensations, neither Draw black conclusions (as we are somtimes apt to Do) under sharp visitations. Remembring y^t god hath told us y^t he chasteneth those whom he loveth, & scourgeth every son whom he Receiveth, & hath commanded us nether to Despise his corrections, nor yet faint when rebuked of him. ye Lord has wise ends in every Dispensation of his providence, & is but fulfilling what he has before Decreed & y^t in infinite wisdom, & he will make every stroak of Divine providence conduce[?] to his own glory, & his peoples good, & y^r in we ought to finde satisfaction. David found y^t it was good for him y^t he was afflicted & Job blessed a taking as well as a giving god, & god hath promised y^t all things shall work together for ye good of y^m that love god, & if all things then y^t [seem to be?] cutting afflictions y^t w^c seems [very?] cross & bitter, & we are apt to [. . .] maybe y^t any other affliction could have been better born y^n such a [one?] yet god knows w^c is best for us & can bring ye greatest good out of ye greatest evil & make y^t turn to o^r salvation. & it is one of ye highest points of glorifiing god to be meek & patient under sharp afflictions, & it is most certainly o^r Duty not only to comply with ye will of god, but also to study how we may glorifie god in the highest way we are capable off, & it will be no Disadvantage to us afterward if we so do, for it will be ye top of o^r glori in heven, if we have glorified god on earth. gods works are all beautifull in his time ecle 3.11.[30] it maybe it Doth not look so to us at present (no affliction being at present joyous, but grivious) yet in y^e [end ?] god will make a Discovery of ye beauty of all his Dispensations to a curcumstance. ye lord make up all o^r Losses in him self.

in perticuler I would commend to poor Sarah y^t scripture psal.68.5[31] a father of ye fatherless & a Judge of the widdows, is god in his holy habitation. & if shee should meet with unkindness from any let her Read Exodus.21.22.23.24. & see how god promises to Defend ye widdow & ye fatherless.

the lord grant y^t you both, & so I, & all of us may patiently & quietly submit to ye will of god in every thing, knowing y^t if we belong to god it will be but a very Litle while before we shall have all o^r tears wiped off from o^r eyes, & we shall meet with all o^r Dear relations & friends & never be seperated any more. the lord prepare us for o^r change, y^t we may be Ready [for death?] if it should come suddenly to us as to others, happy they y^t are Re[ady for y^e?] step they may pass from earth to heaven. I am under much [. . .] write, but my bowels yearn towards you both, & I long to see y[ou, but I know?] not when, nor how I shall get to you, & y^rfore must rest cont[ent to send?] my Dear Love to you & prayers for you, wishing you all prosperity [your most?] affectionate Mother till Death Eliz[abeth Chandler?][32]

In the aftermath of Samuel's death, Mehetabel may have turned to the literature available at the time intended specifically to help women cope with personal tragedy. John Flavel's *Token for Mourners* (1674), for example, which was first imported into Boston in the late seventeenth century and subsequently reprinted several times, describes Christ's advice to a mother who had lost her only son. Cotton Mather's *Companion for the Afflicted* (1701) provided similar guidance; Mather's "intimate tone" and "homely prose," as Kevin Hayes has noted, made his volume particularly appealing to women.[33] (Interestingly, one surviving copy of Mather's *Companion* appears to have belonged to Mehetabel's granddaughter; it is inscribed "Eunice Borllinggames Book Given to hur by hur Mother Chandler [Mehetabel's brother Joseph's wife] in the year 1749.") Because death was such a constant presence in early America, these manuals were often circulated among women and frequently passed down through generations.

It is possible that during this time Mehetabel began recording the several morbid meditations that appear toward the back of her diary along with the recipes and medical remedies. These reflections, which all emphasize the fleeting nature of life, provide additional insight into the wide-ranging nature of Mehetabel's reading.

Wintworth—Sure
twas som stranger—
yes, his stay,—
in helth among us
was but one short day,
then he fell sick,
and langusht but ten more,
Before he payed
Corupted nature's score,
Scorsh't by a fevor
he Refind his breath,
and payed that stated
hommag unto Death.

the Difference betwen
to day, & to morrow

to day man's Drest,
in gold and silver bright,
warpt [wrapped] in a shrowd
before to morrow night,
to day he's feeding
on delicious food
to morrow Dead
unable to do good,
today he's nice
and scorns to fee[d] on crumbs
to morrow
he's a dish himself for worms,
to day he's grand
majestick, all Delight,
gastful and pale,
before to morrow night.
true as the scriptures say,
mans life a span
the present moment
is the life of man.[34]

Two sets of verses from "Solomon on the Vanity of the World, a Poem in Three Books" by Matthew Prior (1664–1721) also are copied out. (Since "Solomon" was not published until 1708, Mehetabel could not have read it until several years after Samuel's death.) Prior's epic poem, which runs to more than 2,500 lines and is divided into three "books," uses Solomon's

inquiries into the true nature of knowledge, pleasure, and power to demonstrate that "all is vanity." Book III, from which Mehetabel's lines are taken,
draws on Ecclesiastes, the Psalms, and Chronicles to underscore the familiar
theme that "Thy Sum of Life must [God's] Decrees fulfill: / What derogates
from His Command, is Ill; / And that alone is Good, which centers in His
Will." (Although "Solomon" is firmly rooted in scripture and in theological
concerns, Prior's other works included love poems, odes to famous people,
and witty epigrams; the inscription on his tombstone in Westminster Ab-
bey reads "Life is a jest, and all things shew it, I thought so once, & now I
know it".)[35]

> *the cradle and the tomb*
> *alass so nigh*
> *to live is scarce distinguished*
> *from to Dye*[36]
>
> *from earth all come*
> *to earth must all Return*
> *frail as the cord*
> *and brittle as the urn.*[37]

Elsewhere in Mehetabel's diary is another poem concerned with death that
appears to have been transcribed by someone else, perhaps the same person
who recorded the "Swe[e]tt Dram" recipe; the handwriting is similar but not
identical.

> *Without a name, forever senceless, dumb.*
> *Dust, ashes, nought Elce Lies within this Tomb.*
> *When T'was I Live'd, or dy'd, it matters not.*
> *To whome Related, or of whom begot.*
> *I was, but am not, ask no more of me.*
> *Tis all I am, and all that you must bee.*[38]

The juxtaposition of Mehetabel's musings upon mortality with the other
material at the back of her diary—the recipes, remedies, and scriptural references—denotes both the variety of her personal experiences and the drama
of early New England life. The celebratory occasions that called for sugar
cakes and currant wine were accompanied by times of serious illness that
required drastic treatment and periods of intense grief that led to gloomy
ruminations. The layering of these elements in the diary also illuminates
how these particular circumstances could contribute to the creation of a dual

consciousness: recognizing the fleeting nature of life, early New Englanders not only concerned themselves with the state of their souls but also placed a high value on certain material comforts, such as good food and drink. The observation made by Janet Theophano about seventeenth-century English-woman Hopestill Brett's manuscript cookbook, which also contains reflections on death, could aptly be applied to Mehetabel's diary: "The placement of admonitions against valuing an earthly life side by side with the sensual descriptions of the pleasures of food and drink" represented for the author the entwining of the "illusory poles of life and death."[39]

While the death of William Coit likely dealt a heavy emotional blow to Mehetabel's sister Sarah, it also presented her with a number of practical considerations, the most pressing of which was how she, as a twenty-six-year-old widow, was to support herself and her two young sons. William did not leave a will, but the probate inventory taken after his death indicates that his estate was fairly small, worth just under two hundred pounds. Although the inventory lists twenty-four acres of land, as well as "5 nurserys of aple trees," among William's holdings, it makes no mention of a house; he and Sarah had, perhaps, lived in John and Mehetabel's former home, with the intention of eventually building one of their own. A large part of the value of William's estate lay in livestock: cataloged on the inventory are two horses and a colt; six oxen, including two at Woodstock that may have represented part of Sarah's dowry or inheritance; seven cows, three steers, and a calf; two swine and a pig; and thirty-eight "old" sheep and twenty lambs. Evidence of William's livelihood as a shipwright is reflected in the tools and lumber in his possession at the time of his death, but also noted are his part ownership of a sloop and a small fishing boat, an investment that would have brought in additional earnings. It appears that Sarah may also have contributed to the family income by taking in textile work; the inventory lists a spinning wheel and carding tools, as well as significant quantities of flax and of cotton and linen cloth and yarn. This at-home business may have enabled Sarah to support her family during her years as a widow.[40]

In the spring of the year following the death of Samuel, Mehetabel gave birth to her fifth child and first daughter; as she noted in her diary: "march 22. 1704 Eliz[th] Coit was born." Both Mehetabel and the baby came through the delivery safely; however, Mehetabel's "lying-in," or recovery, period was likely cut short as the result of the death of yet another family member. Mehetabel recorded in her diary the date of the passing of John Coit's father, which occurred less than a week after Elizabeth's birth: "March. 27. 1704 father Coit dyed." Joseph Coit's death would have ushered in another period of mourning for the family, but it also symbolized the end of an era. As the eldest son, John Coit, who had already become head of the family business, now assumed leadership of the family itself.[41]

The relatively modest nature of Joseph Coit's estate, which was valued at a little over three hundred pounds, may have been due to his having distributed gifts of property to his children during his lifetime and to the fact that his house—an older property that he had inherited from his own father— was appraised at only seventy-five pounds. (John Chandler's homestead, in contrast, had been assessed at over two hundred thirty pounds.) Since Joseph Coit did not leave a will—a surprising omission given his former status as a business owner—John and his brothers Solomon and Joseph came to an agreement on how to divide their father's property. On May 3 they and their mother went before the court to present and sign the settlement, which stipulated that Martha was to have whatever household goods "she may have occasion for" as well as an "Honourable maintenance" to be paid to her by her sons or their heirs for the rest of her life. The balance of the estate was to be divided among John, Joseph, Solomon, and William's children. John, as the eldest, not only inherited his parents' house and home lot, but he also received a double portion of the movable estate. Most notable among this latter property was a black slave known as "old Nanny."[42]

Next to nothing is known about Nanny. That she was estimated by the estate appraisers to be worth a mere eight pounds, at a time when a young, healthy slave commonly sold for several times that amount, seems to offer confirmation that she was of advanced age, while her name also hints at the possibility of a former position as a child-care provider in Joseph Coit's household. The details of Nanny's fate immediately after she became John Coit's property—whether she remained as Martha's servant or was taken into John and Mehetabel's home—are uncertain. One of Joshua Hempstead's diary entries makes it clear, however, that Nanny was living with John and Mehetabel some years later, after Martha Coit had died. Hempstead's single reference to Nanny is on the occasion of her own death; he notes that three days before Christmas in 1717 "old Nanny Jno Coits negro woman was buried in ye evening." John and Mehetabel's "acquisition" of Nanny marked their entry into the realm of slave ownership, a role they would each hold for the rest of their days.[43]

It is likely that after Joseph Coit's death, Martha Coit, who outlived her husband by nearly a decade, remained in her home for a period. Her sons' agreement to provide for her, and the proximity of John and Mehetabel, would have ensured that her needs were met and that she would have companionship. Although neither Martha nor Mehetabel left behind any writings describing their feelings for each other, it is conceivable that their relationship was a mutually satisfying one. The two women may have depended on each other in a myriad of ways—helping each other with housework, nursing each other through illness—and they may also have proved a great comfort to each other in the wake of their personal tragedies. Martha, after all, had no daughters of her own (her only other daughter-in-law at the time was Mehetabel's sister Sarah), and Mehetabel no longer had the physical presence of a mother in her life. Martha may also have formed special bonds with Mehetabel's children. Other than Sarah's two sons, Mehetabel and John's children—one of whom they named in Martha's honor—were Martha's only grandchildren, and she was their only available grandparent.

For Mehetabel and John, the daily demands of work, which for both of them were considerable, may have provided some distraction from the loss of so many family members within such a short time. Mehetabel would have had her hands full caring for her young children and running her household, while the bulk of John's time would have been spent overseeing the extensive operations at the shipyard, where business was booming. In the fall of 1704 alone, at least two large vessels were completed. Mehetabel recorded their launching dates in her diary: "September ye 13 Mr Alfords & vrylands brig. new london was lancht"; "December ye 14. 1704 the Love & Ann was lancht." The latter vessel, which was also built for the merchants Alford and Vryland, may, like the *New London,* have been a brig: a two-masted square-rigger usually weighing at least a hundred tons. Since the shipyard records for this period have not survived, the cost of building the vessels is unknown, as is the original destination of the *New London.* It appears from one of Mehetabel's later diary entries, however, that the *Love & Ann*'s first voyage was to Barbados. If John Coit retained a share in the ownership of the vessels, as shipbuilders sometimes did, he may well have made a tidy profit from their voyages.[44]

Carl Bridenbaugh has described the building of a large vessel (three or four hundred tons) as the "supreme achievement of early American craftsmanship."[45] Although most of the ships produced by John Coit were probably of much smaller size, their construction would nevertheless have been complex and time consuming. The construction of the *New London* and the

Love & Ann would have involved the contributions of carpenters, joiners, carvers, blacksmiths, coopers, and sailmakers, as well as general day laborers. A ship intended for the transatlantic trade could take up to a year to build.

It is not surprising that Mehetabel took notice of the two launchings, as these were celebratory occasions for a shipbuilder, not only representing the conclusion of months of labor but also marking the receipt of a final payment from the merchant. Launchings were often attended by large numbers of the general public, who were supplied with refreshments at the expense of the new owner. The vessel would be christened with a toast, and if an owner were particularly pleased with the finished product, he might present the shipbuilder with a porcelain or silver bowl to commemorate the occasion.[46]

A few months after the *Love & Ann*'s launching, Mehetabel documented the accommodation of a new shipyard apprentice into the household: "April 2: 1705 John Christophs came to live here." John Christophers appears to have been the sixteen-year-old son of Richard Christophers, a New London judge and ship owner who was a client of the Coit shipyard, as his father had been before him. (In two subsequent diary entries for 1705, Mehetabel marked the launching of a Christophers ship: "novem[br] 26, M[r] [Richard] Christophers Sloop was lancht. 1705 twas Rays'd y[e] 1 of august," and "November y[e] 26 the Grac[e] and Hannah was lancht.") Richard Christophers likely arranged the apprenticeship so that his son might learn about shipbuilding as part of his preparation for continuing the family business. Acquiring such practical knowledge was not meant to limit the younger Christophers to the shipbuilding trade but rather would have been useful in his future career as a merchant. New London merchants and ship owners were extensively involved with matters concerning their vessels and occasionally even made sea voyages themselves.[47]

Two months after John Christophers's arrival, Mehetabel and John's household was increased by the addition of a very special member, when Mehetabel's mother came to live with the family. Mehetabel writes that on "june y[e] 15 1705 I came from Woodstock, my mother Chandler Came with me." Whether Elizabeth Chandler, who was then in her sixties, had become frail and unable to care for herself, or whether she simply desired to live out her life surrounded by her daughters and their families, her decision to come to New London was undoubtedly sealed by the outbreak the previous year of yet another war between the English and the French, which once again put Woodstock in jeopardy. Mehetabel must have been gratified at the prospect of having her mother come live with her, given their close relationship and long years of separation. Grown children were expected to care for their aging parents, but Mehetabel may have considered the opportunity to serve her mother as much a privilege as a duty.[48]

One final new member joining the Coit household in 1705 arrived under dramatically different conditions from those that brought John Christophers and Elizabeth Chandler into the home. His name was Mingo, and he was a black slave who had been transported from Barbados. Mehetabel recorded the date of his arrival in her diary—"july 3: 1705 Mingo Came here with Thomas Avery in the love & ann the first voiage"—but provided no additional information as to the surrounding circumstances. (Thomas Avery, now a sea captain, had served an apprenticeship with John Coit a decade earlier.) Mehetabel had previously noted the *Love & Ann*'s return from Barbados in a diary entry—"july 3 1705 Thomas Avery Came in from barbados the love & Ann the first voyag"—but it appears that she had also wanted to separately mark the occasion of Mingo's arrival. Apart from this instance, she never mentioned him again, nor did she ever openly refer to the fact that her family owned slaves.[49]

After enduring what was certainly a harrowing passage to New London from Barbados, a voyage that usually took between eighteen and thirty days, Mingo would have had to adjust to a climate, landscape, and culture that varied radically from what he had left behind in Barbados—and perhaps prior to that, Africa. In addition to having to learn how to meet the expectations of a new set of owners, he may also have had to learn a new language. It is possible that Mingo did not regret leaving behind the plantation system of the West Indies, where an emphasis on obtaining the greatest possible profit and the fear of insurrection fueled by the islands' huge slave population made for cruel treatment, but he may have been torn from family members and friends.[50]

Mingo's age at the time he came to live with the Coits, like much else about him, is unknown, but he was probably a young man, as Joshua Hempstead's diary makes it clear that he lived for many years thereafter. On several occasions, Hempstead employed Mingo for short spaces of time when he was in need of extra labor. Much of Mingo's work for Hempstead seems to have consisted of mowing, raking, stacking, and carrying oats and salt hay, used for feeding livestock—tasks that, according to Hempstead's diary, he was still capable of performing decades after his arrival. John Coit could make a profit by hiring Mingo out, but likely his primary reason for purchasing him was to augment his labor force at the shipyard. In fact, no additional

apprentices are mentioned in Mehetabel's diary after Mingo's arrival. By necessity, most shipbuilders hired such workers as carpenters, joiners, blacksmiths, and general laborers on an as-needed basis. The permanence offered
by slave labor, and the skillfulness the slave subsequently acquired, offered
an attractive alternative to the temporary help provided by apprentices or
indentured servants.[51]

Like slaves in other Puritan households, Mingo would have been considered a part of the Coit "family," over whom the head of the household
exerted a paternal authority. He certainly would not, however, have shared
the same standing as the other family members or even of any hired help.
Despite having close daily contact with the Coits over several decades, and
perhaps even forming personal bonds with them, Mingo would not have
been considered their equal. He may, however, have formed a surrogate
family with the other slaves who eventually came to live in the household:
Nanny, Nell, and Peter.

Joshua Hempstead's diary indicates that Mingo married at some point,
but his wife's name went unrecorded, so her identity is unknown. The couple
may not have lived together, in which case they would have been allowed
occasions to see each other privately and on social occasions. New England
slaves were permitted more opportunities for socialization than their southern counterparts, in large measure because, being so much smaller in number,
they did not inspire the same fears of insurgency they did on the large planta-
tions. New London slaves and free blacks congregated at work parties such as
corn huskings and house-raisings, at church meetings, on training days, and
at funerals. (The latter occasions could be quite elaborate, commemorating
the departed's journey "homeward" with singing and dancing.) There is also
evidence that beginning in the eighteenth century, New London allowed the
celebration of "Negro Election Day," in which local blacks annually elected a
governor to act as a general authority and arbitrate disputes. Negro Election
Day was modeled on New England election day traditions, but it was also
based on slave holidays that paid tribute to blacks of African royal birth. The
position of "Negro governor" carried great prestige among local slaves and
free blacks; in fact, one gravestone in New London's burying ground proudly
declares that the deceased, Florio Hercules, had been the "wife of Hercules,
governor of the Negroes." In general, the concentrated population of New
London blacks and the regular influx of new arrivals from the West Indies
and, to a lesser extent, Africa allowed for the creation of a flourishing black
subculture. Retaining elements of African folkways, and sometimes blending

them with New England customs, local slaves and free blacks expressed their identity through unique manners of speech, dress, work, entertainment, and worship.[52]

Later in the summer that Mingo came to live with Mehetabel and her family, the *Love & Ann* returned to the West Indies. Mehetabel writes that in "August ye love & Ann sett sale for barbados yᵉ second voyage, october she Came in from Antego. this a Seacond voyage." Her next chronological entry, although made in an equally matter-of-fact manner, marked another significant bereavement: "Sepᵗᵗ 23 Mother Chandler dyed 1705 in her 64 year."[53] Elizabeth Chandler had finally "Done with this weary world" and gone "to rest." Her remains were interred in the New London burial ground, and although her gravestone is no longer visible, it is likely that Mehetabel ensured that she was buried near Samuel.

In the little book containing Elizabeth Chandler's poem, Mehetabel's brother Joseph wrote a heartfelt ode to their mother. "Upon the Death of my Dear Mother Mʳˢ Elizabeth Chandler Who Went to Rest on Sabbath day about Sunsett Sepʳ: 23ᵗʰ: 1705," begins with the lines

> *How can I stop the sluces of mine Eyes*
> *Urg'd by the muses I must Sacrifice*
> *A tear of grief, being come to wail her hearse*
> *And vent my sorrows, thô in Countrey verse*
> *Twoul'd be a Crime too great to Let her Flie*
> *Away in Silence, without Eligie.*

Throughout his poem, Joseph extolled Elizabeth's virtues as a Christian, a mother, a wife, and a neighbor, but he also paid tribute to her writings, which, he noted,

> *Plainly prove*
> *That from a Child the Scriptures were her Guide*
> *By which her Faith and Love to Christ she try'd.*

Perhaps Joseph was inspired by his mother's own poetry to compose these lines in her honor.[54]

In the spring following Elizabeth's death, Mehetabel gave birth to her sixth and final child; she remarked in her diary that on "April. 1. 1706. Martha Coit was born." Mehetabel was only thirty-two at the time of Martha's birth, an unusually young age to stop having children. It is not known whether she experienced subsequent miscarriages or whether some physical problem prevented her from becoming pregnant again. Release from the cycle of pregnancy, however, would have provided her with a measure of physical freedom, as well as enabling her to focus more of her attention on the children she already had. Martha, in particular, would come to form a very special attachment to her mother, as their later letters testify, but for the time being she was the youngest, and hence neediest, member of a large and hectic household.[55]

By this point in her life, Mehetabel had begun successfully to fill many of the roles Puritan society expected a woman to perform: she had become a wife, mother, household manager, and dedicated Christian. Moreover, by forging new relationships and meeting new challenges, she had attained a certain standing within her community that was based not only on her membership in a prominent family but also on her own accomplishments.[56]

CHAPTER FIVE

Comings and Goings,
1707–1711

F OR WHATEVER reason, the highest concentration of dated entries in Mehetabel's diary falls in the years 1707, 1708, and 1709.[1] (This does not take
into account the other, *undated* material in the diary: the recipes, medical
remedies, and quotations, which she may have recorded over several decades.) Although Mehetabel certainly did not keep anything approaching a
day-by-day account during this time, the number of entries—more than a
dozen in all—is noteworthy when compared with other periods.

Many of the entries for these years, and throughout the diary as a whole,
deal with the comings and goings of Mehetabel and her family, of travels
taken and visits made and received. This was a common focus for early
American diarists, as travel for both business and social purposes was a regular part of life. In fact, the diary of the eighteenth-century Maine midwife
Martha Ballard contains so many references to the different places she went
and the visitors she received that Laurel Thatcher Ulrich has remarked that
much of the diary's content can be reduced to "a simple grammar of coming
and going."[2] Like Ballard, Mehetabel omitted the particulars of these visits in
many cases, often documenting where and with whom a journey was made
but not necessarily why it was taken.

Mehetabel's first diary entry for 1707 concerns a trip made by John Coit;
she writes that "may 24: 1707 my Husband went to Roadisland." The purpose
of John Coit's journey is unknown, but it is quite possible that he traveled
to Newport, a thriving seaport and commercial center in which boatbuilders
were in demand, on business related to the shipyard. John had a personal

contact in Rhode Island, Benjamin Ellery, a merchant and former sea captain whose stepmother was John's aunt, Mary Coit (who has been described as the first female medical practitioner in Essex County, Massachusetts). There is evidence that John built at least one vessel for Ellery: Joshua Hempstead recorded in his diary on July 15, 1712, that he "helped Jno Coit about Lanching Elery's Great Boat." Years later, Mehetabel and John's daughter Martha paid extended visits to the Ellery family.[3]

Following the entry regarding John Coit's journey to Rhode Island, Mehetabel noted that she herself took a trip. She writes that on "june ye 18 my Husband and Sister Sarah [and?] I went to Stoningtown & brother Joseph Coite was maried to Experience Wheler 1707[.] 21 day we came home." John Coit's brother Joseph did marry Experience Wheeler in Stonington, Connecticut; however, their wedding actually took place on September 18, 1705. Mehetabel's entry regarding Joseph Coit's marriage presents one of the only occasions on which her dating departs from the actual timing of an occurrence that can be corroborated by another source. One explanation for this lapse is that she may have made her first notation about Joseph Coit's wedding some time after the fact and simply forgotten the date; another possibility is that she copied this entry from an earlier diary and erred in her transcription.[4]

The next chronological diary entry focuses on Mehetabel's own brother Joseph. She writes that on "june 25 Joseph Chandler went to portryall [Port Royal, Canada] in 1707[;] September he came home." The twenty-four-year-old Joseph evidently participated in one of the few major North American engagements of Queen Anne's War, which lasted from 1702 until 1713. This latest conflict between the English and the French was triggered by King Louis XIV's intention to claim the temporarily unoccupied Spanish throne for his grandson, Philip de Bourbon, an act that England maintained would create an imbalance of power in Europe. Characterized in the colonial theater by raids on frontier outposts and skirmishes between local militias and Indians allied with the French, Queen Anne's War closely resembled King William's War (1688–1697).[5]

In 1707, about halfway through the conflict, Massachusetts governor Joseph Dudley (who had managed to return to power after the fall of Edmund Andros in 1689), spearheaded a campaign against the French in Port Royal, France's principal settlement in Acadia and a strategic maritime location in the sea-lanes between Massachusetts Bay, the Grand Banks, and England. Though New Englanders' hopes for victory were high, the expedition, which sailed from Boston in May, failed, largely owing to the lack of effective leadership. While the defeated forces regrouped in Maine, Dudley called for reinforcements, an appeal to which Mehetabel's brother Joseph appears to have responded. Despite the pressure to redeem the expedition, the second attack, which took place in August, was also unsuccessful. After a week of fighting the French, whose ranks had likewise been reinforced, the recruits returned to New England.[6]

Joseph's motivation for joining the assault on Port Royal may have been based in part on his having had to live with his own "Garrison fears" as a youth in Woodstock. He was probably also lured by the opportunity both to earn some extra money and to see a bit more of the world. Traveling to Canada certainly enabled him to explore regions of northern New England he had never before seen, as well as offering a brief stay in Boston, early America's most cosmopolitan center.

By the early 1700s Boston was growing increasingly urbanized and sophisticated. Its architecture was gradually becoming more refined, and by 1720 the town would have the best highway system in the colonies. As the leading port in North America, Boston could offer a spectacular array of consumer goods, from clothing and books and furniture to spices and wine and tobacco. It also provided a range of entertainments. Much to the chagrin of the Puritan vanguard, Boston's growth in prosperity had been accompanied by increased secularization and a heightened interest in material pleasures. By the late 1600s ministers could bemoan the existence of "bawdy-houses" as well as the "*enormous number*" of local drinking establishments. No matter what Joseph's interests were, he would have found something to appeal to him in the town.[7]

Joseph's travels in 1707 apparently concluded with a visit to his sisters in New London, an event the siblings were not often able to enjoy. Mehetabel notes that on "Decem[br] 19 he come to n=london[;] y[e] 25 he went home[.] my Husband & Sarah Coit went with him." John and Sarah may have accompanied Joseph to Woodstock for reasons connected with the property left to Mehetabel and Sarah by their father. It was certainly not a propitious time to travel, given the season and the potential dangers connected with the war. Their departure on Christmas Day would not have interrupted any family festivities, however, as neither the Coits nor the Chandlers would have celebrated the holiday. Puritan New Englanders did not recognize December 25 as the actual date of Christ's birth, believing that there was nothing in scripture to substantiate it. They were further disinclined to observe Christmas because the date had formerly marked a pagan Roman holiday, and because it had become characterized by decadent and debauched behavior in old England. As Cotton Mather complained, during the "Saturnalian jollities" of the yuletide season, "men dishonoured the Lord Jesus Christ more" than at any time during the preceding year.[8]

The latest war with the French did not put a halt to New London's maritime pursuits; despite the threat of capture and pillage by enemy vessels, the port continued to bustle with activity. Mehetabel seems to have been mindful of the comings and goings at the waterfront, and she continued to monitor the voyages of some of the vessels built at the Coit shipyard. She records, for example, that on "july ye 7. 1707 the Grace & Hannah sett [sail] for barbados," and that on "August 2 1707 ye love and Ann sett saill for barbados on a satturday." (Mehetabel later added that the *Grace & Hannah,* which she had noted in an earlier entry was "Mr Christophers Sloop," returned in October, a fact seemingly confirmed by the *Boston News-Letter,* which remarked on the early October arrival in New London of a "sloop from Barbadoes, Richard Christophers master.") Several months later, Mehetabel recorded that on "July 22. 1708 the Grace & Hannah set saill for barbados G[e]orge Plumb master. Novem^{br} 13 he came home again." (The *Boston News-Letter* also reported Plumb's return to New London that week, noting that "Plumb and Prentice in two Sloops are arrived in 30 days from Barbadoes.") At around the time of George Plumb's homecoming, Richard Christophers was embarking on another trip to Barbados. Mehetabel writes that "Novem^{br} [10?] Mr Richard Christophers, set saill for barbados in the brig Richard & Joseph the first voyage in 1708 and came home again the 22 of march [1709] & Charls Hill came with him." Although there is no prior mention of the *Richard & Joseph* in the diary, it is quite possible that it was another vessel produced by the Coit shipyard.[9]

It is unfortunate that Mehetabel never elaborated on her attentiveness to the Coit ships' movements. Perhaps pride in her husband's role in the vessels' creation or the fact that he maintained a financial interest in them was partly the reason, but her imagination may also have been stirred by thoughts of the ships' voyages. Although she herself was not able to travel to distant lands, her notice of current events, as well as some of her reading material, attests to her interest in the wider world around her. In a letter she wrote in 1726, for instance, she noted that she was in the midst of reading "the Turkish History," probably an edition of *The Turkish History from the Original of that Nation, to the Growth of the Ottoman Empire,* begun by English writer

Richard Knolles (1550?–1610) and contributed to and reprinted by different authors over the years. Knolles's book was highly regarded by generations of readers, including Samuel Johnson and Lord Byron, and editions remain in print today. Mehetabel's choice of such a volume not only reflects a level of curiosity about an exotic locale and a common attitude among educated readers of her time that the fates of Islam and Christianity were linked, but it also indicates a degree of intellectual sophistication.[10]

There is a suggestion in Mehetabel's diary that she also had an interest in the natural world. Tucked among her recipes is the observation "nine million and three hundred & four Eggs in one fish." There is no context for the remark, but this sort of reflection, like Cotton Mather's fascination with such phenomena as the "Innumerable *Millions*" of stars, may have stemmed from a recognition that the marvels of the physical world "Declare[d] the Glory of God, and show[ed] forth his Handy work." It also mirrored an interest in natural history shared by many educated women of the period. This curiosity ranged beyond the use of herbs for medical remedies to include botany, astronomy, and geography, among other topics. As Kevin Hayes has shown, early American women were known to have read scientific works such as Francis Bacon's *Sylva Sylvarum; or, A Natural Historie;* Aelian's *Variae Historiae;* and Bernard Le Bovier de Fontenelle's *Plurality of Worlds* on the Copernican system, the earliest translation of which was compiled by the seventeenth-century Englishwoman Aphra Behn.[11]

Mehetabel occasionally had the opportunity to make excursions within a few days' travel of New London, In the fall of 1707, for instance, she and John journeyed to Middletown, Connecticut, the hometown of John's mother. Mehetabel writes that in "Septem^br 1707 My Husbend and I went to Middletown[.] October ye 3 we come Home and mother Coit came with us." Upon her return to New London, Martha may have moved into Mehetabel and John's home, as Mehetabel's mother had done a few years earlier.[12]

At around this time a series of developments served to boost New London's standing in the colony. After Connecticut governor and New London resident Fitz-John Winthrop died after falling ill on a trip to Boston, the town provided a new leader (but at the same time lost its minister) when the Reverend Gurdon Saltonstall was chosen by the General Assembly as Winthrop's replacement. Saltonstall's election, which was due in large measure to his having served as one of Winthrop's ablest military advisers, represented the first time a New England clergyman exchanged his pulpit for high public office; during his administration, which lasted until his death in 1724, the meetings of the governor and council were often held in New London.[13]

In 1707 the town also became the home base of the colony's first royal customs agent. The first appointee to the post of "collector, surveyor, and searcher" for Connecticut was an Englishman named John Shackmaple. Two years later, when the British government declared that any vessel sailing from a Connecticut port to another colony or a foreign port needed to obtain clearance from a royal customs official, and Shackmaple remained the colony's only agent, New London became Connecticut's official port of entrance and departure. Shackmaple's presence in New London had a social impact as well as an economic and political one, as he and his family indulged in a more refined and sophisticated style of living and entertaining than was common in the town. Their presence would also ultimately lead to the establishment of the community's first Anglican church.[14]

Mehetabel's next few diary entries provide a little insight into the activities of her children during these years. It appears that by 1708 John junior, who would be twelve in May, Joseph, who would be ten in November, and Thomas, who would be six in June, had begun spending time at their father's shipyard. (The girls were still quite young—Elizabeth would turn four in March and Martha two in April—and were likely kept closer to home.) Despite the fact that they must have been surrounded by adult workers, the boys experienced a few close calls during their time at the shipyard. Mehetabel writes that in 1708 on "Aprell ye 29 a plank fell of[f] the stage upon Thomas Coit & struck him down but gott no grate mater of hurt," and that on "August [12?] 1708 M^r vrylands vessell was burn't upon the stocks, on a thursday, & John coits foot burnt." All things considered, John and Thomas were fortunate that their injuries were not more serious. Both shipyards and docked ships were dangerous places where accidents and even fatalities were common. (Indeed, in late 1725 alone, Joshua Hempstead documented three deaths occurring aboard or near a docked vessel: a "Barbadien Ind[ian] . . . fell off from Gallups Sloops Mast & was taken up dead on the Deck"; a "Stranger . . . got his deaths Wound by a fall from the first Deck of the great Ship into the Hold"; and another "Stranger" was "killed about ye grt Ship by the falling of a peice of Timber from the Sheers.")[15]

Early American households were also hazardous places, particularly for youngsters. All too frequently, children got too close to a fire, a well, or a sharp tool. No matter how watchful a parent, accidents were bound to happen, given the number of children in a typical household and the variety of activities mothers were involved in. On March 10, just a few weeks before Thomas's mishap at the shipyard, for example, Mehetabel writes that her daughter Martha was hurt when her "foot [was] burntt with a warming-pan." Although there seems to have been no lasting damage, the incident must have been upsetting for the entire household. After having already lost Samuel, Mehetabel may have been especially shaken when harm came to one of her children. Clearly, she was sufficiently affected by the injuries to Martha, Thomas, and John to record them in her diary.[16]

The day Thomas was struck by the falling plank his oldest brother was not around to look after him, as the day before, Mehetabel notes, "John Coit went to Middletown with Mr Arnold by water." (Since every time she devoted an entry to one of John senior's trips she referred to him as "my husband," it is almost certain that Mehetabel here meant her son rather than his father.) Young John may have been sent on the trip with "Mr Arnold"—likely John Arnold, a local merchant and ship owner—to gain some firsthand experience in sailing a ship. Inexperienced as John was, he may also have been charged by his father with overseeing the sale of supplies in Middletown. (Several years later Joshua Hempstead sent his fourteen-year-old son Thomas on a similar venture with John Arnold; Thomas "carryed 21 lb of wool & Sold it for 7 bushells of Corn & 3s od in money.") This may have been John's first time away from home; Mehetabel writes that he did not return until "may ye 17."[17]

With so little surviving evidence, it is impossible to know exactly what Mehetabel was like as a mother. Although the letters she exchanged with her daughter Martha reveal that the two shared a close and loving relationship, this intimacy may have only fully developed after Martha grew to young adulthood. When her children were young, Mehetabel, like many of her contemporaries, may have been a strict and even stern parent. Much was at stake in raising children in early New England: in addition to teaching their offspring about avoiding the physical dangers all around them, Puritan parents were also responsible for instructing them on the many potential threats to their soul.

Since Puritan parenting philosophies were closely tied to their religious beliefs, children were viewed as products of original sin rather than as innocent beings to be spoiled and indulged. Parents considered it their duty to curb through strict discipline the sinfulness they believed inherent in every human being. Although some parents resorted to physically repressive measures to control their children, most found a more effective tool in regulating a child's behavior to be the child's own conscience. Parents sought to impress on their children at a young age that God would be greatly displeased by disobedience or misbehavior, and that sinfulness could well lead to eternal damnation. These lessons were reinforced in the meetinghouse, in the community, and in school. Encouraging the development of the child's own conscience was usually effective, sometimes detrimentally so. The diarist Samuel Sewall, for example, records that for a period of months in 1696 his daughter Betty underwent an emotional crisis catalyzed by her fear that she was going to hell because her "Sins were not pardon'd." Sewall's response to his daughter's distress was to pray with her; there were, he writes, "Tears on either part."[18]

Parents could also blame themselves for any willfulness their children showed, as Mehetabel indicated when she recorded in her diary:

> *a wicked wretch Drag'd*
> *his father along the*
> *House. the father*
> *beg'd of him not to*
> *[drag] him beyond such a*
> *place for (said he)*
> *I Drag'd my father*
> *no ferther*[19]

Although these lines appear to be some sort of strange pun, they are actually taken from a passage in John Flavel's "Divine Conduct; or, the Mystery of Providence" (1678), in which Flavel counseled parents to raise God-fearing children and warned children against disobedience to their parents and, by extension, God. Flavel's version of the extract reads, "It is usual with God, to retaliate men's disobedience to their parents in kind: Commonly our own children shall pay us home for it. I have read in a grave Author of a wicked wretch that dragged his father along the house: The father begged him not to draw him beyond such a place; *for,* said he, 'I dragged my father no farther.' O the sad, but just retributions of God!" Perhaps Mehetabel copied Flavel's parable as a way of reminding herself that any acts of defiance her children exhibited might be punishment for whatever resistance she showed her own parents as a child.[20]

The Puritans' concern with their children's spiritual salvation did not preclude the possibility of creating an affectionate home life. Even those ministers who were most concerned with the subject of proper child-rearing advised parents "to win children to holiness by kindness rather than try to force them to it by severity." Mehetabel herself seems to have taken this advice to heart. Included in her diary is a line—"the Child is the father in the second Edition"—taken from a printed sermon on the Ten Commandments by British nonconformist Thomas Watson. In his exposition on the fifth commandment, Watson encouraged parents to "Carry it *Lovingly* to your Children. In all your Counsels and Commands, let them read Love. Love will command Honour: And how can the Parent but love the Child, who is his living Picture, nay, Part of himself? The Child is the Father in the second Edition."[21]

Puritan fathers, though often depicted by their grown children as more authoritarian and remote than their mothers, could also be compassionate and tender. Increase Mather conveyed a sense of both the reserve and intensity of Puritan fatherhood when he observed in his diary, "Little doe children think, wt affection is in ye Heart of a Father." Letters written by fathers following the loss of a child openly acknowledge this love. Samuel Bradstreet, for example, described his late son as "a lovely child[,] Exceeding forward, Every way desireable," who was "most dearly beloved by me in this life and as much lamented since his death." Wait Winthrop wrote to his brother Fitz-John after the passing of his first-born son in 1680 that he had "lost [his] hope, and the greatest part of [his] comfort." Although, as Lisa Wilson has pointed out, "sentiment [would come] to a father's lips easier in the eighteenth century" as modes of expression changed, "seventeenth-century Puritan men also loved their children. Forms of expression—not feelings—changed."[22]

Mothers and fathers worked together to provide their children with basic life skills, religious instruction, and an educational grounding, which was supplemented by formal schooling. The Coit children, particularly the younger ones, were fortunate in that, by the early 1700s, New London finally had an established system of public education. Town records indicate that, in the early years of settlement, schooling was somewhat irregularly provided. Although in 1678 a committee was chosen to procure the town's first teacher, it appears that for many years thereafter school was in session for only a few months of the year. In 1698 the school committee voted that "one halfe peny in mony upon the List of Estate [was] to be raised for the use of a free Schoole that shall teach children to Reade Write and Cypher and ye Lattin Tongue, which School shall be kept two-thirds of the yeare on the West side [New London proper] and one-third part of the yeare on the East Side of the river [present-day Groton]." And in 1701 another vote supported the institution of a grammar school and hiring of a schoolmaster. Revenue from a 1673 bequest to the town for a school was to be used for the education of poor children, while parents and apprentice masters were expected to "make up what more should be necessary." The first schoolmaster whose name appears on record began teaching in 1708; the first school building—"twenty feet by sixteen, and seven feet between joints"—was erected in 1713.[23]

Frances Caulkins observed that, for the first fifty years after the founding of New London, "the business of teaching was . . . principally performed by women. . . . Every quarter of the town had its mistress, who taught children *to behave;* to ply the needle through all the mysteries of hemming, over-hand, stitching, and darning, up to the sampler; and to read from A, B, C, through the spelling-book to the Psalter." Caulkins did not provide her source for this information, but she was likely correct (with the exception that boys would not have learned to "ply the needle"), as dame schools were ubiquitous in early New England. Mehetabel's children would have received a dame school education that in many ways resembled her own. Unlike Roxbury, however, New London appears to have allowed girls to continue their education at the grammar school level. According to Caulkins, they were permitted to attend writing instruction an hour at a time on certain days of the week after the close of the boys' school. The girls may also have received some lessons in "Cypher[ing]," or arithmetic, but it is unlikely that they were taught "ye Lattin Tongue." Even decades later, when a local teacher described by Joshua Hempstead as a "Celebrated School-mistress" taught "Reading writing & Arithmetick & the Needle to ye female," Latin was not included in the curriculum.[24]

The year following Gurdon Saltonstall's election to the governorship, the town of New London took its first major steps toward acquiring a new full-time minister. In June 1708 Mehetabel's uncle William Douglas, accompanied by the other church deacon, went to Boston to consult with the local clergy about a fitting replacement, much as his own father had done decades before. The Boston ministers recommended the Reverend Eliphalet Adams, himself the son of a minister. Orphaned at the age of eight, Adams had been taken under the wing of the Reverend Nehemiah Hobart, a Harvard graduate who sent Adams to his alma mater, where, according to a college historian, he became "the most active offender against the college laws in his Class." After graduating in 1694, the presumably reformed young man taught school briefly in Taunton, Massachusetts, before going on to preach at Little Compton, Rhode Island. In 1698 he was asked to preach to a settlement of Indians, which he did after learning their language. In New London, Adams would employ his language skills to try to persuade local Mohegans to convert to Christianity and to allow their children to be taught reading and writing. He would also make annual "preaching tours" among Connecticut tribes, reporting their results to the Society for the Propagation of the Gospel in Boston, and would sometimes intercede on the Indians' behalf with the Connecticut legislature.[25]

Adams had been assisting the Reverend Benjamin Colman at Boston's Brattle Square Church, the town's most liberal Puritan congregation, at the time the New London deacons approached him. In the late summer of 1708 he accompanied them back to New London, accepting the congregation's formal offer of the ministry in September. Adams was ordained in February 1709, and in December of that year he married Lydia Pygan of New London, with whom Mehetabel and her daughter Martha would develop a close friendship, as their later letters testify.

New London's choice of a new minister must certainly have been of interest to Mehetabel, but her attentions were also likely focused on developments within her own family that summer. In June her twenty-five-year-old brother Joseph was married to Susannah Perrin, a Roxbury woman. Their wedding appears to have taken place in Woodstock, as the town records state that in April 1708, "Joseph Chandler of Mashomoquet and Susanna Perrin of Roxb^r Enter their purpois of Mariage," and that "their marriage was Solemnized June ye 22d 1708." Mehetabel did not mention the wedding in her diary, so there is no way of knowing whether she was present at the ceremony.

Three months after Joseph's wedding, Mehetabel's thirty-one-year-old sister Sarah remarried after five years of widowhood. Mehetabel writes that "Septem^{br} 2: 1708 my Sister Sarah Coit was maried to Mr John Gardiner."[26] Gardiner, whose wife had died the previous year leaving him with seven children, was a wealthy landowner from a prominent family. His grandfather, Lion Gardiner, had commanded the fort at Saybrook, Connecticut, during the Pequot War of 1636–1637, afterward retiring to an island off the coast of Long Island that he purchased from Native allies. Originally called Manchonacke—the Island of the Dead—it subsequently became known both as Gardiner's Island and as the Isle of Wight. In 1686 John Gardiner's father David had obtained a patent to the island that effectively made it a lordship and manor. Sarah's new husband became the first of his family to be addressed as

"Lord" Gardiner, a unique title in colonial America. On the island—which remains in the family to this day—Gardiner reigned not only over approximately three thousand acres of lakes, forests, meadows, and beaches but also over numerous white, black, and Native servants, slaves, and tenant farmers. Through her marriage to Gardiner, Sarah became mistress to a host of adult dependents as well as stepmother to his seven children.[27]

Sarah and John Gardiner spent most of their time living on Long Island, in East Hampton, where Gardiner was a leading citizen. He was also known for his colorful personality and certain life experiences. When in residence on Gardiner's Island in 1699, for example, he received a visit from the infamous Captain Kidd. Later claiming to be unaware of Kidd's outlaw status, Gardiner allowed him to leave behind some of his treasure, such as "Gold, Silver, Jewels and Merchandise," for safe-keeping. When Kidd was soon after arrested for piracy in Boston, Gardiner agreed to hand over the plunder; family legend, however, has it that his wife at the time kept a valuable "souvenir" of Kidd's visit, and to this day some locals insist that treasure remains hidden on the island.[28]

Although Gardiner did not fall under suspicion as Kidd's accomplice, his reputation does not appear to have been entirely spotless. In addition to possessing wealth, the status of a gentleman, and the respect of his community, Gardiner may also have been something of a scoundrel. One of his descendants, a later John Gardiner, discovered on interviewing elderly locals who remembered him that his ancestor had had a liking for "young squaws." The later Gardiner also related an anecdote—the veracity of which he admitted was impossible to prove—in which a man in John Gardiner's service was asked to comment on the nature of his employer's integrity. "Then his character in the main is good?" he was asked. "On the main [i.e., sea] he might pass for a good man," the employee responded, "but on his Island he [is] a devilish rogue."[29]

It undoubtedly took Sarah some time to acclimate to life in a new town, to the isolation of Gardiner's Island, and to her separation from Mehetabel. Although boats commonly traveled between New London and East Hampton, neither Sarah nor Mehetabel would have had many opportunities for visits given their numerous responsibilities at home. A few months following Sarah and John's marriage, John Coit traveled to Gardiner's Island; however, it appears that Mehetabel was unable to accompany him. She writes that on "Decem^{br} 7 my Husband went to ye Ile of wight, Joseph Harris John Mayhew, Robert James went with him ye 12 day thay came home in 1708."

Mehetabel did not record the reason for John's trip, but it likely involved some type of business transaction with John Gardiner (Joshua Hempstead's diary indicates that John Coit built at least one vessel for Gardiner). Regardless of whether the business relationship between John Coit and John Gardiner predated Gardiner's marriage to Sarah, it would only have been strengthened following the wedding, as New England merchants commonly used kinship connections to further their commercial interests.[30]

The business between John Coit and John Gardiner may or may not have included shipbuilding, for, as was typical for the time, John Coit supplemented the main source of his income by other means. John was particularly enterprising: he not only engaged in small-scale farming, but at various times he operated a cider mill, a ropewalk, a ferry service, and a blacksmith's shop. He also accumulated a great deal of land in New London and a significant number of livestock, which he also managed to turn to a profit. By the time of his death he owned 6 cows, 7 pigs, a yoke of oxen, 4 horses, and 145 sheep, the latter of which he leased to his neighbors.

Mehetabel, like many of her contemporaries, also contributed to the family income. Colonial housewives ran stores, inns, taverns, and schools; delivered babies and tended to the sick; took in washing and sewing; and sold dairy products, baked goods, soap, candles, medicines, and other items they produced at home. It is clear that New London women were vitally engaged in the commercial life of their community; Joshua Hempstead's diary is filled with examples of the ways in which local goodwives participated in business transactions and performed needed services. He records, for example, that he bought "5 Bushlls Corn of a Squaw," "a pr of Calimineo Breeches" from Katherine Rogers, a "white horse from Archabald Campbells Wife," and common rights from Love Manwaring. In 1712 alone he writes of hiring Katherine Butler to provide postpartum nursing for his wife, retaining "Goodwife Pember" to treat the "bad swelling" of his son's hand, renting pasturing rights for his cows from "Goodee Atwill," and that "Ms Shapley" was chosen one of the three town innkeepers. Although women often received goods as payment, they were also accustomed to handling currency. Hempstead paid his housekeeper "3s 0d p week & as much mre as I Shall think She deserves," purchased "15s worth of Cakes of Rachell Lewis & 6s 8d of Daniel Shaplys wife," bought wool and oats from "Ms Palmes," and spent £80 on a nine-acre lot of land owned by Elizabeth Crossman. While Hempstead was in Boston collecting payment for a sloop he had built, he transferred a large sum—"£177-16s"—to Mehetabel's sister-in-law Abigail

Coit, who also happened to be in Boston. Hempstead evidently regarded Abigail as the "agent" for her husband Solomon, who had arranged for the vessel's financing.[31]

Many women who were widowed were forced by necessity to support themselves (and, as the case may be, their children), and some were quite financially successful as a result of their business acumen. For example, after Mercy Raymond, the sister-in-law of Mehetabel's brother John's wife Mary, was left widowed with seven children in 1704, she developed into a significant landowner, acquiring thousands of acres in farmland with her business partner, Major John Merritt. Elizabeth Hallam, a widow who appears to have operated both a shop and a tavern, also prospered. By the time of her death in 1736 she had acquired slaves, a diamond ring, a chest made from Bermuda cedar, a "gold chaine necklace containing seven chaines and a locket," and a boat. Although ownership of a vessel was unusual for a New London woman, the extent to which the town's fortunes were tied to the sea ensured that many women had a degree of nautical knowledge, and in at least one instance the parents of a boy to be instructed in the "mariner's art and navigation" by a local seaman specified that in the event of the seaman's death, this role be taken over by his wife.[32]

Perhaps one of New London's most successful businesswomen was the now-celebrated travel diarist Sarah Kemble Knight, who moved to the area some time after her only daughter, Elizabeth, was married to Colonel John Livingston in 1713. Knight herself had been widowed when her daughter was young and had subsequently supported herself in Boston by keeping a shop, taking in boarders, copying legal documents, and possibly teaching writing. Although she was in her mid-fifties when she moved to the area, Knight continued to explore economic opportunities, managing to acquire several properties and operating a shop, a tavern, and an inn. By the time of her death in 1727, her estate was valued at more than eighteen hundred pounds, placing her among the region's wealthiest inhabitants.[33]

Whether Mehetabel personally knew Knight is not known, but she likely knew of her. Knight was apparently a familiar figure in New London because of her personal history, her dynamic personality, and her land dealings, including some boundary disputes she had with neighbors. Knight's financial success and the fame of her travel narrative set her apart from most women of her time, but her strength of spirit and ability to adapt to her environment and circumstances were traits common to her contemporaries.

It is clear from some notes Mehetabel made that she, too, had business dealings with others in the community. On the inside covers and last page of her diary, she kept a running account of different commodities she exchanged with various individuals. Although these entries are now almost obliterated as the result of being crossed out, probably after the accounts were settled, some fragments are still legible. On the inside front cover (see frontispiece), for example, appears:

> mdm Adams mony for [milk?]
> mr hollom mony for [mulases?]
> . . . weight of . . . 3 oo
> [Sould?] . . . of the barell
> 4 3 5 beside what Chamberlin had.

Much of the rest of the endpaper on which the text appears is missing. The only information remaining is a list of names:

> an account of y^e
> Mr Runalds
> to Sam Watters
> to Jams Rogers
> to Thomas W. . .
> to Mr Sha[pley?]
> to m^{rs} Holom
> Capt . . .

The last page of the diary and inside back cover provide a few more details:

> Hannah mannorwing [Manwaring?]
> to [1?] yd of Scotch Cloath
> att o − 5 − o [?]
> to a quart of Rum o −1 − 2 [?]
> to half a quarter Scotch Cloat[h]s − o − 4 [?]
> to cotton w[oo?]ll o − 4 − 2 [?]
>
> Daniell Coit 1 − 5 − o
> to [Daktor?] − 1 − o − o
> m^{rs} Hallam − . . . − 2 − 6
> John to Woodstock - . . . - 3 - oo
> Darrow − 3 − 10 − oo
>
> Hannah mannorwing
> to what was Due − o − 1 − [6?]
> to a pare stockings − o − 5 − oo
> [Below this some lines have been completely blotted out.]

margit fox Due[?]
to 2 yd of garlik – 0 – 6 – 0 ["Garlick" was a type of linen cloth.]
to 1 yd garlik att 4s – 0 – 4 – 0
to ½ yd Dito – 0 – 2 – 0
[An illegible fragment ends this section.]

Unfortunately, the information included in Mehetabel's accounts is so sketchy that it is difficult to draw many conclusions. In some cases it is not even apparent whether the amounts she records—of pounds, shillings, and pence—were owed to her or due to the individual she names, or whether some transactions involved her husband's business. Further complicating the matter is that in New London, as in other areas, systems of exchange could be complex and wide ranging. Joshua Hempstead's diary attests to the variety of links in the local trading network. On one occasion, for example, he notes that he "pd Mr Roe 48s 11d & 21 for a looking Glass & to Capt Philips 36s for ye Salt & to Ben Lester 2s 6d for 2 Sheep Skins & to Ms Fox 1s 0d for vinegar for Ms Williams." Another entry documents his having "Recd of Ms Ab. Coit £25 to be dd [delivered to] mr Wellstead & Moffat & £10 of Ms Hallam to be dd to Jonas Clark."[34] Mehetabel's memoranda only hint at the depth of her involvement in the local system of economic exchange.

Nevertheless, even fragmented, Mehetabel's accounts are extremely valuable, since not a single account book kept by a woman between 1650 and 1750 is thought to have survived. During that period many women kept their own or their husbands' accounts; most, however, did not write them down. Mehetabel's accounts, while brief, do shed light on some of the types of transactions she engaged in. It is clear, for example, that she was involved in the trading of goods such as rum, molasses, cloth, and clothing—items linking her both to home production and to the transatlantic trade. It also appears that her commercial circle was wide, extending from housewives to shopkeepers to merchants. The Hannah Manwaring and "Margit," or Margaret, Fox Mehetabel refers to were likely neighborhood goodwives; "mrs Hallam" was probably the innkeeper Elizabeth Hallam; "mr" Hallam belonged to a family of merchants; and "Jams Rogers" seems to have been a sea captain. The inclusion of "Mdm Adams," the wife of the minister, in Mehetabel's client list exemplifies how women across the social spectrum participated in the broader economy.[35]

Mehetabel's list of reckonings, her notes about Coit-built vessels, and her shipyard apprentice record keeping are a strong indication that she both participated in her husband's business and that she maintained her own trade networks. Her accounts provide a rare example of how some women of her time might be linked to both the "local, personal, [and] largely oral trade networks" of their community, in Laurel Thatcher Ulrich's words, and to the literate, commercial, and male-dominated broader economy that would come to characterize New England over the course of the eighteenth century.[36]

A few weeks after John Coit returned from his trip to Gardiner's Island, it appears that he was off again. Mehetabel writes that "January ye 3 my Husband & Robert James went to Woodstock, ye 10 they came Home." (Although she did not include the year in this entry, it directly follows the one about John Coit going to the Isle of Wight.) Given that Mehetabel did not accompany John, his journey to Woodstock was likely business oriented. John was home in time to attend the ordination of Eliphalet Adams, a festive event that drew people from miles around. In New England's early years ordinations were solemn events preceded by days of humiliation and fasting, but by the late seventeenth century they had become celebratory social affairs. Ordination ceremonies were frequently followed by gatherings at which alcohol was served, and some towns even held ordination balls. Occasionally these celebrations became unruly; in fact, a few years following his own ordination, Eliphalet Adams commented that he had "so often seen such offensive Disorders upon such Occasions as these, People seeming to Imagine that it was a Time when they might allow themselves more Liberty."[37]

Adams's ordination brought Mehetabel's sister Sarah to New London; Mehetabel writes that on "feb^r 8 1708/9 Sister gardiner Came here to Mr Adams's ordination[;] the 28 she went home again."[38] Mehetabel and Sarah likely rejoiced over the opportunity to spend almost three weeks together, quite possibly one of the longest periods of time they would spend in each other's company after Sarah's marriage. At the time of her visit, Sarah was pregnant; that summer she gave birth to a daughter, Sarah. The exact date of her baby's birth is unknown; however, the New London church records report that Reverend Adams performed her baptism in June 1709. Since the baby was evidently born in New London, Mehetabel was likely among those attending to Sarah during her delivery.

The year 1709 brought another major development to New London along with the installation of a new minister: the introduction of Connecticut's first printing press. (The town would have the only press in the colony for the next forty-five years.) In 1710 the press published the first book to be printed in Connecticut, the 116-page *Confession of Faith Owned and Consented to by the Elders and Messengers of the Churches in the Colony of Connecticut in New England,* commonly known as the Saybrook Platform. (Printer Thomas Short's wife Elizabeth is said to have bound the copies, making her Connecticut's first binder.) A synod of ministers meeting at Saybrook (where the institution that would become Yale College was originally located) had produced the platform, which, broadly stated, aimed at standardizing church doctrine and increasing the authority of ministers over their congregations. The platform had the full support of Governor Saltonstall, who was a firm believer in state and clerical authority; however, the New London church and several other Connecticut churches refused to adopt it, believing that it diminished the autonomy of individual congregations and put too much power in the hands of the ministry. The printing of the Saybrook Platform served as a landmark not only in New England publishing history, but also in the history of New England Puritanism, as the controversy and debate it inspired had repercussions that were felt for decades afterward.[39]

For many years after New London's printing press was established, its primary output consisted of laws, proclamations, and sermons. Beginning in 1716, however, the press also began to publish almanacs, which had a more informal, popular appeal. Almanacs were available in New England throughout the colonial period and were the most widely read of any publication after the Bible. In addition to serving as calendars, almanacs included a wealth of both practical and entertaining material: weather forecasts, tide charts, poetry, medical remedies, recipes, proverbs, rosters of public officials, historical narratives, and "compendia of unusual information." Many readers referred to their almanacs on a daily basis, and some even used their blank pages for keeping a diary. (Eliphalet Adams, for example, kept a diary for one year in Thomas Robie's 1717 almanac; his entries consist mainly of notations about the weather and include a brief and dispassionate account of the illness and death of his infant son.)[40]

Few books were printed during the early history of the New London press. In 1715 Thomas Short's successor, Timothy Green, published schoolmaster Eleazer Moody's *School of Good Manners,* which included such chapters as "Rules for Children[']s Behaviour, at the Meeting-house, at Home, at the Table, in Company, in Discourse, at School, Abroad; with an Admonition to Children" and "The Ten Commandments in Verse, with a Compendious Body of Divinity, an Alphabet of Useful Copies, & Cyprian's Twelve Absurdities." Later that year, Green printed another instructional work when he reissued the famous *New England Primer* under the title *A Primer for the Colony of Connecticut.* Both books were kept in print for many years.[41]

The press maintained a small bookshop near the meetinghouse, which, at the time of Thomas Short's death in 1712, carried a dozen primers, three psalm books, two catechisms, eight Bibles, twenty-six "Smal Books," and some "books of divinity." Mehetabel left no record of whether she purchased any books at the shop, but as a dedicated reader she must have been pleased at the increased access to books the press afforded. Up until that time, she may have largely contented herself with borrowing books from neighbors. Most New London households possessed a few books, and some residents were able to amass respectable libraries. Ebenezer Dennis, for example, who ran a "house of entertainment," left behind an inventory of 139 books when he passed away in 1726.[42]

In the early years of their marriage, Mehetabel and John may not have been able to afford to buy many books, but by the time of John's death in 1744, they had acquired a small library. Unfortunately, the probate inventory does not list the titles other than specifying that one was a Bible. (This must have been a fine specimen, as it was valued at thirty shillings; in contrast, two "Large Bibles" in the New London printing press's 1757 inventory were valued at only five shillings each.) The value placed on the books in Mehetabel and John's home at the time of John's death does not necessarily reflect the full range of reading material at Mehetabel's disposal, for inventories often did not take into account small works such as almanacs and pamphlets or books that had deteriorated with use.[43]

In 1710, the year following the establishment of the printing press, New London became yet more important to the colony when it was selected by the British government as the site for Connecticut's chief post office. As a major stop on the main post road connecting Boston with New York and a significant port on the eastern seaboard, New London was fast becoming a communications nexus. The constant flow of shipping and road traffic, as well as the influx of people, information, and commodities, helped, in the words of the historian Chester Destler, to keep the "horizon broad" in New London. Although the town never became as urban or cosmopolitan as Boston, during the colonial period it was a strong secondary commercial center and a vibrant and dynamic community.[44]

For Mehetabel and other New Londoners, the presence of the printing press and the town's appointment as the colony's main postal stop would have meant not only an increased access to printed material and an improved mail system but the expedited delivery of wartime news and information. Updates on the fortunes of the colonial troops would have been eagerly anticipated, particularly since the war with the French had not been going well. In May of 1709 troops had gathered in Boston awaiting another expedition against Canada, but the promised British reinforcements never arrived. That October, Boston finally received official notification that the British government had actually canceled the expedition in July, news that caused many to wonder at the mother country's callousness toward American suffering. Following attacks on settlements in Connecticut, Massachusetts, New Hampshire, and Maine, the colonists' luck finally changed in 1710, when, with British assistance, the New England forces were at last able to capture Port Royal.[45]

Mehetabel, as interested in this major turn of events as she may have been, does not mention it in her diary; rather, her single dated entry for 1710 concerns a journey taken by her son. She writes that "June. 1710 John Coit went to Nyork with Mʳ Arnold." The fourteen-year-old John appears to have been on another sea voyage with the merchant John Arnold, perhaps this time as far away as New York City. Given the wartime conditions, it was dangerous to be on the water, and Mehetabel was undoubtedly anxious until his return. Several months later, in fact, French ships began to be seen so frequently off the New London coast that, according to Frances Caulkins, the town's inhabitants were kept "in a state of constant apprehension."[46]

At about this time Mehetabel may have made the following entry, which is undated but follows the entry about John's trip to New York: "August 10: 17[last two digits missing] the ile of wite taken by the french."[47] Since Gardiner's Island was never invaded by the French, this may have been just a rumor Mehetabel heard. Another possibility is that she accidentally wrote "the isle of wight" instead of "Block Island," located off the Rhode Island coast, which was troubled by French ships in August 1704 and August 1707.

In June 1711, while a constant watch against French privateers was being kept in New London harbor, the governors of the northern American colonies met in New London to plan a raid against Quebec. The governors remained for just a few days, quickly making their arrangements. Despite high hopes for a successful expedition, the fleet that sailed from Boston in late July met with catastrophe. Even with piloting assistance from sea captains familiar with the waters around Newfoundland, such as New London's John Mayhew, several vessels were driven against the rocks. Hundreds of men were lost, and the survivors retreated.

The news of the expedition's failure was greeted with deep disappointment across New England, and some interpreted the catastrophe as a token of God's displeasure with the colonies. This impression could only have been strengthened after Boston suffered the worst fire in the colonies' history not long afterward. Although casualties were minimal, entire streets were laid waste and scores of people were left homeless. Counted among the wreckage were Boston's two most important buildings: the first meetinghouse and the Town House. In his sermon *Burnings Bewailed,* published after the fire, the Reverend Increase Mather implored his readers to be "deeply Sensible" of the "Awful Stroke from God" that was laid upon them, as well as of their "Provoking Evils" that had led to this "Mount of Danger and Distress."[48]

As a devout Puritan, Mehetabel may have shared in the belief that recent events carried a divine message, particularly since they followed on the heels of a series of misfortunes within her family. In April 1711 Mehetabel's forty-six-year-old brother John—who by this time was known as "Captain" and had become Woodstock's first representative to the General Court at Boston—lost his thirty-nine-year-old wife Mary to complications from childbirth. (The baby, a girl named Hannah, perhaps after Mehetabel and John's deceased sister, died a few weeks later.) Left with nine children ranging in age from seventeen years to twenty-one months, John did not remain a widower for long. In November he married Esther Britman Alcock, a well-to-do childless widow of Roxbury, whose first husband had been the son of the Roxbury female healer Sarah Palsgrave Alcock.

Three months following the loss of her sister-in-law, Mehetabel suffered a much heavier blow when her sister Sarah passed away, also after having given birth. The East Hampton church records note that Sarah died on July 3, 1711, "abt. 6 of ye clock in ye morning after she had lain in abt. 3 weeks." Mehetabel did not mark the date in her diary, however, it is doubtless that Sarah's death was one of the greatest sorrows of her life. Apart from her daughters Elizabeth and Martha, Sarah had been Mehetabel's closest living female relative, someone with whom she had shared a unique and lifelong bond. As sisters, they had held a central place in each other's lives, and the special "Respects, Love, & Dear affection" they had felt for each other would be difficult, if not impossible, to replicate.[49]

John Gardiner laid Sarah to rest next to his first wife in East Hampton's South End burying ground overlooking the town green. Sarah's newborn son, named Jonathan, had survived the delivery, and he and his two-year-old sister Sarah remained with their father after Sarah's death. John Gardiner married again and ultimately outlived Sarah by almost three decades. When he eventually died as the result of injuries sustained after falling from a horse while visiting Groton, Connecticut, his body was brought to Mehetabel and John's home for preparation for burial. The grand memorial marking his grave in New London—which refers to him as the "Third Lord of the Isle of Wight"—stands in sharp contrast to the simple, inscriptionless stone that was placed over Sarah's grave.

CHAPTER SIX

Mistress and Matriarch, 1712–1725

A<small>FTER</small> S<small>ARAH'S</small> death, her children by William Coit—twelve-year-old Daniel and nine-year-old William—likely moved into Mehetabel and John's home, as John had been appointed their guardian after their father died.[1] By late that year, then, Mehetabel's household would have been a full one, consisting not only of her five children and two nephews, but probably also her mother-in-law, as well as the Coit family's two slaves, "old Nanny" and Mingo.

Some months later, the Coit household was reduced by one when fourteen-year-old Joseph left for Boston to receive instruction in ship's carpentry. That Joseph was sent out of the colony for training his own father could have provided seems strange, but a nineteenth-century family history states that in going to Boston Joseph was following family tradition. It is not known with whom Joseph apprenticed, but family records indicate that he ended up being unhappy with the situation and was allowed to return to New London.[2]

The year Joseph left for his apprenticeship, Mehetabel made two related but perplexing entries in her diary. On the inside front cover, above a list of accounts, is the fragment "September the[?] 4 1712[?] Mr Waters his. . . ." The paper is torn after "Mr Waters," and Mehetabel drew a line through the notation, which appears to be some type of account. "Sam Watters" appears in the list of names that follow, but the identity of this person has been difficult to establish. Near the back of Mehetabel's diary, a separate entry also concerns Mr. Waters. She writes that on "September 30 1712 I went to Woodstock, & Mr Waters, & Mr John Gardiner & Joseph Coit & come hom y^e. . . .” Since the date of the trip to Woodstock—September 30, 1712—is separated by only a few weeks from the date of the account—September 4, 1712—the two entries are likely related in some way, yet the connection is ambiguous. The motivation for Mehetabel’s trip to Woodstock, as well as her choice of traveling companions—the unknown Mr. Waters, the former husband of her late sister, and her son Joseph—are a mystery. A final entry in which Mehetabel mentions Mr. Waters—“july 1718 Mr Waters went a way”—is equally puzzling.[3]

If Mehetabel returned home by the end of October, she would have heard the good news of the cessation of arms between England and France celebrated with the firing of the New London fort’s great guns. The end of the war was formalized in the early spring of 1713 with the Treaty of Utrecht. The official proclamation of peace made in New London the following August, according to the *Boston News-Letter,* was heralded by a multigun salute by “the Militia, the Fort, and all the Vessels in the [sea] Road, . . . and General Acclamations of Joy.”[4]

The happy news of official peace came on the heels of otherwise difficult times for Mehetabel’s family. In early July 1713 John Coit’s brother Solomon’s wife Mary had died a few days after giving birth to a healthy baby girl. (According to Joshua Hempstead, she died “Suddenly” after having been “brought to bed one week.”)[5] And the week following Mary’s death, John’s mother Martha, then in her early seventies, passed away. Martha had outlived not only her husband but seven of the ten children to whom she had given birth.

Although Martha did not leave a will, some time before her death she made a special bequest to her namesake, Mehetabel and John’s daughter Martha. According to family records, the elder Martha left her granddaughter a silver porringer inscribed with the initials “J. ^C. M.,” believed to signify “Joseph and Martha Coit.” (The style of the inscription, with the initial of the couple’s surname placed in superscript between their first initials, is common to early American engraved objects.) The porringer, which may have been a wedding gift to Martha and Joseph, would have been valued as an heirloom and symbol of the family’s refinement. Martha’s gift of the piece to her granddaughter was in keeping with the custom of deeding land to sons and household items to daughters; since Martha had no daughters of her own, it would have been a logical—and meaningful—choice for her to leave this precious item to her namesake.[6]

According to family lore, the silver porringer survived for many years and continued to be passed down through succeeding generations of girls named

Martha. This pattern of deeding family heirlooms through the female line
of families has been explored in depth by Barbara McLean Ward, who has
found that the practice not only preserved female personal property but sustained kinship networks and served to provide a "constant reminder . . . of
maternal ancestors."[7]

It appears that a few weeks after the deaths of Mary and Martha, Mehetabel
and John sought out the company of their neighbors as a diversion from their
troubles. Joshua Hempstead notes in his diary that on July 30 "in [the] aftern
I went & my wife with Jno Coit & his wife into ye Neck & [to] Minors's &
Ensign Harris's a visetting." The following month they and John's recently
widowed brother Solomon accompanied the Hempsteads on another excur-
sion; this time they "went to Tho Dowglass's . . . to eat watermilions."[8]

Mehetabel did not make a record of the outings with the Hempsteads,
nor, with the exception of her notations about her reading and visiting, did
she ever provide any specifics concerning her leisure-time pursuits. A variety
of recreational opportunities would have been available to her, however, and
it is probable that she, like her contemporaries, enjoyed a bit of fun. Although the stereotype of the New England Puritan as ascetic killjoy endures,
in reality Puritans, like people of any age, valued leisure and recreation. As
Bruce Daniels has so effectively demonstrated in *Puritans at Play,* colonial
New England culture attached great importance to the benefits of "relaxing
pastimes." Even the Puritan ministry recognized that, in moderation, the
regular enjoyment of such earthly pleasures as food, sex (within marriage, of
course), and innocent amusements not only helped steer people away from
sins such as gluttony, lust, and idleness but led to the rejuvenation of the
individual and in the end profited the whole community.[9]

In addition to visiting with neighbors and getting together with friends
to eat "watermilions," Mehetabel likely attended spinning and sewing bees,
berrying parties, house-raisings, and dinner parties. Joshua Hempstead refers
to large-scale "entertainments" occasionally hosted by the Winthrop family,
to local horse shows and races, and even to such a crowd-drawing attraction
as a "Lyon" fresh from touring "N. York [and] ye Jerseys." Weddings also
provided opportunities for socializing, and over the years Mehetabel would
have attended the marriage ceremonies of numerous neighbors, friends, and
family members. As the colonial period progressed, wedding receptions were
often occasions of great festivity. Joshua Hempstead notes, for example, that
at the evening wedding of his son Nathaniel, which was held "in Ms Hal-
lams Hall," "many people held the Entertainment till between 12 & 1 Clock."

Likewise, at the reception he hosted for his son John, there was "a houseful of People [who] Stayed to play till midnight." A party held in honor of a newly married couple from nearby Stonington—at which, Hempstead writes, he was "Entertained Liberally with Plumb Cake & Cheese & Wine & other Strong Drink"—drew more than a hundred people on horseback, in addition to the "Near Neighbours that come on foot."[10]

It is clear from Hempstead's diary that New Londoners also found entertainment value in the spectacle of public punishments. Although disturbing to modern sensibilities, the public dispensation of justice played a significant role in colonial life. Rooted in English tradition, the practice took on added meaning in Puritan New England as a means to both deter crime and impart a moral lesson. Prisoners were marched out to the beating of drums and were addressed by ministers who had prepared special sermons about the offender's misdeeds. The wrongdoer was expected to confess and repent before the administration of punishment, which could come in the form of public humiliation, branding, mutilation, or whipping. Though rare in most places, executions became much-talked-about events and attracted large numbers of spectators.[11]

In New London a range of harsh penalties were meted out over the years. Although very few executions took place, convicted criminals were placed in the pillory or the gallows and were branded, whipped, and mutilated. Joshua Hempstead writes, for example, of going into town "to See a man Branded on ye forehead for breaking open a house in Lebanon & Stealing Sundrys &c" and of being present when "Wm Watkins an Irishman was Branded in ye forehead & had his Right Ear Cut of[f] or Cropt for Burglary." (Watkins may have received a harsher sentence than the other culprit because his crime took place "on the Sabath or lords day.") In 1719 a large crowd was present when Dr. William Blogget, "being Convicted of Adultry with the wife of Lt Timothy Pierce[,] was whipt 25 Stripes & Branded on ye forehead wth [the letter] A & halter put on his neck yr to Remain forever."[12] Blogget was fortunate to escape with his life since adultery was a capital crime, although the death penalty was very infrequently applied. It is impossible to say how often Mehetabel turned out to witness such events, but she would not have been able to avoid them completely, as civil and church leaders encouraged community attendance.

The year 1714 is a significant one for Mehetabel's story, if only because it is the date she inscribed on the inside front cover of her diary with her statement of ownership: "Mehetabel Coit Her Book 1714." Her reasons for dating her diary in this way are unknown, but it is probable that this was the year she began recording entries in this particular volume. Apart from the inscription, the year appears in only one dated entry, in which she writes, "July the 1 1714 my husbend & I went to Wodstock and Come home the 8 day."[13] This visit to Woodstock may have marked Mehetabel's first return since her trip in the fall of 1712 and was likely intended as an opportunity to see family and friends.

A few months after Mehetabel and John's return from Woodstock, the worst measles epidemic in colonial history reached New London. Originating in Newport, Rhode Island, the previous summer, the epidemic—which also gave rise to fatal intestinal, respiratory, and throat infections—had struck Boston in the fall of 1713. By December 1714 it had worked its way down to New London, where it gained strength the following spring. Mehetabel and her family escaped unharmed, but many of their neighbors and extended family members were not so fortunate. John Coit's brother Solomon, for example, lost his second wife, Elizabeth, the former widow of the printer Thomas Short, whom he had married the previous summer. (Eight months later Solomon married his third and final wife, Abigail.) The local mortality rate was extremely high, with some families losing several members in quick succession. The Hill family, for example, lost two young sons and a daughter within a single week; Ebenezer Dennis lost his wife and newborn child on the same day that he buried a daughter.[14]

Most people who came down with the measles were probably cared for by their families, perhaps also receiving some treatment from a local medical practitioner. Several New London residents did acquire some type of medical background over the years, beginning with founder John Winthrop. Winthrop's son Wait-Still also dispensed medical advice and remedies to his neighbors, while Wait-Still's son John appears to have tended to Joshua Hempstead's wife in her final illness in 1716. Hempstead refers in his diary to several active practitioners within the community over the years—including a Dr. Stephenson, Dr. Palmes, Dr. Goddard, and a Mrs. Pemberton—but little is known about their range of skills. Jeremiah Miller, a 1709 Yale graduate who had studied medicine and who also served as the local schoolmaster, appears to have been starting his medical career around the time of the measles epidemic.[15]

The devastation wrought by the epidemic could only have reinforced misgivings expressed by Connecticut's civil and clerical leaders that God was not satisfied with the way people were living their lives. In May 1714 Governor Saltonstall, his council, and the General Court, having taken into "serious consideration the many evident tokens that the glory is departed from us, [and the fact that] the providences of God are plainly telling us that our ways do not please him," had asked church leaders to inquire into the general state of religion and morality. The ministers, reporting back, claimed that, among other evils, they had found neglect in the attendance of public worship, a lack of the Bible in certain households, deficiency in family government, contempt of ecclesiastical and civil authority, and intemperance, as well as evidence of "talebearing & defamation." In the autumn of 1715 Saltonstall responded to these findings by issuing a proclamation intended to reinforce laws made for the "Suppressing and Punishing [of] diverse Immoralities and Irreligious Practices," including lack of church attendance, lying and "pro-phane swearing," drunkenness, and "unseasonable meetings of young people in the evenings."[16]

On the local level, Saltonstall would have found a supporter in the Rever-end Eliphalet Adams; the topic of an election-day sermon Adams had given in 1710 had been, after all, "The Necessity of Judgment and Righteousness in a Land." Like Saltonstall, Adams recognized the need to avoid arousing God's anger through sinful behavior. When a great snowstorm hit New Lon-don in February 1717, for example, he interpreted it as a sign of God's "Judg-ment and Displeasure" and recommended that the congregation "search . . . out what it is that is so Provoking unto God in the midst of us."[17] Adams's style was not fire-and-brimstone, and he was considerably more moderate than some of his contemporaries, but he was deeply committed to the con-cepts of repentance and reformation.

The efforts of Saltonstall, Adams, and others to revive commitment to the Puritan mission of creating a "city on a hill" that would inspire the rest of the world ultimately met with only limited success. Trends toward increas-ing secularity and social permissiveness, which had begun before the turn of the eighteenth century, continued to gain strength in New England. As the first generations of Puritan leaders died, and as New England became a thriving commercial center with a greater degree of contact with the outside world, religion became less of a driving force in the lives of individuals and communities. These changes were more evident in urban than rural areas, yet those living in the countryside were also affected. New England, as Richard Bushman has noted, was changing from a society characterized by pious, inward-looking Puritans to one of shrewd, independent-thinking Yankees.[18]

Mehetabel recorded no diary entries for 1715 or 1716, and only one for 1717. Although brief, it is one of the diary's strangest, both because of its format and because Mehetabel evidently withheld something even as she wrote the entry. The subject is the family's acquisition of another slave, someone who would become a significant part of Mehetabel's life. On the page preceding her notation about Mingo, she writes, "nell Cam to live here in the year 1717 [smudged word] in September she [then?] being twenty years of age." Below this line she wrote the word "she," then crossed it out, and below that she wrote "nell —— ——."[19] It seems that Mehetabel wanted to record something more about Nell but found herself unable to articulate her thoughts.

Nothing is known about Nell's origins; it is unclear whether she was bought from a local owner or whether she was a recent arrival in New London. No local shipping manifests from the period have survived, and Joshua Hempstead, who commonly documented the arrivals and departures of vessels in the harbor, was out of town for part of the month when Nell arrived in the Coit household. Being "twenty years of age"—approximately the same age as Mehetabel's son John—Nell was young, presumably strong, and likely brought into the home to help Mehetabel with the household work. (By this time, "old Nanny" was advanced in years.) While thirteen-year-old Elizabeth and eleven-year-old Martha would have been expected to assist their

Pages from Mehetabel's diary. *Photograph by Robert and Elizabeth Hughes.*

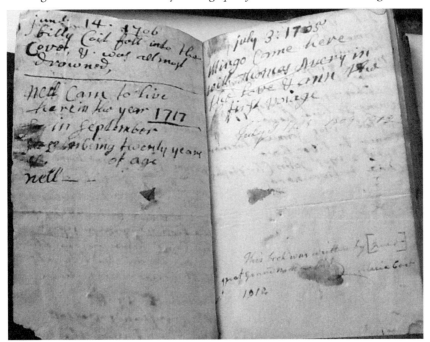

mother with certain chores, the multiple duties associated with running an early-eighteenth-century household meant that there was always extra work to do. In acquiring Nell, Mehetabel could ensure that she and her daughters were relieved of at least some of this labor, particularly the most disagreeable tasks.[20]

Perhaps Nanny and Mingo helped ease Nell's transition into the household, providing instruction on local mores and her new owners' expectations and offering her companionship and support. It is not known whether Nell ever married or had a family of her own. She would remain with Mehetabel for the next four decades, until her death just a little more than two months before Mehetabel's own. On the occasion of Nell's death, Joshua Hempstead described her as a "faithfull Serv[an]t," but as a slave her relationship with her lifelong mistress would certainly have been a complicated one.[21]

After an act forbidding the importation of Indian servants and slaves was passed in Connecticut in 1715, New London relied to a greater extent on black slavery. At the same time resistance to the idea of free black citizenship grew. The year that Nell came to live with Mehetabel, for example, a former slave named Robert Jacklin met with prolonged harassment after purchasing a house and land. Opposition to Jacklin's acquisition of the property became so intense that some townspeople attempted to persuade a resident of Newbury, Massachusetts, where Jacklin had spent his servitude, to claim him as a runaway slave. In April 1717 New London was moved to hold a special town meeting on the issue of blacks and land ownership; the result was a vote to "utterly oppose and protest against Robert Jacklin a negro man's buying any land in this town, or being an inhabitant within s'd town," and to recommend that the colony's General Assembly "take some prudent care that no person of yt colour may ever have any possessions or freehold estate within this government." (A law making it illegal for free people of color to purchase land or even reside in the colony was passed the following year, although it seems to have been infrequently enforced.) Despite these obstacles, Jacklin persevered, and he was ultimately able to record his deed the following year. In 1719 he sold his land at a profit, and several years later he became the owner of 128 acres in Colchester, Connecticut.[22]

Nell's entry into the Coit household did not come at an auspicious time, as by the late fall of 1717 another epidemic, originating in Boston, had spread to New London. Joshua Hempstead described this "Distempr" as featuring a "violent Ague & pain in [the] Bowells & Small of ye back" that was accompanied by a high fever. When Hempstead himself fell ill, he found that taking "Some physick . . . work[ed] kindly downwards & was a Means of Removing the pain"; he treated a remaining sharp ache in his back and chest with "an other gentle purge." Although Hempstead remained in a "very weak & Low" condition for a full two months, he subsequently made a complete recovery. Others in town—including "old goodee Boddington," a mariner named David Chapman, and Richard Christophers's apprentice William Daniels and "Negro man Quash"—were not so fortunate.[23]

Mehetabel's family, which had managed to escape the brunt of the measles outbreak a few years earlier, was not able to elude the distemper. In December, Mehetabel's fifteen-year-old nephew Billy, the son of her sister Sarah and John Coit's brother William, fell ill, and two days later he died. Mehetabel did not mark Billy's passing in her diary, despite the fact that she had earlier taken note of his near brush with death as a child ("june 14. 1706 billy Coit fell into the cove, & was allmost drowned"). According to Joshua Hempstead, who had hired Billy the previous year to help him work on a sloop, he "was buried between 2 & 3 clock" in the afternoon of the day following his death.[24] The funeral must have been an especially sad occasion for Billy's nineteen-year-old brother Daniel, who, aside from his half sister and half brother who lived with their father, John Gardiner, now had no immediate family.

About a week after Billy's death, "old Nanny" died. Nanny's advanced years may have made her especially susceptible to the distemper, which Joshua Hempstead noted had particularly afflicted "ye Aged" when it had struck Boston. After her death, she was likely laid to rest in the Coit family plot in the local burying ground, as was customary in New London.[25]

Although Mehetabel's household suffered no additional losses to the sickness, its ranks grew smaller in the coming months as her children left to make their way in the world. In the summer of 1718, twenty-two-year-old John, who had evidently already met with some success in the family shipbuilding business, built a home of his own. In taking such a step, John may have been looking ahead to the time when he would start a family. This prospect was not far off: the following year he married twenty-year-old Grace Christophers, the daughter of the wealthy New London judge and merchant Richard Christophers. As a wedding gift, John Coit senior, with Mehetabel's consent, deeded John some property that had formerly belonged to his parents. (They later made similar gifts of land to help their other two sons establish themselves.)[26]

In contrast to his brother John's smooth transition to adulthood, Mehetabel's son Joseph's attempts to forge an independent life were beset by difficulties. After the failed Boston shipbuilding apprenticeship, he appears to have continued his training under a series of employers who included his father, Joshua Hempstead, and his uncle John Gardiner. While working at Gardiner's Island in the summer of 1718, Joseph sustained a serious cut to his foot, which "spoilt him for a [ship's] carpenter," according to a memoir he wrote later in life. Joshua Hempstead's son Nathaniel, who was also working for Gardiner at the time, brought Joseph home, where he could be tended by Mehetabel. Once he recovered, he decided to go to sea. Within a few months, however, Joseph contracted a severe case of smallpox while in the Caribbean. To make matters worse, his ship was chased by Spanish pirates on the voyage home.[27]

When Joseph's vessel reached New London, the crew was quarantined, so Mehetabel was unable to care for her son. John Coit, however, was commissioned by the governor to provide the sailors with supplies, so he may have had some contact with him. Joseph had the smallpox "so exceeding bad" that it caused his eyesight to deteriorate. He ultimately recovered, however, and went on to make nineteen sea voyages—"three before the mast, five as mate, and eleven as master"—before becoming a merchant in New London, which appears to have been his true calling.[28]

Although Joseph was a bit of a late bloomer with regard to a career and marriage—he did not wed until he was almost thirty-four—he found religious commitment early in life. In fact, he was made a full member of the New London church in 1718, when he was only nineteen. (His brother John, in contrast, did not join the church until he was well into middle age.) Joseph's status as a church member would have earned him some respect in the community; it would also have been a source of pride for Mehetabel, who had likely spent many hours in the religious instruction of her children. Mehetabel must have been equally pleased when her son Thomas was taken into the church the following year, just a few weeks shy of his seventeenth birthday. The boys were unusually young to take on the responsibility of full church membership; in most communities throughout the colonial period, fewer than 10 percent of new members were under twenty years of age.[29]

Two years after John and Joseph moved out of the house, Mehetabel's daughter Elizabeth left to get married. At the time, she was only sixteen. Any reluctance Mehetabel may have felt at allowing her daughter to marry at such a young age was possibly alleviated to an extent by Elizabeth's choice of a mate: Captain Samuel Gardiner, a son of John Gardiner's by his first wife. Samuel, who was about nine years older than Elizabeth, not only inherited the prestige that came with the family name—although as a second son he was not heir to the title "Lord"—but he also possessed a significant amount of land in East Hampton, where he and Elizabeth settled. Although Mehetabel had commemorated John's wedding day in her diary—"July 2. 1719 John Coit was Marryed to Grace Christophers"—she did not record the date of Elizabeth's ceremony, which took place in New London on November 8, 1720.[30]

In the spring of 1720 John's wife Grace had given birth to their first child; Mehetabel observed in her diary, "April 7th: 1720 John Coit was born." Her grandson's birth signaled a new stage of life for Mehetabel, one that must have provided her with a certain amount of satisfaction. To live to see one's children's children was considered to be "the crown of mothering."[31]

At the time of her grandson's birth, Mehetabel was almost forty-seven years old, well along into middle age. Her active period of mothering had almost come to an end: only fourteen-year-old Martha and eighteen-year-old Thomas were still at home. (Although Mehetabel's nephew Daniel may also have been in the house, he would have been gone by the spring of 1721, when he married Lydia Christophers, the sister of John's wife Grace.) Thomas was probably away from home much of the time, working at the shipyard and, according to Mehetabel's diary, occasionally traveling. The month following Elizabeth's marriage, for example, Mehetabel writes that "Thomas Coit went to Woodstock Decemb[r] the 28th 1720 and Came home the 4th day of January following."[32] Mehetabel did not specify whether the journey was for business or pleasure, but it likely had elements of both. In addition to spending time with his Chandler cousins, Thomas may have been sent to do some trading on his father's behalf, as his brothers had done before him.

Although Mehetabel was probably absorbed by the changes occurring in her family during this time, she also would have been aware of various events occurring in her community and beyond. During the early months of 1721, for example, she could not have failed to notice a series of disturbances in the New London meetinghouse involving the Rogerenes. On several Sabbath days, John Rogers, the seventy-three-year-old founder of the sect, and his "Crew" disrupted worship and attempted to hold their own services in the meetinghouse in the break between morning and afternoon meetings. Rogers was not deterred by the punishment he received for these actions, which included fines and on at least one occasion temporary imprisonment. This series of confrontations with the New London church would be Rogers's last, however, as not long afterward he contracted smallpox on a trip to Boston (again in the throes of an epidemic). In the fall of 1721 Rogers succumbed to the disease, and several members of his family soon followed.[33]

Given their convictions regarding divine retribution, many in the New London congregation would have believed that John Rogers had ultimately received what he deserved. This impression may have been reinforced by the fact that few outside the Rogers clan contracted smallpox. (In reality, the disease's failure to spread was undoubtedly due to the quarantining of the family.) Reverend Eliphalet Adams does not appear to have belabored this point from the pulpit, but he probably felt some relief at the passing of his long-time adversary. Over the years, Adams seems to have tried to defuse the situation with the Rogerenes and to temper his behavior toward Rogers—on one occasion even sending him a bottle of spirits while he was imprisoned during a cold spell. The group's provocations, not to say its very existence, however, could not have been easy for Adams to bear. After Rogers's death, the Rogerenes continued to practice their faith, but their relationship with the New London church was marked by less conflict.

With the threat of smallpox looming, and the many dangers of child-birth well known to her, Mehetabel likely greeted the news of her daughter Elizabeth's first pregnancy with a mixture of concern and joy. Happily, how-ever, Elizabeth was safely delivered of a baby girl in November 1721. As her mother and Chandler grandmother had done before her, Elizabeth named her first-born daughter Elizabeth. Although Mehetabel would record various items about her granddaughter in her diary over the years, she did not enter the date of her birth.

A few months following the new baby's arrival, Mehetabel's daughter Martha sent her sister Elizabeth a letter that suggests that she may not yet have met her niece. Written when Martha was fifteen, it is the earliest of her extant letters; unfortunately, Elizabeth's letters appear not to have survived.

New-London. February the 23. 1721/2

Dear Sister:

We are by providence Sepperated far asunder and Therby Deprived of a Considerable part of that Comfort which we might Justly Expect to Take in the society of Each other. it therefore becomes us Since we are capable, to be Sending to Each other Every opportunity, and I am confident you will be Carefull So to Doe[.] we have no other Such friends, as methinks we Should be, what Like an only Sister, may I truely Say, but you have a Nearer Relation but I Trust you are verry mindfull Still of pore Martha and cant forgit your fathers house. and your old acquaintance past wherof are Married viz. Tho: Manwaring & Ester Christopher's Clem: Miner & Abigal Turner &c. Samual Richards Corts Moly Hallam. Hanna Pressan hath Lost her Child very sund-ing.[34] we Expect you & you littel Daughter over the first good opportunity, O I Long to [see you?] ten times as much as ever I did if possibel, this winter hath bin a Thousand year Long every body wants to See you & your Child very much

[written vertically on left-hand side of paper] it is very Late & I must not in-larg at this time, give my Dear kind Love to your Spouse & except the Same your Self from your only Sister M C[35]

Martha's age at the time helps to explain the letter's content; likewise, her notation about the lateness of the hour having prevented her from writing at greater length accounts for the haste with which she evidently composed it. She would have written by candlelight after the day's chores and lessons had been completed and perhaps in preparation for a boat leaving for East Hampton the following day. It being February, there would have been fewer boats making the crossing between the two towns, and thus fewer opportu-nities for the two sisters to communicate.

Martha's letter recalls the one written to Mehetabel by Sarah many years earlier, in its expression of yearning for a missing sister. While Sarah con-veyed to Mehetabel her "Dear affection yᵗ longs to vent it self into yʳ boo-som" Martha declares to Elizabeth, "O I Long to see you ten times as much as ever I did if possibel." Like Sarah, Martha asks that her sister write fre-quently ("it therefore becomes us Since we are capable, to be Sending to Each other Every opportunity, and I am confident you will be Carefull So to Doe") and to keep her close in thought ("I Trust you are verry mindfull Still of pore Martha"). Sarah and Martha both seem to have believed that "we have no other Such friends . . . what Like an only sister," and each appears to have regarded this relationship as one to be treasured.

One significant difference distinguishes Sarah's letter from Martha's: their circumstances at the time they were writing. Sarah was terrified at the pros-pect of an Indian attack on her community, while Martha wrote from a posi-tion of security and comfort. This distinction is underscored by the chatty tone of Martha's letter and by the gossip she chose to include. Far from having to worry about her safety each day, Martha could afford to focus her attention on such matters as local romance.

· · · · ·

Several months after Martha sent her letter to Elizabeth, Mehetabel made two entries in her diary. The first marked the birth of John and Grace's second son—"july 8. 1722 Richard Coit born" (the baby was likely named after Grace's father). The second is rather long by the diary's standards and encompasses several pieces of information: "October 20. 1722 Thomas Coit went to Rhod=Iland, yᵉ 26 day he came hom again, the 29 my husband went to the ile of wight and East hampton and Came home the first of novemᵇʳ: on a fryday the 2 day Thomas Coit was taken sick very bad all that weak, the next weak went a brod again." After Thomas returned from his short trip to Rhode Island, he seems to have fallen ill with what was commonly known as the "bloody flux": diarrhea, dysentery, or some other type of intestinal infection. According to Joshua Hempstead's diary, the flux afflicted several New London households about this time, and on November 2 a nine-year-old boy named John Truman died from it. The flux could leave sufferers in a weakened state for some time even after their condition improved, and Mehetabel's comment regarding Thomas's decision to go "a brod again" after having been "taken sick very bad" for a week could imply that she felt he was rushing his recovery. Before he left, she may have treated him with her own remedy for "all sorts of f[l]uxes," which she included in her diary. The concoction calls for "2 quarts of new milk, 2 nutmegs, eighteen peppercorns, eighteen Cloves, [?] peneworth of sinemon [cinnamon, and] twise as much of the outward bark of an old oak." Mehetabel recommended that it be administered "at 4 times[;] the first time as hot as you can Drink it. the next time not so hot[. . .] att 4 a clock in the morning at 4 in the afternoon and at night."³⁶

By the next year, Mehetabel's daughter Martha had also begun to travel, although her trips appear to have been social in nature. In August 1723 Martha left on a prolonged visit to the Ellery family in Newport, Rhode Island. Although Mehetabel recorded no entries in her diary for 1723, a letter she received from Martha during that time survives:

New-port A.t the 13 1723

Honᵈ: mother

I was very glad to hear from you[.] I felt uneasy that I did not hear from you in So Long atime I did not know but every body was dead, I had not heard whether father had got home. I Thot I Should had a Letter by Mʳ Willson but had not, I am very glad we have heard from Bro. Joseph, I felt concarn'd about him when we heard the Dolfull news about Cap: Manring & John Christophers[.] it was very Surprising to me when I heard of it.

Mad: Elery Say's I munst not come home this two month's, I am going to flower her a doubel nightdres wide and narrow, & one thing or other, when I have don them I will come home becaus I know how very Lonsom it is for you now I am hear, She Talk's of giving me a Caleco peatcoat to quilt, and several things.

She woud be very glad of a bottel of Rosewater if you can Spar it, She intends to Send you Some more of her waters we have ten gallons of it.

I Long to See you very much. [sentence crossed out: give my love to bro. John & sister Grace?] give my Duty to father & your self & Love to brother Jnº. & Sister. I want to See the Children verry much—no more at present from your Dutyfull Daughter—

Martha Coit.[37]

The Ellery family was, as previously noted, distantly related to Mehetabel's husband: John Coit's aunt was Benjamin Ellery's stepmother. Joshua Hempstead's diary indicates that John Coit and Benjamin Ellery—who at various times was a merchant, sea captain, privateer, judge, and member of Rhode Island's General Assembly—maintained a business relationship over the years. Martha's letter suggests that Mehetabel and Abigail Ellery had a trade network of their own, exchanging homemade medicinal waters. "Mad[am]" Ellery was the former Abigail Wilkins of Salem, whose relatives had played an active role in the 1692 witchcraft crisis.[38] Four years younger than Mehetabel, Abigail had married Benjamin Ellery in Gloucester in 1696. It is unclear whether Mehetabel and Abigail first became acquainted through their husbands or were somehow already known to each other.

At the time of Martha's visit, the Ellerys' son and two of their daughters were married and living in Newport; another daughter, eight-year-old Mary, remained at home. (The previous year the Ellerys had lost a son about Martha's age, Benjamin junior, who appears to have died from smallpox.) The Ellerys were quite wealthy and were counted among Newport's social elite. As a mark of their status, they had had their portraits painted by Nehemiah Partridge in 1717. The full-length paintings depict the couple in formal dress, each standing against a velvet-draped window. Benjamin rests one hand on a cane, a sword's hilt evident beneath the drape of his coat and a three-masted ship, perhaps one of his own, visible through the window, while Abigail holds a flower, suggesting refinement or gentility. On Abigail's death in 1742, the *Boston Evening-Post* carried her obituary—an unusual tribute for a woman—reporting that she had been a "Gentlewoman who adorned the Character of a Christian, in every Branch of Female Li[f]e, so

Nehemiah Partridge, portraits of Abigail Wilkins Ellery and Benjamin Ellery, ca. 1717. *Courtesy Newport Historical Society.*

that she was cordially respected by all sorts of People, and the Poor do in a particular Manner regret a Loss they must sensibly feel."[39]

Newport had a population of about four thousand and was New England's second largest urban center after Boston. In addition to being a religiously tolerant community that harbored Quakers, Jews, and Baptists, Newport was also one of New England's most cosmopolitan centers, with a thriving maritime trade, a diverse population, a cultivated upper class, and numerous shops, taverns, and social clubs. During her stay with the Ellerys, Martha would have had an active social life, paying visits, attending dinner parties, and perhaps even going to balls.[40]

In spite of the excitement offered by this change in scenery and society, the seventeen-year-old Martha seems to have sorely missed her family. This homesickness may account in part for the distraught opening lines of her letter—"I felt uneasy that I did not hear from you in So Long atime[.] I did not know but every body was dead"—but her distress may also have been caused by the "Dolfull news" she mentions having recently received. A few weeks earlier, two New London mariners, Captain Peter Manwaring and

John Christophers (who had once served an apprenticeship with John Coit), had lost their lives when their ship was wrecked in a storm off the coast of Long Island. Since none of the crew survived, the tragedy only became apparent after bodies and debris began washing ashore. Given these circumstances, Martha's relief at having received word of her brother Joseph's safety is not surprising.

One other event that may have indirectly contributed to Martha's anxiety was the public execution of twenty-six pirates that had occurred in Newport just a few weeks earlier. The pirates had been captured after a battle with a British man-of-war off the Newport coast, and after being tried and convicted, they were hanged as a group under their "Jolly Roger" flag. Their execution constituted the biggest mass pirate hanging in New England's history and attracted hordes of people from the surrounding countryside. If Martha had arrived in Newport by the time of the hangings, she and the Ellerys almost certainly would have attended them. No executions had been carried out in New London during Martha's lifetime, and the experience of witnessing what was probably the first hanging she had ever seen—particularly one on such a large scale—may have been as unnerving to her in its own way as receiving the news of the shipwreck.[41]

It is likely Martha returned to New London in time for her brother Thomas's wedding, which took place on November 5 at New London's Congregational church. Thomas's bride was Mary Prentis, the daughter of Jonathan and Elizabeth Latimer Prentis. (Jonathan was a New London justice and prosperous former mariner who served as a deputy to Connecticut's General Court; Elizabeth was the woman previously mentioned who was considered sufficiently knowledgeable about the "mariner's art and navigation" to be designated as a surrogate instructor to her husband's apprentice.) Thomas and Mary, who were both twenty-one, settled in New London. Although Thomas may have worked for a time at his father's shipyard, he seems to have ultimately taken up the trade of blacksmith after John and Mehetabel deeded him John's "Smiths Shop" the following year.[42]

Several months after Thomas's wedding, Mehetabel noted in her diary that she was able to visit her daughter Elizabeth, then expecting her second child. She writes that "feb^r 20: 1724 on a thursday my Husband and I went to gardiners Iland, the next day to East-Hampton. we went up from the fire place a foott to the towne[.] the 25 day Samuell gardiner was born." Mehetabel and John's stop at Gardiner's Island may have involved business with John

Gardiner, as well as an opportunity to see Mehetabel's sister Sarah's children, fourteen-year-old Jonathan and twelve-year-old Sarah. Their traveling conditions were far from ideal; according to Joshua Hempstead's diary, the day they left for the island was cold and windy, and the day they sailed to East Hampton was marked by "Snow & Rain all day & att night."[43] Mehetabel and John's decision to travel by boat during the dead of winter may have been precipitated by more than just Elizabeth's approaching delivery date; it is possible that she had been experiencing a difficult pregnancy and they feared for her safety.

In any case, Mehetabel must have felt relieved to be with her daughter at the time of her delivery. She was also fortunate to be able to spend the next several weeks with Elizabeth and her family—according to her diary, she did not return home until the end of March. (John Coit returned to New London less than two weeks after they had landed, by Joshua Hempstead's account.) When Mehetabel finally did take her leave, she was accompanied by her two-year-old granddaughter. She and little Elizabeth returned to New London by way of Gardiner's Island, where Mehetabel collected her niece Sarah to take home with her as well. As she noted in her diary, "march 28 I came ["Home" crossed out] from East hampton and stayd 4 days att the Iland, Sarah Gardiner & Lize Came Home with me." Fortunately for the three traveling companions, the weather for their sea voyage was fair.[44]

The presence of Sarah and "Lize" (probably pronounced "Lizzy") in her home doubtless brightened Mehetabel's days and helped ease Martha's longing for her absent sister. It is not known how long the girls stayed with Mehetabel, but it is evident from a surviving letter Mehetabel later wrote to Elizabeth and Martha (who was then visiting Elizabeth while her husband was away) that Sarah and Lize had returned home by early summer. The letter, which is the earliest extended piece of writing in Mehetabel's hand, provides insight into her character, personality, and emotions that the diary entries, because of their brevity and focus on occurrences, do not.

New-London. june 24. 1724

Dear Children

this comes to bring you my very hart to be divided amoung you, so you may tak your shares & send the Rest back to your poore brothers, I long to see you all, my affections are allwaes upon the wing, Ready to fly[.] tis a Tryell to live so Remote; I find my self sumthing incline[d] to impatience, and am sometimes hardly capable of any modaration, and am Ready to wish the time to fly swifter, that we may meet again[.] you know sumthing of the yarnings of a mothers bowels, you could not part with your Dear littel Lize a few days, without dying, how then doe you think I can contented[l]y live without you allwayes, I want poore Martha att home very much, but cant expekt her before your husband comes home; I hant had one line from her since she went away, I should be very lonesum ware itt not for your sister Molly[;] she is pretty well gott over late indisposition[.][45] I supose you will have your fill of one another[.] I hope you love better then ever anybody did[.] [Two lines crossed out.] I want to talk with you about some things Relating to Martha which is not proper to writt, my hart is very full and longs to tell you all its Akeings

Dear Children mind the one thing neadfull that good part that can't be taken away, persue the best things, seek first the kingdom of heaven and the Riteousness thereof, and then all other neadfull blesings shall be added,

from your Dear and Most affectionate Mother till death Mehetebel Coite[46]

Mehetabel's letter reflects an almost palpable sense of longing for her absent daughters. She equates this separation to a kind of death; as she asks her daughter Elizabeth, "you know sumthing of the yarnings of a mothers bowels, you could not part with your Dear littel Lize a few days, without dying, how then doe you think I can contented[l]y live without you allwayes[?]" In its focus on the trials of being separated from loved ones, Mehetabel's letter mirrors those her own mother had written to her years earlier. The two writers' approaches do have marked differences, however; foremost of which are the ways in which the two women dealt with the subject of religion.

Elizabeth Chandler loaded her letters with biblical allusions and quotes from scripture; in fact, they contain more spiritual advice than personal material. Mehetabel's letter, by contrast, is devoid of religious content apart from her final admonition to her children to "mind the one thing neadfull"—a phrase Elizabeth Chandler herself used in one of her letters to Mehetabel—and to "seek first the kingdom of heaven and the Righteousness there of." Whereas Elizabeth Chandler wrote of looking forward to a "Joyfull meeting" with loved ones "at ye resurrection," Mehetabel expressed a wish that time might "fly swifter" to the moment when she and her daughters would be reunited on earth. Such an attitude reflects the growing secularity of the age. By the early decades of the eighteenth century, religious commitment had become, for many people, a significant aspect of their life rather than its defining force. Although Mehetabel may have been as devout in her own way as her mother had been, she evidently felt free to express herself in ways that had nothing to do with her religious beliefs.

Mehetabel's letter is addressed to both her "Dear Children"; however, it contains some remarks that are clearly directed at Elizabeth alone. Aside from commenting on Elizabeth's ability to understand the "yarnings of a mothers bowels," Mehetabel refers to a confidence she is looking forward to sharing with her eldest daughter about "some things Relating to Martha which it is not proper to writt." Subsequent letters exchanged by Mehetabel and Martha indicate that this confidence concerned a romantic relationship involving Martha of which Mehetabel did not approve. Although Martha's later letters indicate that she was trying to avoid a particular suitor, her earlier letter to her sister reveals an interest in the subject of romance, and at eighteen she may have already become involved in a love affair. If Martha found herself attracted to an "unsuitable" young man, Mehetabel would rightly have worried, since at the time the nature of courtship was evolving to include a greater emphasis on sex. (In 1722 a Harvard College club even chose as its debating topic "Whether it be Fornication to lye with one's Sweetheart [after contract] before Marriage?")[47]

Couples engaging in premarital sex were not necessarily immoral or rebellious. In the seventeenth and early eighteenth centuries English law did not set clear parameters for marriage, and although the colonies had instituted their own marriage laws, some ambiguity remained. As a result, it was not uncommon for couples to perceive their married state as beginning after they had pledged themselves to each other or the marriage banns had been posted ("after contract"), but before the actual wedding ceremony had been performed.[48]

At the time Mehetabel wrote her letter, punishments for couples who engaged in sexual relations before marriage became milder, and rates of premarital pregnancy, which had been increasing since the seventeenth century, continued to rise until they reached a high of 30 percent in the mid-eighteenth century—the highest of any period in American history.[49] In New London premarital sex and pregnancy were a standard feature of life by the 1700s. In the 1720s alone, for example, Joshua Hempstead refers in his diary to a number of instances in which sex had evidently occurred outside of marriage: Rebecca Richards made a "publick Confession of her fault & had her Son (Born in fornication) Baptized"; Ann Stebbins had an "Illegitimate" child; Susanna Trowbridge was taken into the church after making "a publick Confession of her fault in having a Child before marriage"; John Eams confessed for having "Comitt[ed] fornication wth his now wife before their marriage."[50]

The details of Martha's entanglement have, unfortunately, been lost to history. Ultimately, however, any fears Mehetabel had proved groundless, as Martha appears to have escaped the relationship unscathed and to have remained the "Dutyfull Daughter" she signed her letters as.

Martha was almost certainly home from East Hampton by the time her sister-in-law Grace gave birth to her and John's third child and first daughter. Mehetabel took note of the occasion in her diary: "Nov: 30th Elizabeth Coit Born in 1724." The baby was christened the following week by Reverend Eliphalet Adams, whom several months earlier New London had almost lost to Yale College, which had invited Adams to assume the presidency. The town, however, refused to let him go. As Joshua Hempstead recorded in his diary, "wee had a Sort of Town meeting to Consider if wee were Willing to part with Mr Adams. I was most of ye day on it & it is Negatived."[51]

New London could do nothing to prevent its loss of another leader, however, when that autumn Governor Gurdon Saltonstall died suddenly of what appears to have been an apoplectic fit. According to the *Boston Gazette,* his funeral, which was held in New London, was attended by a "vast Concourse of People" and was marked by full civic and military honors. Joseph Talcott of Hartford was chosen as Saltonstall's successor, bringing to an end the decades during which New London had served as the governor's home base.[52]

Less than six months after Governor Saltonstall's death, the local Mohegans also lost their leader with the death of Ben Uncas, sachem since the death in 1722 of his predecessor, Cesar. (He was succeeded by his son, Ben Uncas junior.) By this time the Mohegans' numbers had dwindled since the first settlement of New London, in large part owing to the ravages of infectious disease. Over the years the tribe had also faced a range of other challenges, the primary one being the erosion of their landholdings: financial need had forced the dispersal of large tracts of property. In 1710 the sale (for a mere fifty pounds) of several thousand acres between New London and Norwich to a small group of proprietors had angered many townspeople, who viewed this territory as an extension of New London. The selectmen of New London subsequently attempted to manipulate the young and inexperienced sachem Cesar (the son of Owaneco, who had authorized the sale), persuading him to sell them the same acreage for a hundred pounds and to state "that all former conveyances were void, having been fraudulently obtained by 'taking advantage of the old age of my father Owaneco.'" Governor Saltonstall, however, opposed this maneuver, remonstrating with the town that "it would be more for their interest as well as credit, to improve that to which they had an undisputed title [some seventeen thousand acres of common, undivided land], than to go about to make a purchase of Mohegan, while the title of it was under discussion in the common pleas." (The colony's leaders believed that only the Connecticut government—not the Mohegans—had the right to determine the fate of Native territory.) Although the General Court ultimately refused to confirm this second sale, the townspeople were likely pacified by the provision made by a committee convened to settle all claims to the Native lands, which stated that those lands reserved for the Mohegans' personal use would revert to New London upon the tribe's extinction.[53]

Ben Uncas senior died during a time of devastating illness in the New London area, what Joshua Hempstead described in early March of 1725 as "the Most Sorrowfull time yt Ever was Seen in N. London for Mortality." The exact nature of the epidemic is unknown: Mehetabel did not mention it in her diary, Joshua Hempstead referred to it generically as a "sickness," and Martha, who wrote two surviving letters to her sister Elizabeth during this period, described it as a "distemper." Treatments for the illness probably varied, but when Hempstead's son fell sick in January, Dr. Jeremiah Miller decided to "Bleed [him] in ye Morn & Bathed his Breast with ointment of Marsh Malloes."[54] Dr. Miller's services appear to have helped, or at least not impeded, Hempstead's son's recovery, but they were ultimately ineffective in combating the epidemic, for within a few months scores of people had died. Martha's two letters provide a glimpse into these "Dolfull times":

New London Feb: 19 1724/5

D[r] Sister Betty

    I know you Expect to hear from us all Opertunites Therefore tell you we are all well unless [except] Brother Thomas who is Often out of Order[.] has now a very Bad pain in his face with other Infirmity that atends him[.] Sister Grace has bin very Sick But is now much better. Poor Liz: Dart is Raving Distracted as much as 2 or 3 men can hold her[.][55] Molly Butler is Like to Die, wth a Consumption.[56] no other news but what Jos: has Told you. you know without my telling you we all Long to See you and your Dear Sweet Littel Children, but Spring is at hand & then I hope we Shall See you hear with them.

    Mother give's her D[r] Love to you and Sent the Stockings she has been so Long about. Tis very Cold and Late and no fire and an ugly pen and I not very well so that I must Conclude with my Dear Love to you and honest Brother. Wishing you Both Happy & well.

    I am Your Loving Sister Martha Coit[57]

March 8th 1724/5

Dear Sister

   Since I wrote to you Last thare has Died[:] Jonathan Hill, Thomas Dou-glass, & his Son Thomas, Jonathan Haines Old Sam:^{ll} Harris, & His Son Petter, Moly Buttler, Bethiah Taylor that Lived at ant Coit's Jno Plumb's Son George Butlers[?] Son, & Severall Negro's. eight Lay Dead at wonce.

   Uncel Douglass is very Like to Die. O Sister Poor Brother Thomas has got the Distemper[.] This is the ninth Day, and 'tis not yet Broke[.] I am afraid you will never See him alive again poor Soul

   Bro: Joseph saild the 2 of this month A very Bad Storm the next Day. Tis Dolfull times here the Bell Constantly Tolling, Dayli hearing of peopel being Sick. I Hope This Distemper has not got with you. I Should Run Distracted if I should Hear you or your Husband was Sick with it; I Long to hear from you very much.

   Mother would have you send her half y^d of that Black & whit stuf for Cuf's. she is all most worn out sitting up nights[.] give's Her Dear Love to you all. as Duse you[r] Only Sister.

Martha Coit

I ask't tomma what I s[h]ould tell you[.] he said I must tell you how Bad he was & that he prayed God would Bless you & your [page torn: children?] and that you would never see [page torn: him again?] O Sister tis very hard⁵⁸

The day after Martha wrote her letter, her brother Thomas succumbed, as he had feared he would. He was not yet twenty-three. Thomas's prolonged illness and untimely death would have been devastating to Mehetabel and her family, and to his wife Mary, who was then expecting their first child. (Thomas junior was born that summer.) A few weeks later the family's loss was compounded by the death of Mehetabel's son John's six-month-old daughter Elizabeth. In her diary Mehetabel made a simple acknowledge-ment of these bereavements: "Aprill 25: 1725: Elizabeth Coit dyed: march 10: my son Thomas Coit died."⁵⁹

   In addition to suffering the loss of Thomas and Elizabeth, Mehetabel also lost friends, neighbors, and relatives. (As Martha writes, these extended family members included Mehetabel's cousin Thomas Douglas and his son Thomas, and Mehetabel's uncle Deacon William Douglas, the last of her mother's siblings.) The sickness and deaths of so many—heralded, as Martha describes, by the tolling of the town bell—must have completely preoccu-pied the family. Mehetabel and Martha probably spent much of their time nursing others, taking breaks only to see to necessary chores and to attend funerals.

New London's epidemic abated not long after little Elizabeth's death in late April. Afterward, Mehetabel's family and the community tried to get on with their lives. Indeed, the demands of daily living, as well as deep-seated spiritual beliefs about resigning oneself to divine dispensation, left them with no alternative. Mehetabel's ability to continue to attend to practical matters, even during times of despair, is highlighted by Martha's comment about Mehetabel's having sent Elizabeth a pair of stockings and her request that Elizabeth send her mother a "half y^d of that Black & whit stuf for Cuf's." Even though Mehetabel was "all most worn out sitting up nights" nursing Thomas, she managed to attend to such mundane matters as the production of clothing. Her workload, her responsibilities to her family, and her conviction that she must accept God's will kept her from yielding to her grief.

A few months after the deaths of Thomas and baby Elizabeth, Mehetabel's faith and fortitude were put to perhaps an even greater test. On October 1 her daughter Elizabeth died in East Hampton of unknown causes. Possibly she contracted the same "distemper" that had killed her brother Thomas. There is no evidence that Mehetabel was with her when she died. Elizabeth was laid to rest in the South End burying ground in East Hampton, near the grave of Mehetabel's sister Sarah. The horizontal brownstone tablet marking her grave was inscribed with the simple memorial: "Here lies bured ye body of Mrs Elizebeth Gardiner wife of Cap^tn Saml Gardiner who died October ye 1 1725 in ye 22 year of her age." The young children Elizabeth left behind, Elizabeth, nearly four, and Samuel, not yet two, appear to have remained with their father for the time being.[60]

In her diary, Mehetabel recorded the date of Elizabeth's passing in the same paragraph in which she noted the deaths of Thomas and her granddaughter Elizabeth, concluding that entry with "October the 1 day my Daughter Elizabeth Gardiner Died att East hampton."[61] Mehetabel provides no clue in her diary as to how she dealt with this latest bereavement, but a letter she wrote to Martha a few months later suggests that she was suffering through a depression. Martha herself was surely grief-stricken over the death of her only sister, the prospect of whose loss she had earlier claimed would make her "Run Distracted."

CHAPTER SEVEN

Letters from Martha, 1726–1730

Mehetabel and John sent Martha on a visit to friends in Boston the spring following the death of her sister. The trip is documented by a series of six letters, which have miraculously survived, that Martha wrote to Mehetabel between May and July 1726. During this time, Martha stayed with John Slaughter, a sea captain, and his wife, Elisabeth Bradstreet Slaughter, who lived several blocks from Boston Common on the corner of Essex Street and Rainsford Lane (now Harrison Avenue). The basis of the Coits' relationship with the Slaughters is uncertain; unlike with the Ellerys, the two families do not seem to have been linked by kinship or commercial interests. Martha's letters do imply, however, that a long-standing friendship existed between Mehetabel and Elisabeth Slaughter, and that Mehetabel was also well known to Elisabeth's sister, Hannah Bradstreet Hall. It is a mystery how and where these friendships developed, since the Bradstreet sisters were originally from Essex County, Massachusetts, and were more than twenty years younger than Mehetabel. Mehetabel and John both had relatives in Essex County, and it is possible that Mehetabel first became acquainted with the women through these connections.[1]

Martha's first writings to Mehetabel from Boston report on her arrival and settling in and recount her efforts to purchase some clothing. (At the time, she and Mehetabel were still dressing in mourning.) Mehetabel did not receive Martha's first letter right away, as she herself had recently left New London for Woodstock, and when Martha discovered this, she directed a follow-up letter to Mehetabel there. The first one Martha sent still bears traces of its red sealing wax and carries an inscription later added by Mehetabel: "a letter from Martha Coit May 15: 1726 from boston, the firstt letter."

Boston May 15

Hon^d: Mother

    I have nothing to right, but only to tell you I got Down very well by sater-day noon not very much tire'd[.] found Mrs Slaughter very well[.] She had got home but the saterday before, I was recived with as much kindness as was possabel. I have not concluded what Close to git yet, have not been out of the gate so cant recomemend the place before I have seen it. I Long to see you all very much allredy, but Liz:[2] I die to see, I'll right every Opertuny

[written vertically down left-hand side of paper:] have not seen ant Coit yet Jonathan Came to see me[.] I am Your Dutifull Daughter Martha Coit[3]

The reverse side of this letter reads "Service to Mrs Eunis & Mrs Red tulap &c."

A little more than two weeks later, Martha followed up with another:

Boston May 28th 1726

Hon^d Mother

    I Sent word by Mr Hunting to you how I got down but you missing of him, I shall give you an Account in this, we got here by Saterday noon, not very much tire'd. Mrs Miller held out beyond expectation. I have been very Much Disorderd with the teeth ach, but am now very well, but have not been a visiting any body yett.

    I have gott me a Sutt of Black grassett at 5^s - 5^d p^r yard & a SearSucker gownd, which I hope you will Like, its as gentill as any thing I could gitt in mo[u]rning or out[.] Mrs Slaughter is extrodinary kind byond w^t I could expect, & Mrs Hall is her one Sister, I was very glad to here you gott to wood-stock [&] want to know how Long you Design to stay. pleas to give my Duty to Uncle Chandler[4] & thank him for his kind Letter, I would have rite to him but my Letters will not bare to be Scan'd there fore must Omitt it. My Duty to your Self & Love to all frinds. I am your Dutifull Daug^r Martha Coit[5]

Martha's first days in Boston were likely made more comfortable by the sight of several familiar faces; her letters indicate that her cousin Jonathan Gardiner may have been in town as was her "ant Coit," her uncle Solomon's wife, Abigail. Also staying in the area was Mary Miller, a daughter of the late governor Gurdon Saltonstall who was married to Jeremiah Miller, New London's schoolmaster and physician. There was one resident of New London whom Martha was happy to be some distance from, however, as her subsequent letters indicate that at least part of her reason for remaining in Boston was to avoid an unwanted suitor back home. His identity is unknown, but he may have been the cause of Mehetabel's concern two years earlier. By this time, at least, any romantic feelings Martha may have ever harbored for him appear to have evaporated.

Visitors from New London were not the only people Martha knew in Boston. Her later letters mention a number of other acquaintances, despite this being her first visit ("have not been out of the gate so cant recomemend the place before I have seen it"). The letters imply that Mehetabel also knew these individuals, although in most cases the exact nature of the relationship is unclear. Since extensive genealogical research has not revealed any evidence of kinship—even with those whom Martha refers to as "cousin"—it appears that these connections were likely an outgrowth of Mehetabel and John's social and commercial networks, and perhaps of Mehetabel's earlier residence in Massachusetts. That Mehetabel knew so many people in Boston without having lived there for any length of time is bewildering, but it is also intriguing, suggesting that she had widespread social bonds and that she had done more traveling than is documented in her writings. It also signifies that the extent of her life experiences reached beyond the confines of New London and her household and belies the traditional image of the circumscribed world of the colonial housewife.

The remaining four letters Martha sent Mehetabel from Boston illustrate that she enjoyed an active social life while she was there; even her trips to Sunday meeting were made in the company of friends. Although she writes of occasionally doing "one thing or [an]other" for Mrs. Slaughter, her visit, overall, appears to have been a leisurely one, and she seems to have greatly enjoyed herself. This enthusiasm comes across clearly in her writing, as does her lively sense of humor and her irreverence. Although Martha's letters are marked by erratic spelling, punctuation, and grammar—her fear that her uncle John Chandler might find her compositional skills lacking ("I would have rite to him but my Letters will not bare to be Scan'd") was certainly well founded—they also exhibit a flair for self-expression.

Boston, June 5th 1726

Hon^d Mother

I Send this Scrip by Jonathan (knowing that you Infallablely expect a Letter) tho I have not much to right about unless tis to tell you I this moment came from Mrs. Brookses where I saw kings & queens & the whole Royall family[;] notwithstanding I was so much of a Stoick soul[,] there presents made me tremble.[6]

I was to See Mrs. Miller yesterday[.] She was well but Longs to gitt home & I Long to see the folks att home very much, even beyond expression but dont want to come yet for One Reason—which I chall not here insert. I was last Sabeth at Church where I heard the Organ, which I think is Divine Musick if tis not wicked to Say so,[7] pleas to give Service to M^ad Starling & Mrs Eunies & tell them I am Distracted for their coming[.] I have been to

M[rs] Wates Mrs. Walleses & M[rs] Brownes[.][8] they are all charming Peopel, extreem kind to me.

Chandler[9] is to go to Roxburo to Show me where you was born this week[.] pray give my Duty to father & thank him a thousand times for the preasen[t] Sent by Sweetlin[10] which was very exceptable. I must conclud with my Duty to your Self & Love to Jn[o].[11]

[written vertically on left-hand side of paper:] I long to here from Jo[n] and am your Dutifull and only Daughter

Martha Coit[12]

A line at the top of the following letter has been cut off.

Boston June 6th 1726

Hon[d] Mother

I Recived your Letter & am glad to here you are gott well home. I have not been out very Much yet by reason of my being indispos'd[.] I went to see coz: Ruby[13] onece but no more of my coz[n] yett[.] I Saw Jn[o] Ellery & his wife pass by Mad[m] Saltonstalls but they did not know me.[14] I have not done much yet but fixx my Cloth and one thing or other for M[rs] Slaughter.

I dont know how Long I Shall Stay[.] I must ask you, I' am wellcome to Stay here for ever, if you Could Spair me. When I think of father & you & Dear Betty[15] [partial line crossed out] I think all the world should not make me stay another week, but when I think of other folk's I Am Resolve'd not to come home this seven year. I have gott me a pair of gold buttons, M[rs] Miller and every body think I have done as well about Cloths as was posable, wont you send money to buy you a Sute of Cloths due, dark grassett lind with dark persion is very pritty you want them[.] Mrs Lucretia Christophers[16] Sent to me to buy her 2 pair of Silk Stockings, & if you will tell her that I have been to Severall Shops & cant gitt none I Should be glad, but I design to gitt them if above ground before I come home & please to tell her they make gounds whole before for young wemen[;] if Stuff 14 yards in one, if calico 7 yards, She Desired me to send her word[.][17] I think I Must Conclud with my Duty to father & your Self and Love to all frinds. I am your Dutifull Daughter Martha Coit[18]

Capt Slaughter & wife gives thier hearty Service to father and you & so dus Molly[19]

The first page of the following letter, written between June 6 and June 28, the date of Martha's final letter, is missing:

. . . not gitt me a Scarf, but I can't Reasonabley Desire aney more Since you cant Accomplish you Businiss at Woodstock. I have been to See Coz[n] Burnall[20] thay was Redey to eat me, Coz Sarah is an Old Maid, Coz Rubey is a very pritty woman, Coz Noris is a fat woman. I was at a wedding of Coz Burnalls, Sun's Daughter;[21] he is a very pritty man & his wife an Innesent

Soul[.] She Says if I knew how well She Loves my Mother I Should not Stay from the house one moment[.] we had Sackposit[22] & wine &C And I think thay are Charming folk's[.] I Design to be more with them quickly[.] Mad[m] Elery has been Sick & I dont know the way there[.] M[rs] Slaughter is very Bussey jest now by Reason he is jest going to Sea[.] he Sayl next week then we Shall be all at Liberty.[23] Mad[m] Saltonstall & M[rs] Kathrin[24] is very kind to me & knows me as well as if thay had See[n] me a thousand times[.] I have not seen M[rs] Mears & M[rs] Buckley[25] yet. M[rs] Hall is a very pritty woman & the other of M[rs] Slaughters Sisters[.] M[rs] Hall gives her Duty to you & wants to See you more then any body in the world[.] M[rs] Slaughter Desires to know if M[rs] Adams[26] Likes her Calico[.] I have got a trunk I due rite something every day[.][27] I have not heard M[r] Mather yet but Design to go & hear him to morrow[.] I have been to Church once the Orgains is heavenly musick, I hear M[r] foxcraft & sett in M[r] Browns pew & Dine there a Sundays they are extrodinary kind[28]

I Did rite you word about [Be]thiah that She was Married to One Demmon has been Married this Six Months Lies in 3 Months hence[.] She Lives very well her Husband is a panniell-Maker She is a Littel alterd[.][29] I have not Seen M[rs] Harris & M[rs] Proctor yett[.][30] I have Recived the Cup but who brot it I cant tell [.] I Design to git it Dun.[31]

Poor M[rs] Eunice I pittey her with all my heart She has a Charming Mother at home who Dies to See her cant Mention her without tears. I am very glad you ware [?] her Mother tis Dredfull to Live Abord Ship her Mother is uneasey about it[.] I wish you would urge her to be at our house as much as you can[.][32] her Mother is extrodinary kind to Me so kind I am quite a Shamed. I Must Conclud with my Duty to Father & your Self a thousand times over & Love to every body. I am your Dutifull Daughter——Martha Coit[33]

You Must send me word when I Must come home[.] I am uneasey about your being alone but I hope my staying here will brack the nott & Lett me fly.

Martha's final letter ends quite abruptly; the lack of a closing indicates that a page may be missing, or that she never actually sent the letter.

Boston June 28th 1726

Hon[d] Mother

I rote last week by M[r] Wallis but he Stay's Till this week & I have a Littel more to right now, which is to tell you that I have been to hear Mr Mather preach[.] his text was, [Viz ?] Josua 2 Chapter & 21[v] & She bound the Scarlet thread in the window![34] it was Surprising to me to hear him extend his voice to such a degree as he did some times, but I Like't his preaching very well, & I bleave the better becaus you so much admire him, ware it not so far I Shou[ld; paper torn] go to hear him every day,[35] I Sat with Coz[n] Sarah in the gallery went home with her and stay'd all night & the next day went to Coz[n] Jonathens[36] their Sun's, Lydia Procter sent for me from their very kind to me[.] She Lives extrodinary Handsome. Last night I came to Mr Browns where I now am thay are the prittest folks in the world[.] I am to Stay this night also[;] they say I must never go home. I here the Gentlman' his new house[37] is quit[e] Demolish't[38]

In addition to illustrating aspects of her own personality, Martha's letters also provide insights into the type of person Mehetabel was. For example, the sentiments expressed by Mrs. Hall, who wanted to see Mehetabel "more than any body in the world," and by Elizabeth Burnall Greenleaf ("Coz Burnalls, Sun's Daughter"), who, Martha writes, "Says if I knew how well She Loves my Mother I should not Stay from the house one moment," indicate that Mehetabel was highly esteemed by her friends. The "extrodinary kind[nesses]" and hospitality shown to Martha by her Boston acquaintances are also signs of the high regard with which these people held Mehetabel: in so warmly welcoming Martha, they were, in effect, paying their respects to her mother. Mehetabel's decision to let Martha go to Boston in the first place—and to permit her to remain for such an extended period—shows that, as a mother, she was capable of acting selflessly. Although she must have missed Martha terribly, particularly given the recent loss of two children, she managed to place Martha's needs and interests ahead of her own and allowed her the time to enjoy her holiday.

Like Martha's Boston sojourn, Mehetabel's trip to Woodstock involved a high degree of social activity, but it does not appear to have had the same spirit-lifting effect. In fact, throughout her twelve-day visit, which she documented day by day in a letter to Martha, Mehetabel frequently complained of feeling "Dull," "weary," and "Malloncholy." The two days of travel to Woodstock seem to have exhausted her, and she was evidently suffering from a series of headaches; however, her despondency could also be attributed to the recent deaths of so many loved ones. (Mehetabel added a rather animated postscript to her letter several weeks later, which suggests that by then she was feeling somewhat better.)

Mehetabel's letter gives the impression that she first documented her trip for her own purposes, then decided later to send her mini travel diary to her daughter. There is no salutation to the letter, but following Mehetabel's synopsis of her stay are a few paragraphs clearly addressed to Martha. The two-page letter is divided into two columns; it is unclear why Mehetabel chose this format.

July 4, 1726

May 19: 1726 I set out to goo to woodstock, and before we got to bowlses itt Rain'd a smart shower and we faint ["were fain," obliged] to go in thare for shelter[.] when the showr was a littel over we satt out again[.] gott to norwich stay'd att Lothrop's that night had fry'd veall for supper, Susannah Moris and I lay to gether.[39]

fryday 20 we dind att Cady's had beef & pork and Herbs, began to be very wery[.] I Rid behind Sam[ll] Moriss most of the way[.] gott to woodstock a littel before night all most Tyr'd to Death[40]

Sattarday 21 keept house all day not able to stir,

Sabathday went to meeting com home very weary att night brother Joseph [paper torn: and?] wife Come to see me

munday 22 half dead still but went to brother Joseph's a foott, betty Chandler went with me. I stay'd thare all night[41]

Tusday 23 I came back again went to Richardson, grigsis, parkers, peeks, perrins, Childs, Aspinwals, and Soo to brothers very very [weary?]

wednesday 24 Election day, we went up to Town See trayning[.] went to dinner att Coz Johns billy and his wife thare too[.][42] wee, that is, sister, coz hannah and coz billys wife, and I went to Abbits, James Corbins, Mr Dwights Jos bacons, Jabez Corbinns, Deacon Morris, and M[r] Carpinders and so home to brothers[.] the same day coming home Sister fell Down and brake her arm, thay sent for parker to sett itt[43]

thurdsday 25 Sister Susannah Chandler set out to goo to boston, Rainny wather, Dull and Malloncholy long to gitt home, I went to M[rs] Homes she is not married yett[.] att night M[r] Dwight and his wife and M[r] Morris here to see us[.] sister very bad with her arm

fryday 26 a bright Charming morning, in the forenoon I Read in the Turkish History[44] in the afternoon Brother, coz Hannah, and I, went to Sam[ll] Morrisis Eate Trouts, to coz billys and Drank Syllibub,[45] came home wery, and Dull, a pain in my face, I hate to Ride, the Horse start[ed?] 3 or 4 times, I wish't to be att [paper torn: home?]

Satterday 27 we made dyer bred,[46] I had the head Ake very bad, we went up the lott to see the folks cutt bushis, went to M[r] Carpinders, Came home wery and Malloncholy, would give all the world to be att home

Sabathday 28. went to meeting on foot, the text happy are the people thatt are in such a case, (I could not think my selfe happy, if I was in his peoples Case,)[47] I went to diner att Johns, brother Joseph thare too, my head full to the brim all day[.] att night Mr perrin and his wife to see me

munday 29 brother Jonh went with me to west hill, we went to mercyes, paysons, Coys & Rites[48]

tusday 30 I sett out to Come home, brother Chandler come with me as far as chenys[.] brother Joseph came with me as far as plainfeild, thare we met sister Abigail Coit, we went to Dinner thare stayd an hour or 2 then set out for norwich[.][49] brother coit came with us as far as quinnibauge thare we came over in a connow, Coz Sam[ll] Chandler came home with us, we Rid over Shistuckill alone came to norwich about Dark, lodge'd att lathrops[50]

Wednesday 31 we got home about 10 a clock, not very wery, found all well except the gardin, and that was overRun with weeds, Sam Chandler went home the next saturday, so much for woodstock, till I see you,

M[rs] Sarah Shakmaple come to see me she Longs to see you, M[rs] Eunice can tell you all the nuse,[51] I would[?] have you Rite to your father, and acknowledg his kindness to you, and desire him to lett you stay longer, I know he would take itt well, send me word if you have been to Roxbury and Charlestown and who you went to see att Dorchester.[52]

tis now Monday night and the 4 day of july, we had a letter from your Brother Joseph last week, and an other to day by Thomas Mumford, who is come home. he is gone to Anguila, or saint martins for salt and we shall look for him hom in a bout a fortnight[.] your uncle Joseph Chandler is gon home to day, I have sent your pettycoat, and apron by him, to coz Chandler, who I Suppose will bring itt to you, Mary Truman was married last night,[53] if you would have me be easey in your absence you must write to me often and tell me every thing[.] give my service to Cap[tt] Slaughter and tell him I wish him a good voyage. to M[rs] Slaughter & to M[rs] Hall a thousand times[.] I hant seen M[rs] adams since I had your letter[?], But I know she likes the chimise[?] very well—she had itt made up in a minit[?]

the man says he has sent you a letter in my name. if he has I know nothing of itt. he brought me a coppy of itt to day which I have just now bin a Reading, if he has send me word, and Say Sum thing that I may tell him[.] he'll[?] be distracted to know what you say, thare is some very good counsil[?] in it, so far as is applicable to you I would have you apply itt to your self. Dont expose itt to be sure.[54]

Mehetabel's final lines to Martha, regarding "the man" who sent her a letter in Mehetabel's name, are perplexing. This individual does not seem to have been Martha's persistent admirer, as Mehetabel encourages her to respond to his letter, yet Mehetabel's claim that he would be driven to distraction waiting to hear Martha's reply indicates that he cared deeply for Martha. He must have been in some position of authority to have presumed to write to Martha in Mehetabel's name and to have offered her some "very good counsill," which Mehetabel advised Martha to apply to herself. Why, then, did Mehetabel avoid naming him, and why did she sign off with the caution "Dont expose [his letter] to be sure"? Clarification, unfortunately, is not provided in any of Mehetabel's or Martha's later letters, and subsequent events in their lives do not furnish an adequate explanation for this strange passage.

In addition to describing her visit to Woodstock in a letter, Mehetabel also wrote about it in her diary. Two brief, consecutive paragraphs summarize the main points of her journey. The entry appears to have been made retrospectively, as Mehetabel confused some of the dates: she denoted May 25 as Election Day instead of May 24, and the day she arrived home as June 1, rather than May 31.

> may 19: 1726
> I sett out for Woodstock

stayed att norwich that
night, gott to Woodstock the
02 day on a fryday allmost
tyred to Death
the 25 day Sister Chandler
fell Down and broke her
arm, Election Day

june 1 I Came Home again
itt was butt a malloncholy
visitt, I being not very
well all the time that
I was thair[55]

In committing her travel experiences to paper, Mehetabel was engaging in a practice common among her contemporaries. Early New Englanders' custom of making a record of their trips, like their fondness for diary keeping in general, was an outgrowth of the Puritan belief that external events would ultimately show themselves to be part of a preordained divine plan, and that all types of occurrences were worthy of documentation. Many writers included travel-related entries in their diaries, and some even began a diary for the express purpose of describing a journey.

One of the most famous early American travel diaries was that kept by Sarah Kemble Knight, Mehetabel's New London neighbor, during the course of her 1704 journey from Boston to New Haven and New York. Knight's entertaining narrative exhibits many characteristics of contemporary travel accounts in its focus on such details as the people she encountered, the accommodations she met with, and the meals she was served. Although Mehetabel's travel letter is much briefer and less descriptive than Knight's account, she also apparently felt moved to document whom she visited, where she spent the night, and what she ate for dinner ("fry'd veall" at the Lathrops', "beef & pork and Herbs" at Cady's, trout at Samuel Morris's, syllabub at "coz billys"). Like Knight, Mehetabel had to share a bed during her journey ("Susannah Moris and I lay to gether"), and experienced the challenges of traveling by land and water (both women, in fact, were forced to cross rapids in a "Cannoo").[56]

Of significant interest is the fact that the journeys of both Knight and Mehetabel were prompted by financial interests. Knight traveled to New Haven and New York to help settle the estates of her brother-in-law and brother, and Martha's undated letter from Boston indicates that Mehetabel was also tending to some business, although she does not specify its nature. Knight's and Mehetabel's circumstances were not unusual; women in early America were accustomed to traveling for financial reasons and were sometimes required to make journeys on their own.[57]

Not long after returning from Woodstock, Mehetabel may have had an opportunity to return the hospitality her brothers had shown her. An undated diary entry notes that "july 1 my brother john Chandler Came here[.] the 2 day my brother Joseph Came[.] the 8 day thay went home fryday." (July 8, 1726, did fall on a Friday.) A later entry would seem to support this possibility: "july 2 1726 Susannah Chandler [Joseph's twelve-year-old daughter] Came to live with me."[58] Complicating matters, however, is the fact that in her letter to Martha about Woodstock, Mehetabel wrote that "tis now Monday night and the 4 day of july, . . . your uncle Joseph Chandler is gon home to day." One possible explanation for this discrepancy is that John Chandler and whomever he had traveled with ("thay") went home on the eighth, and that Mehetabel did not record Joseph's earlier departure; another possibility, of course, is that this visit did not take place in 1726. There is no way of knowing for sure.

What is certain is that a few weeks after she returned from Woodstock, Mehetabel's niece Susannah came to see her and stayed for such a long time that Mehetabel described Susannah as having come "to live" with her. (Mehetabel's use of "to live with me" rather than "to live here" suggests that Susannah was her particular guest.) Although Mehetabel did not provide a reason for Susannah's visit, one might speculate that, given Mehetabel's depressed state of mind on her recent trip to Woodstock, her brothers may have thought that a young companion might help lift her spirits in Martha's absence. Whatever the reason, Mehetabel likely welcomed Susannah's presence in her home. Another of Mehetabel's diary entries dated years later suggests that the two remained close, and perhaps as a tribute to her aunt, Susannah named her first child Mehitable, a name belonging to neither her mother nor her mother-in-law.

Mehetabel made another entry concerning an individual's travels that July: "july 22: 1726 Mᵣ Winthrope wentt to England."[59] She was referring to John Winthrop (1681–1747), great-grandson of the first governor of Massachusetts, grandson of the first governor of Connecticut, and son of Wait-Still Winthrop, who had served as chief justice of Massachusetts. Wait-Still had died intestate in 1717, leaving John and his sister Ann as his only heirs. Although Connecticut law held that intestate estates were to be divided equally among all children—with the exception that the eldest son receive a double portion—John Winthrop filed a suit arguing that, under the English law of primogeniture, he was entitled to all of his father's real property. When the colony upheld the right of Ann and her husband to a share of the property, Winthrop went to England—on July 22, 1726—to dispute the decision. Although his appeal was granted in 1728, and despite the fact that he had left behind his wife and children, Winthrop remained in England until his death almost twenty years later. (During that time his wife, Ann Dudley Winthrop, daughter of former Massachusetts governor Joseph Dudley, managed the family's sizable estate.)

The British court's decision, which challenged Connecticut's laws of intestacy, sparked widespread anxiety with regard to the security of land titles. The colony's statutes on intestacy, in fact, would not be officially reestablished until 1745. Mehetabel's interest in Winthrop's departure for England likely resulted not only from the drama generated by his lawsuit against his sister and his decision to seek an appeal overseas but also from the possible repercussions should his appeal be granted. Her entry about Winthrop stands as further testimony to her attentiveness to significant social and political developments.

Mehetabel left no other writings dating from 1726, but Joshua Hempstead's diary notes that in September he attended a "Church meeting at Mr Coits." He does not describe the meeting at Mehetabel and John's home, but it may have featured a sermon by Reverend Adams, group prayer, and an element of socialization. If its composition was similar to the meeting held at the New London home of the Chapman family a month later, at which, according to Hempstead, were present "9 or 10 Men 23 or [2]4 women," the female attendees greatly outnumbered the males. By the early decades of the eighteenth century, most congregations had more female than male members, a trend that continued throughout the colonial period. While power remained firmly in the hands of male church leaders, female congregants played an active role, as Mary Maples Dunn has suggested, as "keepers of the covenant and protectors of the [Puritan] idea of mission."[60]

Puritanism remained the dominant religion in New London, but other faiths were also beginning to gain a foothold. By 1726 the town was home to both Anglican and Baptist societies, as well as to the Rogerenes. After the death of John Rogers senior in 1721, adherents of the various faiths coexisted more or less peacefully, although conflicts did occasionally arise. In June 1727, for example, Eliphalet Adams and some of his colleagues engaged in a public debate on points of doctrine with a group of Baptists in Lyme,

Connecticut. And in 1736, John Shackmaple and other members of the Church of England were tried for "feasting & playing" on a Congregationalist fast day. Argumentative religious tracts also appeared in New London: in 1725 Peter Pratt published a diatribe against the Rogerenes (*The Prey Taken from the Strong . . . Dangerous Errors of Quakerism*), and the following year saw the junior John Rogers's *Brief Account of Some of the Late Sufferings of Several Baptists Inhabiting New London County.* These sometimes heated debates and disputes did nothing to halt the trend toward religious pluralism, which would become a hallmark of the eighteenth century.[61]

Mehetabel did not record anything dated from the early months of 1727, but a letter she received from Martha that summer is still in existence. Martha wrote from Newport, where she was paying another visit to the Ellerys. This letter is written in a more stylized hand than her usual script:[62]

> Newport July 8.th 1727
>
> Mad[m]
>   I rote the enclosed Letter to have Sent by Mr Parnell[63] but he went without, & therefore Send it now thô tis allmost out of Date. I Rec'd yours by Way which which [*sic*] I was very glad of Thô very Sorry that your hand's grows wors. Mad[m] Ellery's Ears I Think are very Bad but she Dus not Do any thing to them, I am afraid of that Lime water. I am Greve'd that you Should be so Consern'd about my Eye when it has been well so Long[.][64] it Look's as well as Ever & is I Think as Strong, I am also very well in Health, & Fancy my Self begin to grow Fatt
>   I Should have Come home with Starr[65] had not you Seen an apperishon, but that Confounds me very much & I Dread the Thoughts of itt. I am more avers't then Ever, & if it should Continew, do Beleve it would bring me into a Consumption, Peopel have very wrong notions about things here, & will not be beat out.[66]
>   I have heard that you have had Benj:[a] Unkus to visit you. LAW, they Put in here but did not Come a Shore—what's apointed will Come to pass
>   Bro:[th] Jos: saild Last Thursday was a week to S[t]. Kitts & from there is to Come Directly home, they think. have not heard from Boston have wrot to M[rs] Slaughter once.
>   I Long to See you very much & the Dear Children. I have Sent Lize a fan by M[r] Starr. My Love & Serv[ice?] to all that you think will Except it. to M[rs] Adams in pertick[l]er[.] I did not think I Should want to have see her so much
>
> from Your Dutifull Daughter Martha Coit
>
> I think this has an abrupt Conclushon but you know how it is w[th] me some times[67]

While Martha's letter contains much of interest, its most provocative line alludes to the possibility that Mehetabel received a visit from the sachem of the Mohegan Indians, "Benj:ᵃ Unkus." Since Martha provided no context for this statement, and since neither Mehetabel nor Benjamin Uncas left a record of it, it is necessary to piece together various bits of information to reconstruct the circumstances.

As the leader of the largest tribe in Connecticut, Ben Uncas was arguably the most powerful Native in the entire colony. The grandson of the legendary leader Uncas, who had forged an alliance with some of the colony's first set-tlers, Ben Uncas had succeeded his father, also named Ben Uncas, as leader of the Mohegans after the latter had died during the sickly period of 1725. At the time of his alleged visit with Mehetabel, the younger Ben was undergo-ing a life change, exploring a newfound interest in the colonists' religion and attempting to curb his drinking and his temper, both of which had caused problems for him in the past. By his own account, he had a problem with alcohol; he had also engaged in some notable incidents of violent behavior. In 1720, for example, he had participated in a mob that, according to colony records, "did severely whip a Pequod Indian squaw . . . because she had in-formed the superiour court that she saw Wampaneags son load a pistol, and heard him speak threatning words, as if he would kill Ashcraft, lately acquit-ted on his tryal." (Daniel Ashcraft, a white man, had killed Wampaneag, a Mohegan, by striking him on the forehead with a stone, yet had been found not guilty of the crime.) Two years later Ben Uncas publicly executed a Pe-quot named Robin, shooting him "Through ye Body," according to Joshua Hempstead, "for Scalding [his father's] Sister in a drunken frollick." By the late 1720s, however, Ben Uncas was making serious efforts to "reform," in the eyes of his white neighbors.[68]

In a letter to Connecticut governor Joseph Talcott in the spring of 1728, Eliphalet Adams reported on a meeting he had had with Ben Uncas, in which Uncas had discussed his plans for leading a more temperate and religious life. Adams explained to Talcott that Uncas had "a while since in a time of sick-ness been very much awakened and concerned to think what would become of him if he should die in his state of ignorance and sin: but God being pleased to spare him and his distress continuing he applied himself to me for some instructions in religion." According to Adams, Uncas pledged to attend Sabbath meetings, a resolution he had "*pretty tolerably*" kept, and to "leave off drinking and quarrelling." Uncas was not always successful in meeting his avowed goals—in 1742 he confessed before the New London congregation of being guilty of "excessive drinking"—yet he did eventually become a full church member. He also encouraged other Indians to take up Christianity, an endeavor that Adams fully supported, believing that it was the Puritans' obligation to make "overtures" to the Indians for their "spiritual good" ("who can tell whether a door may not be opened for the bringing some of them to the acknowledgment of the truth, who have so long sat in darkness"). As Adams observed to Talcott, ministering to the Indians would be one way of showing gratitude to God for the good land the colonists had obtained from them at relatively "easie rates."[69]

Given his growing commitment to the Puritan faith, it is possible that Ben Uncas attended church meetings in addition to Sabbath services. Perhaps his visit to Mehetabel's home was for the purpose of attending such a meeting. Another possibility is that he came on a social call in the company of Eliphalet Adams, whom he occasionally visited. In any case, Ben Uncas may well have been the first Native guest in Mehetabel's home. Although she may have previously employed an Indian servant or purchased goods from a Native trader, it is highly unlikely that she had ever before interacted on a social basis with anyone of Native descent. Indians were a steady presence in New London throughout the colonial period; however, their social contact with whites—particularly with those of Mehetabel's status—was limited. It is compelling, then, to imagine the meeting between Mehetabel and Ben Uncas, an Indian with sufficient power to approach the colonists on an equal footing.

While the meaning behind Martha's remark about Ben Uncas is far from obvious, the lines that follow are even more challenging to decode. "LAW, they Put in here but did not Come a Shore—," she writes, "what's apointed will Come to pass." Martha seems to be expressing relief that a ship coming into Newport did not unload its passengers—from the statement's context, apparently Indians—but she appears apprehensive about the ultimate outcome of the incident. Unfortunately, specific information about this event has not been discovered.

Within two weeks of the date of Martha's letter, Mehetabel made an entry in her diary indicating that she had left Newport. Martha was soon on the move again, however; Mehetabel writes that "july 20 1727 John Coit Martha and Joseph went to norwich[.] the same day Lydia Star married to John Bowles[.] the 25 day Joseph and Martha came hom again." From the way the entry is written, it could be surmised that John, Martha, and Joseph went to Norwich to attend the wedding of Lydia Starr and John Bolles. The couple was married in New London on July 20, however, so John, Martha, and Joseph's trip must have been made for another purpose, which Mehetabel neglected to record. It is highly possible that they went to Norwich to visit their cousin Hannah Draper Gore, the daughter of Mehetabel's late sister Hannah. The younger Hannah, both of whose parents had died by the time she was about seven, had been raised as the ward of her father's brother. At the age of seventeen she had married Samuel Gore of Roxbury, where the couple had lived for several years before moving to Norwich. At the time of Martha, John, and Joseph's visit, Hannah and Samuel's four children were in their teens and early twenties, and two of them were married themselves.[70]

Several weeks after the Coit children's Norwich trip they and their parents may have traveled to attend the wedding of another cousin: Sarah Gardiner, the daughter of Mehetabel's late sister Sarah. The ceremony took place in the East Hampton meetinghouse on Long Island, and was likely followed by a reception hosted by Lord John Gardiner. Sarah was only about seventeen at the time of her marriage, while her new husband, Charles Treat, a 1722 graduate of Yale College who had trained for the ministry, was thirty-one. Treat's grandfather, Gershom Bulkeley, had been an early preacher at New London and one of New England's most noted alchemical physicians. (Treat's mother Dorothy had apparently inherited this fascination with alchemy, as there is evidence suggesting she wrote a surviving medical receipt book.) Charles Treat ultimately pursued neither theology nor medicine but agriculture, purportedly because the wealth and lands Sarah brought to their marriage freed him from having to pursue a profession. The couple made their home in Glastonbury, Connecticut, on what had been Charles's late father's large farm.[71]

A few weeks after the wedding, Joshua Hempstead noted in his diary that he and John Coit senior were in New Haven for the occasion of the colony's official proclamation of the ascension of King George II. (George I had died in June.) Hempstead does not mention Mehetabel, so she likely missed the historic event, which, the diarist observed, was attended by throngs of spectators and marked by great celebration: "the Troop & Eight foot companys in Arms" fired off volleys and a great-gun salute, and the revelry, complete with bonfires "& other Signals of Joy," continued into the evening. When Hempstead became ill while attending a court session a few days after the festivities, "Mr Coit" helped him back to his lodgings.[72]

Although Hempstead almost always used the deferential "Mr." when referring to John Coit, his diary indicates that they maintained a friendship despite their differences in social station. John's act of kindness is just one example of the many ways the two men assisted each other over the years, lending each other equipment and the services of their respective slaves, and working together on various projects on their properties. In early New England, as Anne Lombard has demonstrated, a system of neighborly labor exchange, trade, and credit "bound household heads into networks of mutual dependence" that generated goodwill and bonds of camaraderie. Such appears to have been the relationship of John Coit and Joshua Hempstead.[73]

Like Mehetabel, John continued to remain active and productive throughout his middle years (in October 1727 he was almost fifty-seven years old; Mehetabel was fifty-four). Hard work provided a man with financial resources and a sense of self-worth, but it was also considered vital on cultural and religious grounds: men were expected to have a "calling" both to serve God and to pursue a particular occupation. John Coit continued to run the shipyard with his son John for many years, and a few months after his trip to New Haven he was authorized by New London's selectmen to build a new wharf and oversee the town ferry, a significant achievement. John appears to have been a shrewd businessman, and over his lifetime he amassed a considerable estate that included land, livestock, and capital.[74]

Mehetabel made only one dated diary entry for 1728, documenting a trip her daughter Martha took in the spring. She writes that on "A[p]rill 6 : 1728 Martha Coit went to glasonbury with Mr Treat and his wife"—Martha's newly married cousin Sarah and her husband Charles. A surviving letter Martha wrote Mehetabel on April 8 supplies a few details of the visit; however, it also contains several facetious remarks that are difficult to interpret. Martha's letter possesses the same informal, confidential quality of her previous letters, but its tone is even more casual and gossipy—as if she were writing to a friend rather than a parent. Evidently, Martha's relationship with Mehetabel was sufficiently open and relaxed for her to feel comfortable addressing her "Hon^d Mother" in this manner. Martha's perception of Mehetabel as a confidante was no doubt strengthened by the liberties Mehetabel allowed her: rather than keeping Martha close to home, she provided her with the freedom to travel, to socialize with different groups of people, and to find her own way in the world.[75]

Glassenbury Aprill 8th 1728

Dear Mother

    This comes to tell you we got up very well sun an hour high att night, the Day we Left NL—we meet with no adventers in the way[.] I Long to know how you do & how you come off wth the Plague of Plagues[76] & whether the Soleits[?] gon to Boston to Ease his Distress't Soule[77]—I went to Meeting this afternoon & sat perch't up in this 2[d] Seat, was a mear witch[.][78] Sarah is the Most Polite Gential woman I ever saw[.] they all take there fashons from her Ladyship O! Stink—well, I Shall go to middeltown about the middle of the weak, Shall want to git home in a fortnight very Much[.] My Poor worke Suffers Exceedingly[.][79] I Dout I Shall want things before I cant posably git them dun—

    I hope I shall git Rid of my Stomackach before I come home[.] I shall go to Naog to-morrow to See Dolley[.][80] She is gon to Dochester poor Soule: I shall not add any farther att this time then Duty to Father & your Self Love to Johnne not D——t[81] & am Your Dutyfull and Only Daughter Martha Coit

P.S becauss this Letter Shuld not be insiped I add this posscript which is that Sarah gives her Duty to you. M C[82]

It appears from her letter that the twenty-two-year-old Martha may have thought her teenage cousin was putting on airs since having married into a prominent family—although as the daughter of Lord John Gardiner, Sarah would have been used to being considered a member of the local "aristocracy." Martha describes Sarah as polite and genteel, yet she also sarcastically refers to her as "her Ladyship," a comment she follows with "O! Stink." Perhaps Martha's impatience with her cousin prompted her to interrupt her visit with a side trip to Middletown, the home of several family members of her late grandmother, Martha Harris Coit. In any case, she writes that her wish was to be home within a fortnight.

That summer Martha was back visiting the Ellerys in Newport. During the course of her stay, she sent Mehetabel two letters that have survived. The first is a brief note that announces her arrival; the second, sent a few weeks later, provides a more detailed account of her activities.

Newport June 14th 1728

Mad[m]

    I have but a moment to wright therefore Can but jest tell you, that I had a very Long & uncomfortable voiage down, was very Sick but I hope that I Shall be the Better for it, I am now very well Except my Eye which which [*sic*] is Bad[.] Shall go to the Docters to Day

    I Cant give any Guiss when I Shall Come home, they want me to Stay all Summer, I have been to See Mr Ellery[83] [o]nce[;] they are very kind and pritty.

The widdow Hum:$^{[b]le}$ Serv:^{t} meet with very Poor Success, I hope he has done Tormenting,[84] I Shall not add any farther then Duty to Father and your self & Love to all that you Think will Except of it

from Your Dutifull
   Martha Coit

a Small baskett off Eggs would be Extreemly well accepted by Mad^m Ellery.[85]

Newport July th 5.th 1728

Dear Mother

I Beleive you will Think it very Strange that you have not heard from me in so Long a time & Especally when Joseph's Letter's came, when he wrot he knew of no Opertunity but Mr Bebe happen'd to be going that moment therefore I had not time then nor have know of any Opertunity Since. there has been Severall Peopel from New London Viz^t. Starr, Harris, Cotten, but I have not Seen them to Enquire how you Doe.

Bro:th Jos:^{ph} Saild Last thirsday & had a fine time of[f?] they think[.] he had a Letter & Some Pistoles for a venter from New London by Mr Cotten, but they Came too Late.[86] if he went to London he was to take his Orders from me what to Lay it Out in &c —— which makes me willing to Stay Longer then I intended. I was Rejoy'st that you Escapt so well, I hope there is no Relaps. Pleas to Give my Duty to Mrs Adams & Tell her I will Obay her Command, in Saying of NO, thô tis to the minester himSelf[.][87]

I was very glad to See Mrs Kathrina Win[.][88] I Think She dus not answer Peopels Expectations of her[.]

I must not forgitt to tell you my Eye is perfectly well, & that which I Took to be a wart, prove'd to be a Boy'l which Broke & My Eye grew Emediatly well without going to the Docters, which I think is a very Great mercy, there is a poor young woman here that has almost Lost the Sight of Boath her Eys with a Sort of a Felm that is growing over them, my'n might have been as bad.

I am now Drawing Mary a Robe in Larg Sprigs to be work't in Cruiel which I think will Look very handsome if Dun well.[89] I have Draw'd Stomechers Severall, & workt one for Mary, which they Like very well, they thinks by it as Mrs Burnham dus by ho[p]ing that it is a Gift.[90] I have begun my Pinners att Last I think they are tollarable. Mad^m Thinks Tis' nonsence to think of going home yett, I wait for your Orders, I have mett with nothing Extrodinary Yett.

Tis a mighty Fashion here to ware your Black Beaver Hats, & when Joseph went a way he gave me 3 pound to Buy one, & Mad^m Ellery Say's She will give me Lutshing[91] to Line itt. & if you think tis Best I'll gitt one.

I have Rid out twice Since I have been here once a Horsback with about a Doc:^{tr} [?] more of the Top [?] & once in Willm Ellery's Shayes with Mrs Almy.[92] I Long to here frome you very much & to See you more[.] Lize and

Sam[ll] are the best and most Orderly Children in the world —— & Nell is very good. My Duty to Father & your Self Love to brother John & sister Grace & I hope the Talk is over & they have peace.[93]

[written vertically at bottom left-hand side of letter:] I am Your Dutifull & only Daughter Martha Coit[94]

Among the different subjects touched on in Martha's July 5 letter was Mehetabel's state of health. As in her April letter from Glastonbury, Martha expressed concern about Mehetabel's well-being, although she did not specify what her mother was suffering from. Martha's vague references to Mehetabel's physical condition—"I Long to know . . . how you come off wth the Plague of Plagues," and "I was Rejoy'st that you Escapt so well, I hope there is no Relaps"—might be an indication that Mehetabel was experiencing general health issues rather than a particular illness. Mehetabel was almost certainly not afflicted with a real "plague," since there were no incidents of epidemic illness in the area at the time. Moreover, Martha's almost jocular use of the term "Plague of Plagues" implies that it was some sort of euphemism. Since Mehetabel was fifty-five at the time, she may have been grappling with the physical challenges brought on by menopause.

Mehetabel's health issues, whatever their source, may help explain why Martha took her sister Elizabeth's children, six-year-old Elizabeth and four-year-old Samuel, along with her to Newport. By this time, it is quite possible that Elizabeth and Samuel were living with Mehetabel and John; if not, they probably moved in with them several months later after the death of their father, who had not remarried. In taking the children with her, Martha may have been trying to give her mother some respite. Nell's presence in Newport, however, is a bit more difficult to understand, as her absence from the Coit household would have left Mehetabel shorthanded.

Martha's report on Nell's behavior—"Nell is very good"—as if she herself were one of the children, belies the realities of Nell's existence and the extent of her responsibilities. In addition to being required to attend to the Coit family's various needs, she may also have had her own family to care for. (On Nell's arrival in 1717 Mehetabel had written that she was then about twenty years of age, so she would have been in her early thirties at the time of the Newport trip.) Female slaves with families were placed in the terrible position of being caught between two sets of duties, and they were frequently required to put their owners' needs ahead of those of their loved ones. Notwithstanding this imposed dedication, however, the slave was always aware that at any moment she could be sold and possibly separated forever from

husband and children. Indeed, even after Nell had served the Coits for decades, John Coit stipulated in his will that "[his] Negro Woman Called Nell"
should be left to Mehetabel, unless he "Should Sell S^d Negro woman."

The leisure time and material comforts Martha alludes to in her letters
present a vivid counterpoint to the harsh circumstances of Nell's life. Although Martha's visit to Newport seems to have been timed in part to deliver
her from the persistent attentions of her admirer, its primary purpose appears
to have been a social one. While Nell's days would have been taken up with
watching the children and making herself available to answer Martha's needs,
Martha herself was free to pay visits and go out riding. During her stay with
the Ellerys, Martha associated with Newport's wealthy, elite, and powerful;
she would have been lodged in a comfortable room and served lavish meals.
Nell, by contrast, was more than likely housed in the garret (along with the
Ellerys' own black servants), offered the simplest of fare, and allowed limited
opportunities for socialization.

Martha's letters indicate that she worked on clothing both for herself and
others on her trips to Newport: she writes of "flower[ing] . . . a doubel nightdres wide and narrow," quilting a petticoat, making pinners, and "draw[ing]"
a robe and stomachers. In general, these garments were ornamental pieces
intended to symbolize the wearer's high status and refined tastes. Stomachers were decorative panels worn at the front of a bodice of an open-robed
gown (also known as a "robe"), while pinners were women's headcoverings
distinguished by long, hanging folds of material. The fact that Martha was
"draw[ing]," or designing, her own patterns indicates that she possessed
some skill as a needlewoman, as does the fact that she was working in crewel,
a type of embroidery using a variety of stitches and done in worsted wool
yarns. All of Martha's female contemporaries were taught to sew at a young
age so that they would be able to satisfy the clothing and linen needs of their
families, but only girls from wealthier families had the leisure time and the
resources to pursue the type of decorative needlework Martha describes. Her
efforts were evidently of good quality, as she reports that the stomacher she
had completed for Mary Ellery was "Like[d] very well," and that another
stomacher was appropriated by a "Mrs Burnham," who looked upon it as a
"Gift."[95]

It is evident that Martha continued to have the interest in matters of fashion which she had expressed in her earlier writings. Her trips to Boston
and Newport—among the colonies' most stylish and sophisticated centers—

certainly provided her with plenty of opportunities to pursue one of her apparent main objectives: to "conclude . . . what Close to git." To that end, she purchased a "Sutt of Black grassett"—urging her mother to also consider buying one—as well as a "SearSucker gownd" and a "pair of gold buttons." She also welcomed her brother Joseph's generous gift of money—the three pounds he gave her would have been considered a substantial sum—to buy a stylish "Black Beaver Hat."

Martha's letters illustrate an early American phenomenon known as "proxy" shopping, by which several individuals—friends, neighbors, acquaintances in other cities—might be involved in the execution of a single purchase. For example, Martha was charged by Lucretia Christophers with an order for "2 pair of Silk Stockings," and she seems also to have been instrumental in forwarding some calico on behalf of Elisabeth Slaughter to Lydia Adams. Her brother Joseph's offer to "take [clothing] Orders" from her should he go to London demonstrates how proxy shopping often took on a transatlantic dimension, and how the sex of the shopper did not dictate the sex of the proxy. In fact, proxy shopping could transcend gender, race, and class, as both women and men shopped for each other, and servants and slaves carried out commissions for their masters and mistresses. Regardless of the proxy's background, if he or she made decisions that fit the commissioner's taste and budget, his or her contribution would be valued. Martha evidently took her promise to procure silk stockings for Lucretia Christophers quite seriously, as she wrote to her mother that she would strive to find them if "above ground."[96]

Taste and refinement were important factors in the purchases Martha describes. While writing from Boston, she assured Mehetabel that the black grasset suit and seersucker gown she bought were "as gentill [genteel] as any thing [she] could gitt[,] in mo[u]rning or out," and that Mary Miller and "every body" else thought she had "done as well about Cloths as was possible." This sanction by other members of her social circle, as well as their exchanges of fashion intelligence—such as when Martha asked Mehetabel to tell Lucretia Christophers about gowns being made "whole . . . for young wemen"—demonstrates how standards of taste were established by elite women. These ideals also trickled down to women of lesser social rank, as Martha noted when she wrote that the women of Glastonbury, Connecticut, took "there fashons" from her cousin Sarah Gardiner Treat, whom Martha mockingly referred to as "her Ladyship." As society became more secular and increasingly commercial during the eighteenth century, people of all classes developed a greater interest in novelty and in changing fashions—often to the dismay of their social superiors.[97]

If Martha wrote Mehetabel other letters during her time in Newport, they have not survived. The following month, however, Mehetabel received a letter from Elisabeth Slaughter, her Boston friend with whom Martha had stayed. The letter is the only extant piece of correspondence between the two women. That Mehetabel preserved it for so long—storing it alongside the letters she received from her mother and sister and daughter—suggests that she highly valued their relationship.

> August ye 27 1728
>
> Mdm:
>   I hop you will pardon my neglect in not wrighting to you altho you have Just reson for it: your repeeted favors calls for my thankfull remembrance for the last agreable present[.] I return you many thanks
>   I have sent you Doctt Mathers pictur: my husban this day arived hear: I hope C^{uz} Martha is wall [well][.] pleas to give my cind love & humble service to hur[.] I long to se hur: my duty to your espoues [spouse] and acept the same your self which is all from mdm your humbl servit
>
> Elisabeth Slaughter[98]

Elisabeth Slaughter's letter makes it clear that she did not possess the same degree of literacy or writing proficiency as Mehetabel or Martha. While Martha's letters are characterized by poor spelling and jumbled syntax, these deficiencies may be at least partly attributable to youthful exuberance and do not mask her ability to express herself through writing. Elisabeth Slaughter's letter, by contrast, gives the impression that she labored over the wording of her brief note, which is marked by several corrections. (In the first sentence, for example, she added the word "not" above the line between "in" and "wrighting"; in the second, she crossed out "your" and added "my" before "thankfull remembrance," replaced "of" with "for" before "the last agreable present," and inserted an "a" between the "e" and "b" in "agreable.") To be sure, her letter could have been written in haste, particularly since, according to local shipping news, her husband had just that day returned from a Newfoundland sea voyage, but the letter also plainly conveys the author's lack of experience and ease with putting her thoughts to paper.

Although Elisabeth Slaughter did not identify the "agreable present" she had received from Mehetabel, or the nature of the "repeeted favors" Mehetabel had done for her, she did describe the gift she was sending Mehetabel in

Peter Pelham, portrait of Cotton Mather, 1727.
Courtesy American Antiquarian Society.

return: "Doctt Mathers pictur." This likeness of Cotton Mather was based on a portrait painted the previous year by Peter Pelham, a painter and engraver (and the stepfather of artist John Singleton Copley), and it was widely purchased after Mather's death in February 1728.[99]

No correspondence between Mehetabel and Martha from the following few years has survived, nor did Mehetabel leave any dated diary entries for this period, but other records shed light on an important development in their lives—particularly in Martha's. In December 1730 Mehetabel and John received a letter from a recent Yale graduate named Daniel Hubbard requesting Martha's hand in marriage. The letter makes it plain that Daniel, who was preparing for the ministry, had been courting Martha for some time, but it has been difficult to pinpoint when and where the two first became romantically involved. Daniel seems to have spent his childhood in New Haven, and after graduating from Yale in 1727 he remained at the college for a few years to tutor and teach the freshman class. At the time he wrote to Mehetabel and John, he had recently moved to nearby Stonington, after having been proposed as a possible candidate to fill the town's pulpit. Daniel hailed from a long line of clergymen: his father, John Hubbard, had preached at Jamaica, Long Island, until his death shortly before Daniel's birth in 1706; his mother's second husband was the Reverend Samuel Woodbridge of Hartford; and his great-grandfather, William Hubbard, had been a minister and early New England historian.

Martha's nineteenth-century descendants who compiled and published her letters believed that Daniel may have been the suitor who had pursued her so relentlessly and that Martha had simply changed her mind about him. Whether or not this is actually the case—there is not enough surviving evidence to either support or dismiss their theory—it is clear from the letter Daniel sent Mehetabel and John that he was completely smitten with their daughter. He refers to Martha in passionate and adoring terms, calling her "ye f[ai]r Creature, who next to Heaven holds the Empire of [his] Heart" and his "Partner Soul." Daniel expressed his love for Martha in a self-consciously literary style, employing florid prose and dramatic imagery. As a minister-in-training and a Yale graduate, Daniel certainly would have been well-read, and he clearly took pains to portray himself as a man of letters.[100]

To Mr Jhon Coit
att
N—— London

Honoured Sir & Madm I blush & tremble on my knees while I study how to approach your Presence, to ask of you a Blessing for which I have long address'd ye Skies. From my first Acquaintance at your House I have wish'd my Happiness thence; nor have I yet found it in my Power to seek it from an Other. My careful Thoughts with ceas'less Ardors commend ye Affair to that Being, who alone inspires a pure & refined Love. The Eye-Lids of ye Morning discover me in my secret Places, with my first Devotions solliciting ye dear important Cause; and ye Evening-Shades are conscious to ye Vows I make for ye fr Creature, who next to Heaven holds the Empire of my Heart. And now while I write I pray ye great Master of Souls to incline yours to favour my Address. By ye Love of God I beseech you—Ye happy Parents of my Partner Soul—but I forbare till I may be honoured with ye Oppertunity of a personal Application. In ye mean time I consecrate my best Wishes To ye Interest of yr Family—& with ye hig[h]est Respect subscribe my Self, Sir and Madam, yr most devoted most humble Servant

D. Hubbard
Stonington December, 1730[101]

Regardless of what Mehetabel and John may have thought of Daniel's letter, they were likely pleased by the proposed match. Daniel was evidently deeply in love with their daughter, his prospects were good, and he came from a distinguished family (his forbears included Massachusetts governor John Leverett, Connecticut governor George Wyllis, and other eminent members of New England society). They gave their blessing to the union, and Daniel and Martha became engaged.

CHAPTER EIGHT

Transitions, 1731–1744

Prior to their marriage in the summer of 1731, Martha received at least two love letters from Daniel, who at the time was in New Haven finishing his tutoring obligations at Yale. Like his earlier letter to Mehetabel and John, whom he here refers to as "yᵉ tender & dear Arbiters of my fate," Daniel's first to Martha, dated January 15, is notable for its display of both physical and spiritual passion. Since Daniel was considering the ministry as a career, his use of religious imagery is not surprising (nor is his counsel to Martha to always "improve in Virtue, & study to make as good a Figure in yᵉ Eyes of Angels, as you do in mine"). What is startling, however, is his candor in alluding to his longing for their "mutual Exchange of Passions," to the "flaming Wishes of an impatient Lover," and to his visualization of "yᵉ Scene of [their future] Blisses." Daniel was clearly anticipating the physical joys of marriage, a fact that he seems to have been eager to share with Martha.

To Mrs Martha Coit att N London

Dear Creature

does Absence teach you to love? do you look and find but Half yourself at Home? do yᵉ pleasant Cares & sweet Anxieties of Seperate Lovers at all perplex your gentle Bosom? Alas, my virtuous generous Fair, methinks you should feel some of these Solicitudes to requite what I endure: all yᵉ painful Ills of impatient Love & distant prospects sit heavy on my Soul. I love, I love, my Anguish, I cherish my Torments, till yᵉ bright Moments yᵗ fly to my Succour hurry my enraptured Spirit to a mutual Exchange of Passions with yours. To hear from you were Half yᵉ Pleasure of Injoyment; but this your Severe Prudence denies! Well, I will call you cruel, but esteem you discreet. The liberty of writing you indulge me I will faithfully use. Nothing will I tell you of Faith & Constancy; but what is greater yᵗ your Beauties continually improve on my Fancy! In every new Idea you are still more lovely. Thus my

Dear, improve in Virtue, & study to make as good a Figure in ye Eyes of Angels, as you do in mine. Allways shall it be my Ambition to assist you in so noble an Attempt. Here I cannot forbare calling to Mind the Ten-Thousand ardent Vows, which are sacred to this great Design: & I assure my self y^t ye Day approaches when I shall bow my Soul in thankful Adoration to ye Author of my Hopes & Happiness y^t he sets me in a Capacity for ye Prosecution of it. By the Power of this Imagination an innumerable Choir of bright Ideas crowd upon my Soul, & paint me amost eligant Prospect of an happy Life. Suffer me then my Fair One to open to you ye Scene of Blisses which are already present to my foreboding Thoughts. The flaming Wishes of an impatient Lover shall hurry me in a noble transport over ye uncertain joys (y^t lie between) to y^t auspicious Hour when Heaven & Fate shall assure us each others Hearts. Then will we swear in ye Presence of our friendly Angels y^t ye Love of God shall be our Happiness, his Glory our Business, ye Imitation of his Holiness our Study, his Power & Goodness our only Confidence. Then Shall our united Vows conspire to pray down a Blessing on our tender Hours. Thus with Devotion shall we begin our Life; & y^t God we worship shall cherish us in ye Arms of a careful beneficent Father. While we deal faithfully in his Covenant we cannot want ye Smiles of his Providence. In a day of Adversity if such he ordains he will soften our Cares & relieve our Sorrows. In ye meanwhile with what inimitable Pleasure shall we daily behold each other with this sweet Reflection, the Beloved of my Soul is a Favourite of Heaven, & ye Owner of my Heart has an Interest in ye Bosom of a God. O my Life, my All; but my God, when shall we begin ye utmost of our joys. I chide, I chide, ye winged minutes: they fly too slow while my Hope's defer'd while I am not with you; joyn, joyn your Wishes with mine to haste ye promis'd Day; bid me, bid me fly to your dear Imbrace! This, This will fill ye vast Desires of your impatient Lover & very humble Servant

D. Hubbard
N.H. Jan 15th 1730/1

P.S. I am allways mindfull of my Duty to ye tender & dear Arbiters of my fate.[1]

Given the intensely personal nature of Daniel's letter, one wonders whether Martha shared its contents with Mehetabel. Martha obviously cherished the letter, since she kept it for the rest of her life, but whether she replied to it is not known, as no letters from Martha to Daniel have been discovered. In truth, she may never have sent any, since Daniel's January letter indicates that her "Severe Prudence" was preventing her from writing to him.

The second letter from Daniel to Martha, written in late April 1731, is structured around a comparison of the beauties and charms of springtime with those of love. Although less sexually charged than his previous letter, it still anticipates the "nameless joys of Love" the two will share following their marriage.

Dear Creature:

My tenderest wishes are that the fair Soverign of my Hopes and Fears be now as happy as the season looks gay and joyful: it is a most beautiful and charming hour! every favorable circumstance of Nature conspires to crown it with Honour and Delight. The Happiest Period the various year can boast now hovers toward us in all the radient airs of genial Light, attendant on the approaching Sun. The youthful morning unveils her rosie blushes: and the faithful Day is so far risen that I have already visited a neighbouring Verdant Field where I have given it in charge to all the choicest Herbs and Flowers, by the ministry of Ten Thousand sun-beams which alite to paint their colours, or drink their juices, to offer up a sacrifice of pure Incense to the gracious Power who indulges us mortals so much Pleasure in his excellent Works. The Heavens are all serene; The clear air perfumed with the sweet odors of opening Flowers and spreading Blossoms of faithful Trees.

The face of the earth smiles; everything seems pleased and all the creatures in good Humour; in a word, my Dear, my charming all, this once the whole creation looks like you. All these Beauties I severally admire in proportion of the Resemblance they bare to you; and none of the Pleasures errising from the contemplation of them shall I ever want while I may call you mine. This prerogative is the highest distinction my ambition aspires after. When what I now write comes to your hand, walk into your garden and imitate the pleasure I have now been enjoying.

There view with curious eye the fair and elegant structure of your Tulips and Twenty more little Darling vegetables, for which I have no names, and the beautiful light of colours which hover over them: and assure yourself that there is less harmony in the nice arrangement of their lights and shades than there is in a sett of generous Passions, regulated by the Love of an ingenious and virtuous woman. Think withal what Improvements in Happiness we may hereafter help one another to make when with the sweets of nature and the nameless joys of Love we shall possess the superior Blessing of a Daily Intercourse with the great Original of Bliss, who amidst the Temporary Delight his goodness shall indulge us, will prepare us for a state of immortal youth and Pleasure in the fairest garden of his own planting in the Paradise above. To that happy Place my fair, my dearest Soul, we'll travel Hand in Hand. The virtuous joys of all our tenderest Hours shall shoot up into Divine Transports at the expectations of an eternal Possession of all the Good an infinite Benevolence has to give. The Duty of my station calls me off: I must forbare writing: My regards, &c. Martha, do'nt forget me: for as never other man was, intirely and by your own condescending choice, I am forever yours,

Danl Hubbard
N. H., April 27, 1731[2]

Daniel's raptures over the glories of nature were obviously a by-product of being in love, but they also reflect a pure joy at the coming of spring. Mehetabel expressed a similar sentiment by copying in her diary a poem titled

"Child of the Summer" written by Mathias Casimirus Sarbiewski (1595–1640), a Polish Jesuit and celebrated poet who was also known as "the divine Casimire" and "the Polish Horace." From the mid-seventeenth century on, Sarbiewski's verses were translated from the original Latin by such prominent British writers as Isaac Watts and Abraham Cowley, the latter of whose works Mehetabel also quoted in her diary. Exactly when Mehetabel copied Sarbiewski's poem is unknown, but it may have been as late as or after 1750, when an eighth edition of James Hervey's two-volume *Meditations and Contemplations,* which included both Latin and English versions of Sarbiewski's poem, was published in Boston. Mehetabel's transcription follows:

> *Child of the sumer*
> *Ch[a]rming Rose*
> *no longer in confinment Lie*
> *arise to light thy form disclose*
> *Rival the spangles of the sky*
>
> *the Rains are gon*
> *the storms are ore.*
> *winter retires,*
> *to make the way*
> *com then thou swea[t]ly*
> *blushing flower.*
> *com lovely stranger come away*
> *the son [sun] is Drest*
> *in beaming smiles*
> *to give thy beauty*
> *to the day*
> *yong zephyrs wait*
> *with gentlest gales*
> *to fan [thy] bosom as thay play*
> *Casimire*[3]

"Child of the Summer" appears about midway through Mehetabel's diary, after the bulk of her dated entries and at the beginning of the section that includes the medical remedies, recipes, and literary quotations. The poem provides a bright counterpoint to the somber pieces that bracket it, Mehetabel's enumeration of the ten plagues of Egypt and the "Wintworth" elegy:

> *Wintworth – Sure*
> *twas som stranger –*
> *yes, his stay, –*

> *in helth among us*
> *was but one short day,*
> *then he fell sick,*
> *and languisht but ten more.*[4]

Several pages later, Mehetabel transcribed some additional verses commemorating the beauty of a flower. The lines are taken from a section in Book I of "Solomon on the Vanity of the World, a Poem in Three Books," Matthew Prior's epic poem on the vanity of man.[5]

> *take but the Humblest*
> *Lily of the field,*
> *and if our prid[e]*
> *will to our Reason yeald,*
> *it must by sure*
> *comparison be known.*
> *that on the Regal seat*
> *grate David's son,*
> *arayed in all his Robes*
> *and tipes of power*
> *shines with [less] glory*
> *then that simple flower.*
> *prior*[6]

Mehetabel's motivation for recording these particular lines about the lily is uncertain: was she merely struck by the way Prior illustrated his message about human vanity, or was she also moved by his assessment of the flower's beauty? In any case, her inclusion of these lines and of "Child of the Summer" suggests that she may have had an affinity for flowers. Daniel's remarks regarding the "fair and elegant structure of [the] Tulips" in Martha and Mehetabel's garden and the "harmony in the nice arrangement of [the garden's] lights and shades," lends credence to this theory, as does the fact that a decorative flowerpot was listed among Mehetabel's and John's possessions at the time of John's death.

August 18, the day of Martha's wedding, was a Wednesday and a "fair" day, according to Joshua Hempstead's diary. Although neither Martha nor Mehetabel (nor Joshua Hempstead) left an account of the wedding, it likely involved a reception for family and friends held at Mehetabel and John's home. According to two letters later written by Martha to Mehetabel, she and Daniel took an extended trip afterward. This trip would not have resembled the romantic honeymoon taken by today's newlyweds but rather was a journey to see family members who lived at a distance. The couple first went to New Haven, where they apparently stayed with Daniel's brother John and his family and where they remained until after Yale College's September 8 commencement ceremonies. (At this point Daniel's tutoring responsibilities were officially transferred to another recent graduate.) John Hubbard may well have been an interesting host: although he himself did not attend college, he had been awarded an honorary master of arts degree by Yale College the previous year for his proficiency in Latin, Greek, philosophy, medicine, poetry, and belles lettres. He evidently put his learning to good use over the course of his varied career as a doctor, judge, and military leader.[7]

A few of Daniel's other relatives also may have attended the commencement. As the result of his mother's and grandmother's several marriages, Daniel had numerous step-siblings and half cousins. His grandmother, who was known as both Mehitable and Mabel Wyllis, had married three times and had had children with each of her husbands. After the death of Daniel's grandfather, the Reverend Daniel Russell, she had married Isaac Foster, the minister of the First Church of Hartford; after Foster's death she married his successor, the Reverend Timothy Woodbridge. Daniel's mother, Mabel Russell Hubbard, had married Timothy Woodbridge's nephew, the Reverend Samuel Woodbridge, after Daniel's father's death. She and Samuel, who was a founder of Yale and was appointed a trustee in 1732, had several children together before she died in 1730.

In a letter Martha wrote Mehetabel two days after commencement, she did not reveal what she thought of the exercises, but she may have found them tedious, as they would have lasted for several hours and consisted largely of orations given in Latin and of student thesis defenses. Her letter does indicate, however, that she enjoyed the occasion's social aspects. The event typically attracted throngs of spectators, including members of Connecticut's leading families, and provided a good opportunity for people watching, a pastime of which Martha was clearly fond.[8]

New Haven Sep^t th 10th 1731

Mad^m

I know you Expect to hear from me by Mr Adams[9] therefore shall acquaint you that I am very well & have been ever since I Left you[.] believe we Shall not come home by Hartford as we intended but the same way we came & by that means shall have an Opertunity of Seeing Aunt Rugels[10] again who is one of the finest women I ever Saw[.] we have had Opertunity of Seeing a

Sister Woodbridg[11] hear at Commincment[.] She is a young woman grown & I think very Pritty. M[rs] Eunice Tallcott & Severall other Lady's Grace'd the Seremony[.] Brother Joseph would not [have] been Sorry if he had been with us,[12] I Conclude he is at N-Port or I Shuld have wright to him[.] the house is full of People and nothing but noys and hurry there[.][13] Must begg you would Excuse this Letter's being so short

    My Duty to Me Father & your Self

    With Love to Brother John. Serv'[ice] to Aunt Ad——s and L——n &c from[,] Mad[m14]

Your Dutyfull Daughter
Martha CHubbard[15]

Your Son gives his Duty to Father & you

It appears that Martha and Daniel had originally intended to stop in Hartford, where Daniel's stepfather, Samuel Woodbridge, had a "noble House," according to the diarist Samuel Sewall, but they decided not to make the journey. Perhaps it would have been a melancholy visit for Daniel, owing to the recent death of his mother (and the fact that his stepfather had already remarried). Instead, Martha went to Woodstock, where she was able to reconnect with Chandler relatives and friends, and Daniel traveled to Boston for an unnamed reason. Martha wrote to Mehetabel from Woodstock:[16]

Woodstock Octobr th 4th 1731

Mad[m]

    When Broth Joseph came home he Left me at Uncle's,[17] where I Stay'd till Saterday night, & then came to Cozn John's where I now am with one of the best of women, who is hearty, good, and kind, and Seams more like a Sister than any thing Else.[18] Old Mr Morris[19] was here this day and inquired after you & invited me to his House, where we Design to go tomorrow.

    Cozn Chandler this Day went to Boston & is Expected back next Saterday[.] I hope Mr Hubbard will come with him[.] if he dus, believe we shall be at home next tusday. My Duty to My Father & your Self with Love to Brothers & Grace & Cozn Lydia.[20] &c—I should be very glad of a Line or two by Cozn Thos.[21] to know how you do which if you would favour me with would add very much to the Satisfaction of your Dutyfull and only Daughter

Martha Hubbard[22]

Martha provides no clue as to why it was necessary for Daniel to travel alone to Boston so soon after their wedding, or why her brother Joseph, rather than her new husband, accompanied her to Woodstock, but she seems to have enjoyed her visit. Within a few weeks, she and Daniel had returned to New London, where they may have rented a house—they did not build their own home until a few years later. Daniel began teaching school in New London, and he also started a law practice. Although he occasionally preached to the New London congregation when Eliphalet Adams was away, he did not ultimately pursue the ministry.[23]

After Martha left to get married, Mehetabel's household was the smallest it had ever been, consisting of just her and John; her grandchildren Lize, who was almost ten, and Samuel, who was about seven; and Mingo and Nell. Yet at about this time, Mehetabel and John acquired another slave. In the spring of 1731 Joshua Hempstead made the first of several references to "Mr Coits Peter," who occasionally worked with his own slave, Adam. It is not clear how Mehetabel and John came into possession of Peter—whether he came from Barbados like Mingo or was purchased from a neighbor—but he may have been brought into the home to help John, then in his early sixties, with the farming and other physical chores.[24]

The particulars of Peter's life, like details of the lives of Mingo and Nell, are vague. He was probably in his twenties when he came to live with Mehetabel and John, as Joshua Hempstead noted that he was "50 or over" at the time of his death in 1758. He was thus a good deal younger than Mingo, who undoubtedly was middle aged, since he had been the Coits' servant since 1705. (Nell was in her mid-thirties at this time.) Joshua Hempstead's diary makes it clear that Peter, like Mingo, eventually married, but the timing of his marriage and the identity of his wife are unknown.

Ten months after Martha's marriage to Daniel, in June 1732, Mehetabel's thirty-three-year-old son Joseph ended his longtime bachelorhood when he married nineteen-year-old Mary Hunting of East Hampton, Long Island. (The couple had probably not been together for very long, given Martha's comment in her September 1731 letter that Joseph would "not [have] been sorry" to see all the attractive young ladies gracing Yale's commencement ceremonies.) Joseph and Mary were married in East Hampton by Mary's father, Nathaniel Hunting, the town's minister. Following the wedding, Joseph and his new bride took up housekeeping in New London.

The day after Joseph's wedding, Martha gave birth to a baby boy whom she and Daniel named Russell, which was Daniel's mother's maiden name. Russell's baptism a few days later at the New London meetinghouse would have been especially meaningful for Martha, since she had become a full church member just a few months earlier.

In the fall of 1732, as the colony observed "a publick Thanksgiving," Mehetabel had much to be grateful for. She and John were apparently enjoying good health and financial security, her surviving children had made successful marriages and were living close by, and grandchildren were enriching her life. In addition to Martha's son and Elizabeth's children, this latest generation included John and Grace's four boys, then between the ages of four and twelve, and the son of Mehetabel's late son Thomas. (Although young Thomas lived in Lebanon with his mother Mary and stepfather Ebenezer Gray, the two families maintained close contact over the years; in fact, a daughter of Mary and Ebenezer's would one day marry Martha's son Russell.) Also at this time, Mehetabel's nephew Jonathan Gardiner, the twenty-one-year-old son of her sister Sarah and Lord John Gardiner, built a house in New London, perhaps in preparation for his marriage to the daughter of Eliphalet and Lydia Adams, which would take place the following autumn. Mehetabel was no doubt pleased by the prospect of this union, which would add the ties of kinship to her long-standing friendship with Lydia Adams.

As was so common in colonial days, however, moments of celebration could be closely followed by occasions for mourning. In late March 1733, almost nine months to the day after Mehetabel's son Joseph's wedding, his young wife died in childbirth. Their infant son Jonathan soon followed.

Contrary to prevailing practice, Joseph did not remarry until several years later. He instead focused on his career as a merchant, becoming quite successful selling goods brought in from Europe, the West Indies, and Boston, and by the late 1730s he had his own wharf in New London. Joseph had retired from maritime life in 1731, after having spent, according to his calculation, "1100 days on the high seas, which is 3 years & 5 days." He observed in his memoir that what was "very remarkable . . . in all these voyages" was that he "never lost but one white man, who dyed on ye Island of Barbadoes, viz, Andrew Denison, and an Indian boy before we left England." Joseph did not comment on how many nonwhite men (or women) had been lost on these voyages, but enslaved Africans and West Indians were undoubtedly passengers on some of them. From the time he was a young adult, Joseph himself owned several slaves, including, according to various entries in Joshua Hempstead's diary, a "Negro man" who died in March 1725, another "negro man" who died in April 1733, and "a Negro Woman . . . [who] died in child bed" in 1750. Later in life Joseph had at least four additional slaves: Violet, Eunice, Pero, and Bristol Barney, the latter of whom he ultimately freed in 1785.[25]

In contrast to her brother Joseph's, Martha's new family flourished. Two years after Russell's birth, in June 1734, Martha delivered a daughter she named Lucretia, perhaps in honor of her friend Lucretia Christophers Brad-dick (for whom she had vowed to purchase silk stockings if she remained "above ground" while in Boston). Martha and Daniel were not only blessed with children, but they were also prospering materially; Daniel was honored with the appointment of high sheriff of New London County the following year. (Joshua Hempstead, who attended the "Entertainm[en]t" the couple hosted to celebrate the appointment, noted that Daniel "Sent for his Neighbors to Rejoice with him.")[26]

A few months after Martha's baby was born, Jonathan and Mary Adams Gardiner had their first child, a boy named John. At his son's baptism Jonathan "own[e]d the Coven[an]t" and officially joined the church. He was not to enjoy parenthood or church membership for very long, however; a few months later, Jonathan left on a sea voyage from which he never returned. After months passed with no word from the vessel, its occupants were presumed dead.[27]

In addition to being sorrowed by Jonathan's disappearance, Mehetabel may also have wondered about its providential import. As part of her belief system, she would have pondered the significance behind all types of occurrences, even as she realized that it was beyond human ability to comprehend that meaning. The next two entries Mehetabel made in her diary reflect this curiosity about God's workings. In the first, she simply notes, "feb[r] 1734/5 Richard Dowglass Died very Suddenly." Douglas, who was in his early fifties at the time of his death on February 26, was Mehetabel's cousin, the son of her mother's brother William and his wife Abiah. Joshua Hempstead, who was also struck by the suddenness of Douglas's death, elaborated on the circumstances surrounding it: "[was] at Mr Prenttiss's house holding a Court to Try Several Delinquents who were presented for disorders &c. Capt Richard Douglass was there with the many Spectators & went away about 4 or 5 Clock well & went over to Mr Winthrops point to help his people with a Scow Load of hooppoles & Lumber & before he got to Mr Stewards wharff as he was Steering the Scow [he] fell down Dead So that he never Spoke a word more and was Carryed in by daylight & never moved."[28]

Even to people who thought frequently about their own mortality and who lived in a world where lives were often brief, the swiftness with which death might strike could be unsettling. To Mehetabel and Joshua Hempstead, Richard Douglas's sudden demise may have been made even more poignant because of their high regard for him. According to the *New England Weekly Journal,* Douglas was "well beloved in his life" and "much lamented by all Ranks and Ages of People among us."[29]

Mehetabel's second entry, dated seven months later, focused on an incident that left many in New London full of questions about God's motives. On the same page on which she had written of Richard Douglas's death, she noted, "September 1 1735 a Dreadfull storm of thunder and Lightning which struck the meetinghouse and killed ned birch Sabath Day." (The date of this entry is in error; the episode actually occurred on August 31.) While afternoon services were being held at the meetinghouse, a bolt of lightning struck the church spire, causing large timbers to drop from the ceiling. Several people were injured and others were burned. As Joshua Hempstead described it, "when Mr Adams Stood up & began prayer a Terable Clap of Thunder & Lightning Came[,] Struck ye meeting house in Divers places & struck Divers persons. it pleased God to Spare al our Lives But Edwd Burch a young man newly for himself [Burch had just turned twenty-one] . . . was Struck more fatally & Died. . . . [Those struck] by bleaded & propper means . . . Recovered. Divers others Mazsed & Litely hurt. it is Suposed yr was about 40 Struck Down."[30]

Even though members of Mehetabel's family apparently escaped unharmed (she did not remark otherwise in her diary), the incident must have left her stunned and upset. As Eliphalet Adams recalled, the "pitiful and affecting" cries of "dear friends" calling for assistance were terrible to hear, and the sheer intensity of the experience was something he believed people would remember until their "Dying Day." The death of the "modest [and] promising" young Edward Burch was so widely lamented that there was almost "universal" attendance at his funeral. Even if Mehetabel had not been to services the day of the lightning strike, she could not have failed to wonder at its implications for her church and her community.[31]

It was Eliphalet Adams's duty to interpret the calamity's providential meaning for his flock, and by the following Sunday he had composed a suitable sermon. Titled *God Sometimes Answers His People by Terrible Things in Righteousness. A Discourse Occasioned by that Awful Thunder-Clap which Struck the Meeting-House in N. London, Aug. 31st, 1735,* it was later published by the New London press. Adams's sermon attracted a large crowd, many of whom were, he noted, "(doubtless) being led by their Curiosity to . . . observe what our Sentiments and Dispositions were under such an Awful hand of God." According to Adams, the lightning strike was a call for people to examine their actions, to "Search and try [their] ways and turn again unto the Lord." He recommended "several particulars for the Amendment of our Conduct": namely, the need to spend more time in personal devotions, to pray as a family each morning and evening, to show mercy and compassion to others, to speak out against sin, to be more diligent with regard to communion and baptism, and to "Let wildness & Extravagance cease from this Day forward." While acknowledging that the congregation had received a severe dispensation, he also encouraged them to marvel at the fact that the vast majority of those present had been "remarkably Preserved." Overall, Adams took a measured approach to interpreting the disaster, attempting to open people's hearts to self-reflection rather than to intimidate them with threats of damnation. Addressing those outsiders who might be tempted to regard New London as a particularly sinful place to have been so providentially censured, his advice was to "Judge not that ye be not Judged."[32]

Not long after Eliphalet Adams's sermon was published, the New London press reached a milestone when it printed its first work by a female author: *An Account of Some Spiritual Experiences and Raptures and Pious Expressions of Elisabeth Mixer . . . Together with the Relation She Gave of What God Had Done for her Soul, in Order to Her Admission into the Church of Christ in Ashford.* The seventeen-year-old Mixer's descriptions of her visions of heaven, angels, and the "Lovely JESUS" and the depth of her faith in the face of serious illness had so moved her minister, the Reverend James Hale, that he arranged for the publication of her conversion narrative, which Mixer first related before the Ashford congregation in 1720. Some circumstantial evidence raises the possibility that Mehetabel read Mixer's narrative. In addition to being a wide reader with the means to purchase this landmark publication from the New London press, Mehetabel also had extensive connections to Mixer's hometown of Ashford: her nephew Robert Mason and cousins William and Nathaniel Abbot lived there, as did several acquaintances who were former Woodstock residents. Coincidentally, Mehetabel's brother John, who was early on a major proprietor of Ashford, had sold Mixer's father the family's home lot.[33]

A family connection may also have led Mehetabel to read a work similar to Mixer's published in Boston a few years earlier, in 1733. *An Address to Young People, or Warning to Them from One among Them, Yet May Be Called Warning from the Dead* was the account of the "signal and remarkable" deliverance from total physical incapacitation experienced by Mercy Wheeler, a devoted young member of Mehetabel's brother-in-law Joseph Coit's congregation. Following a bout with the "burning Ague," Wheeler had been left barely able to speak or move for more than five years, when one day "it pleased GOD to open her Lips . . . [to] shew forth his Praise." Although Wheeler's recovery was limited, it appeared to her family and friends that the "Divers Days of Fasting and Prayer" orchestrated on her behalf with the assistance of Reverend Coit and neighboring ministers had produced extraordinary results. As Reverend Hale had with Elisabeth Mixer's, a family friend and church deacon named Samuel Stearns saw the potential of Wheeler's story of forbearance in the face of adversity to influence other young people and so arranged for its publication. Wheeler herself believed that God's restoration of her power of speech laid upon her a "Duty" to address others of her generation "by way of Advi[c]e, Counsel & Caution." In the course of her narrative, she drew on a phrase that both Mehetabel and her mother had used when counseling their daughters: *"the One Thing needfull,"* she maintained—and Mehetabel and Elizabeth Chandler would have agreed—was to "Remember your Creator and . . . Redeemer."[34]

Given the importance of religion to many colonial New Englanders, it is not surprising that the majority of publications written by women during these years were of a devotional nature. Narratives of spiritual growth, like Mixer's and Wheeler's; volumes of deathbed counsel, like that of Grace Smith of Eastham, Massachusetts (*The Dying Mother's Legacy,* 1712); and even captivity narratives, like those of Mary Rowlandson (*The Sovereignty and Goodness of God,* 1682) and Elizabeth Hanson (*God's Mercy Surmounting Man's Cruelty,* 1728), reflect their authors' connection to faith. Perhaps one of the most significant early female authors to write in a spiritual vein, however, was Jane Colman Turell (1708–1735). Turell was, from an early age, encouraged in her literary pursuits by her father, Benjamin Colman, the leader of Boston's progressive Brattle Square Church, where Eliphalet Adams had once been his colleague. Colman had seen to it that both his daughters had a broad education and access to a wide range of books. As a young adult, Jane Turell wrote poetry, hymns, personal essays, and letters in addition to keeping a diary. After her death at the age of twenty-seven, a collection of her writings was published by her father and her husband, the Reverend Ebenezer Turell of Medford, both of whom considered her a *"Poetic Genius."*[35]

One tragic way a woman's words might find their way into print was through the publication of a criminal conversion narrative. During the 1730s, at least three of these personal accounts of repentance by a condemned woman were published in New England. Patience Boston, a young, part-Indian woman living in Maine, had murdered her master's eight-year-old grandchild; Rebekah Chamblit, a white Boston servant, and Katherine

Garret, a Pequot Indian working in a minister's house in Saybrook, Connecticut, had both been convicted of murdering their illegitimate newborns. The twenty-seven-year-old Garret, who was descended from "one of the best Families" among the Pequots, according to Eliphalet Adams, was convicted of infanticide by the New London court, imprisoned in the town for several months, and then executed. Her hanging on Town Hill in May 1738 was the county's first execution and attracted spectators from miles around.[36]

In Garret's two-page "Confession & Dying Warning"—the warning to young people to heed their consciences, and to children and servants to obey their parents and masters lest they come to a similarly bad end—she admitted to "the Crying Sin of Murder," acknowledged the justice of her sentence, and expressed her desire to be reconciled with Jesus Christ. Garret also thanked God that she had the ability to read, so that in her last days she could reap the benefits of the Bible and other "good Books." Garret's account was published in New London together with the sermon Eliphalet Adams preached before her execution. Adams had ministered to Garret during her months of imprisonment—the authorities had allowed her this time to prepare her soul for death—in an attempt to convince her of both the need to repent and "the greatness of Gods mercy and that there is forgiveness with him." After making an open confession of her offenses before the New London church, Garret was baptized and taken into the congregation. During this time, she was allowed to attend Sabbath meetings, lecture days, and prayer sessions held in private homes.[37]

Whether or not Mehetabel witnessed the spectacle of Katherine Garret's execution—which, according to Adams, was attended by a crowd "more Numerous, perhaps, than Ever was gathered together before, On any Occasion, in this Colony"—she likely followed the case with interest and may have read Garret's confession and Adams's sermon. She was probably in attendance when Adams gave a preliminary sermon on the Sabbath before the execution, since that day Martha's fourth child, a daughter named Elizabeth, was baptized. It is, of course, impossible to know how Mehetabel felt about Katherine Garret's hanging, but perhaps she, like Adams, was moved by the repentance and faith Garret showed even to the end, when she passed out of this life "with her hands lifted up, . . . *in the posture of one praying.*"[38]

In early 1740 Mehetabel's son Joseph married Lydia Lathrop of Norwich. Mehetabel must have been delighted to see Joseph, now in his early forties, settled and with the prospect of having a family of his own (he and Lydia

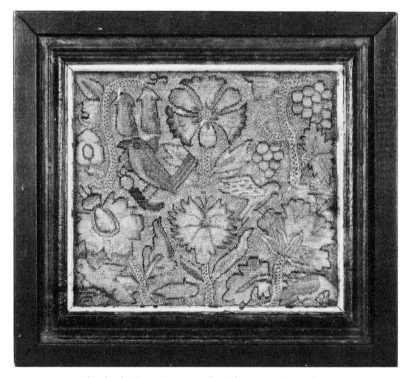

Elizabeth Gore Gager embroidery, ca. 1637–1643.
Courtesy Connecticut Historical Society, Hartford.

eventually had nine children together). Not much is known about Lydia, other than that she had a "reputation for virtue and religion," according to a family genealogy, and that she brought to the marriage a piece of needlework created in England by her great-grandmother Elizabeth Gore Gager (born circa 1627). Lydia would pass the embroidery on to her and Joseph's first-born daughter. (This child, also named Lydia, married her first cousin William Hubbard, a son of Martha and Daniel's.) The heirloom continued to be handed down through the female line for generations and was ultimately donated to the Connecticut Historical Society in 2003.[39]

The coming months brought additional changes to Mehetabel's family. Following a winter so cold that ice extended across Long Island Sound to Fisher's Island and local residents were able to hold a barbecue in the middle of the river between New London and Groton, the area was hit with an epidemic known as the "long fever." The fever was probably typhoid, which is typically spread through food or liquids contaminated by someone carrying the *Salmonella typhi* bacterium. Among those stricken was Martha's husband Daniel.[40]

Like others who contracted the disease, Daniel may have exhibited the symptoms of a high fever, headache, diarrhea, and even delirium. Any measures taken to ease his discomfort ultimately proved unsuccessful, and Daniel died in late March.

Daniel's death prompted Mehetabel to make her first dated diary entry since 1738, when she had made a notation about a trip taken by her granddaughter ("novem[br] 17 1738 Lize Gardiner Came home from Boston with Joseph printis"). At the bottom of a page on which she had recorded the deaths of several family members, she noted, "march 24 1741 my son M[r] Daniell Hubbard Died in the 3." (Mehetabel's nineteenth-century descendants who compiled the printed volume of her writings speculated that, had she known Daniel's age, she would have concluded the entry "in the 35th year of his age.") Mehetabel's references to Daniel as both "my son" and "M[r]" hint at both affection and respect for her son-in-law.[41]

Daniel was buried in the New London burying ground near other Coit family members. Martha evidently spared no expense in arranging for a headstone—Daniel's is much larger than the surrounding grave markers. She may also have spent a significant sum on the reception after the funeral, which would have been well attended, given Daniel's position as the county's high sheriff.

Although in his brief life Daniel had amassed a respectable estate, Martha's future was far from secure; in Daniel's will she was left only the traditional third of these assets (which included an unnamed "Negro Girl . . . to be at her disposal forever"). The balance of the estate was to be distributed among their children, including approximately four hundred pounds Daniel specified should go to their eldest son Russell, three hundred pounds each to Daniel and William, and two hundred pounds each to Lucretia and Elizabeth. After Daniel's death, according to Martha's nineteenth-century descendants, she began to keep a shop in New London to help make ends meet. She may also have begun teaching school—for a while she was in possession of the Elizabeth Gore Gager embroidery belonging to her sister-in-law Lydia, and it has been suggested that she used the piece as a model for needlework lessons.[42]

Less than a week after Daniel's death, Mehetabel's nineteen-year-old granddaughter Lize was married to her twenty-two-year-old cousin David

Gardiner. (Lize's father Samuel and David's father David were both sons of Lord John Gardiner by his first wife.) David's father had succeeded Lord John as proprietor of Gardiner's Island, but since David himself was a fourth son, there was little chance that he would ever hold that position. A graduate of Yale College, he instead made his living as a merchant, eventually forming a partnership with Lize's brother Samuel. Happily for Mehetabel, Lize remained in New London, enabling them to maintain their close relationship and Mehetabel to play a role in Lize's children's lives.

At the time of Lize's marriage, New London, like the rest of New England, was experiencing a religious revival that would become known as the Great Awakening. The principal actors behind the Awakening included the Reverend George Whitefield, a British Anglican; the Reverend Gilbert Tennent, a Pennsylvania Presbyterian; and Jonathan Edwards and James Davenport, Congregationalist clergymen from New England and New York, respectively. Unlike traditional Calvinists, these ministers believed that salvation was not preordained and that it could be attained by being "reborn," a process involving, according to Whitefield, an "inward Change and Purity of Heart, and Cohabitation of the holy Spirit." Also setting them apart was their emotional, spontaneous style of preaching, which was designed to stir their listeners to immediate expressions of repentance. The resulting scenes could be quite dramatic, as members of the audience screamed, collapsed, and even went into convulsions. Joshua Hempstead, who heard the Southold, Long Island, minister James Davenport preach several times in the summer of 1741, wrote of women fainting and "being Ter[ri]fied [and crying] out Exceedingly." Hannah Heaton, a young woman who also attended Davenport's lectures described "sinners crying out for mercy for their souls[,] some saints a praising god[;] some exhorting and praying over poor sinners."[43]

In the early 1740s New London County became swept up in the religious fervor, receiving visits from some of the most famous revivalist ministers. During the week that Lize and David Gardiner were married, for example, Gilbert Tennent preached several sermons in New London—including some in the evening by candlelight—attracting crowds from miles around. Soon scores of people began joining the church. In June Joshua Hempstead, returning from a few days away, observed in amazement the "wonderfull work of God made Evident in the powerfull Convictions Conversion of Divers persons in an Extreordinary manner." That week, he wrote, "hath been kept as a Sabbath most of it, & with the greatest Success Imaginable & beyond what is Rational to Concieve of it by the Account tht I have of it by all hands." Hempstead concluded that there had "Never [been] any Such time here & Scarce any where Else."[44]

A total of 81 new members were admitted to the New London Congregational church between the spring and fall of 1741, increasing the prior membership of 57 men and 112 women by almost 50 percent. Eliphalet Adams certainly rejoiced at the growth of his congregation, particularly since membership had fallen off dramatically over the years. In 1740 only about 16 percent of all New London parish residents (a population of about 1,100) were Congregational church members.[45]

Unfortunately for Eliphalet Adams and for other ministers whose churches experienced similar growth, the surge did not continue. In fact, many of the ministers who had welcomed the revivalists to speak before their congregations soon found themselves to be the subject of their criticism. Influential in this change was Gilbert Tennent's *The Danger of an Unconverted Ministry*, published in 1740 by Benjamin Franklin, which highlighted the need for religious leaders themselves to be "born again." While George Whitefield and other evangelicals spoke out against unconverted clergymen as a class, the Reverend James Davenport, among others, began passing judgment on specific ministers—including Eliphalet Adams, whom Davenport denounced as a "carnal Pharisee." Soon Davenport and like-minded evangelicals took their arguments one step further when they called on the newly converted to leave their congregations and start new churches under revivalist leadership.[46]

Such developments caused deep divisions within churches across New England, giving rise to camps of so-called New Lights, who supported the revival, and Old Lights, who disapproved of the revivalists' "enthusiastical" exhortations and their attacks on clergymen. (There would also come to be disagreements between moderate and radical New Lights.) In New London this rift first became apparent in the fall of 1741, when five members of Eliphalet Adams's congregation, one of whom was Joshua Hempstead's son, stopped attending services because of what they termed the "deadness of the church" and the "legal [i.e., spiritless] preaching." The group formed a separate society under Davenport's general leadership, meeting at members' homes as well as in barns and in fields and other outdoor spaces. This new society, the Separates, which eventually included about 115 members, tended to be composed of individuals who were younger, poorer, and less involved in town and church affairs than those belonging to the Congregational church. In fact, one of the hallmarks of the revival was that it appealed to people from all walks of life, including servants, slaves, and Indians.[47]

In addition to overseeing the Separates' new church, Davenport, along with his colleague the Reverend Timothy Allen (who would be dismissed by his West New Haven congregation in 1742 for excessive revivalism), formed the Shepherd's Tent, a New London school for training young men—and, possibly, women—to become teachers, ministers, and exhorters. Students at the Shepherd's Tent were, perhaps, active participants in the Separates' lively displays of their newfound enthusiasm around town. One observer wrote that he had heard that Davenport "goes singing to Meeting & about the Streets with his Armour bearers & by some other oddities. The People in New London are set into a Mighty Ruffle & disturbance, but especially by his treating Mr. Adams as an unconverted Man & praying for him Publickly as such." Davenport favored disorderly demonstrations that drew public attention; in fact, one Boston writer described him and his followers as appearing "more like a Company of *Bacchanalians* after a mad Frolick, than sober Christians who had been worshipping God."[48]

In response to the turmoil developing within Connecticut churches, a council of ministers and representatives from each town in the colony met to consider, as Joshua Hempstead wrote, "what may be thought most Expedient to be done with Reference to the Traveling ministers." The council agreed that no clergyman should be allowed to preach in another minister's parish without first having obtained his consent. This recommendation was upheld by the colony's General Court, which in May 1742 passed "An Act for Regulating Abuses, and Correcting Disorders in Ecclesiastical Affairs." Recognizing that "sundry Persons, some of whom are very Illiterate and have no Ecclesiastical Character, or any Authority whatsoever to Preach or Teach, have taken upon them Publickly to Teach and Exhort the People in matters of Religion," the act made it a requirement for visiting ministers to obtain permission to preach from the settled minister and the majority of the congregation. In June 1742 the general association of Connecticut ministers met in New London to officially endorse the new law.[49]

Joshua Hempstead's writings indicate that, throughout the Great Awakening, Mehetabel and John remained Old Lights, retaining their allegiance to the established church and to Eliphalet Adams. During the height of the crisis, they actively offered Adams their support by hosting church meetings and lectures at their home. Hempstead, who attended these events "at old Mr Coits," also remained an Old Light, even though his son had joined the Separates.[50]

Hempstead noted John's presence among a group of local officials who called on Timothy Allen at the Shepherd's Tent in February 1743. This visit, probably meant to see what was transpiring at the school—which, along with the Separates' church, was protected under the colony's 1708 religious toleration act—was evidently "to no purpose," for, as Hempstead noted, "Mr allin was up with the Schoolars & would not come down to Speak with us." Although Allen's wife Mary "Carryed [their] message & brot word he would Soon come," he failed to appear. Mary Allen subsequently "Excused his delay by Reason She Said it was a day of fasting wth ym."[51]

Not long after John Coit attempted to visit the Shepherd's Tent, James Davenport returned to New London, where he would carry out what has been described as "the most remarkable event of the Great Awakening in New England." On Sunday, March 6, after Davenport had lectured local Separates on the importance of forming a "pure church" and thereby "cast[ing] away every kind of idol"—particularly "certain religious books" which "had been worshipped as guides, and exalted into standards of faith"—he and his followers built a bonfire on Christophers's Wharf. They commenced to throw into the flames classic works of Puritan theology by Increase Mather, Benjamin Colman, Matthew Henry, and Eliphalet Adams. Reportedly singing "*Hallelujahs* and *Gloria Patri* over the Pile," participants were heard to proclaim "*That the smoak of the Torments of such of the Authors of the abovesaid Books as died in the same Belief as when they set them out, was now ascending in Hell in like Manner as they saw the Smoak of them Books rise.*"[52]

The following day Davenport and the Separates gathered with the intention of subjecting their "fine apparel" to the same treatment, as Davenport believed that "some of them made Idols of their gay Cloath[e]s." Accordingly, as the *Boston Evening-Post* reported, the "Women brought in their Scarlet Cloaks, Velvet Hoods, fine Laces, and every Thing that had two Colours," while the men contributed "Wigs, Velvet Collars, &c., &c." Some people supposedly stripped off articles of clothing where they stood. Davenport himself was said to have gone so far as to remove his trousers, when, according to the *Boston Post-Boy,* a "young Sister, whose Modesty could not bear to see the Mixture of Cloaks, Petty Coats, and Breeches, snatch'd [them] up . . . and sent them at him, with as much Indignation, as tho' they had been the Hire of a Wh[ore]." At this point, the crowd began to reconsider their involvement, and one man spoke "warmly" to Davenport, telling him that he was "*making a Calf,* and that he tho't *the D——l was in him.*" Davenport is said to have responded that he "*tho't so too;* and added That he was *under the Influence of an* evil Spirit, *and that God had left him.*"[53]

Those who read about the bonfires were shocked by the actions of Davenport and his followers and by Davenport's claim that he had been "under a Notion of a special and immediate Direction of the Holy Ghost." Ultimately, as a result of these "late extraordinary Proceedings at New-London," Davenport lost credibility with the public and with his fellow New Light preachers. On March 30 a council of New and Old Light ministers gathered at the home of Eliphalet Adams to discuss what might be done to prevent similar disturbances. The next day the New Light leader Jonathan Edwards gave a sermon that Joshua Hempstead described as being "very Suitable for the times to bear Wittness against ye prevailing disorders & destractions yt are Subsisting in the Country by means of Enthusiasm."[54]

Davenport was banned from returning to the colony, but he apparently did not need any inducement to refrain from itinerant preaching in New England. The next year he published an apology for his "*Errors* and *Misconduct,*" among which he counted his maligning of the ministers, his encouragement of lay exhorters, his acting without benefit of scripture, and his orchestration of "the awful Affair of Books and Cloaths at *New-London.*" Several of Davenport's New London followers, some of whom had been assessed small fines by the court for profaning the Sabbath, also reevaluated their commitment to their new church. The Shepherd's Tent was ultimately disbanded, and many Separates left to join other denominations, such as the Baptists. Within a few years, the society seems simply to have ceased to exist.[55]

The book-burning episode lived long in the memory of New Londoners, as did the divisions caused by the Great Awakening. The democratic nature of the Great Awakening and the challenges it posed to traditional forms of authority—which some historians have claimed laid a foundation for the American Revolution—were a clear indication that New England society was transforming itself. For Mehetabel, who was nearing her seventh decade, such signs were no doubt becoming increasingly visible.

One reflection of Mehetabel's advanced stage in life was her children themselves growing middle-aged. In 1743 John turned forty-seven, Joseph forty-five, and Martha thirty-seven. For Martha, the aging process and the challenges life had thus far presented seem to have produced a moderation of the high spirits so evident in her early writings. A more conservative outlook is revealed in a letter she sent Mehetabel in the spring of that year from Boston, where she may have gone to make purchases for her shop. This is the last of her letters to Mehetabel that has been found.

Boston May 9th 1743

Hon[d]: Mad[m]:

    thro' Divine goodness we are all well—had a Comfortable Journy Except the last day which was Extreem Hott, Coz:[n] Gardiner Held out beyond Expectation, She talks of going to School to Learn how to wright you a Letter against Next Post[.] She Setts Goking & Loping about & I cant make her touch a Pen all I can do,—Dear M[rs] Slaughtr is well gives her Love to you is Hearty & Sincear to the Last Degree. I Long to hear from you, & my Little Flock, Please to bid Russel & Cretia Right to me, My Duty to Father & Your Self Love to Bro:[ths][.] I Expect an Epestel from Jose[ph] [illegible word] Post[.] I have writ something Large to M[rs] Molly, which She I suppose will Shew you therefore have not time to add farther att Present then to begg your Rememberance of me at the throne of Grace that I may be keep from Sin & Return'd in Safety to the Armes of My Dear Parents—

from Hon[d] Mad:[m] Your Dutyfull Daughter[56]

[signature torn off]

While in Boston, Martha apparently stayed with her former hostess, Elisabeth Slaughter, leaving her children under Mehetabel's care. The identity of Martha's traveling companion, the illiterate "Coz:[n] Gardiner," is unclear.

Martha's experience of hardship and her growth in spiritual devotion, manifested by her having joined the church and in the religious references sprinkled throughout her letter, may have altered the nature of her relationship with Mehetabel, creating an added sympathy and understanding between them. Mehetabel no doubt drew on this relationship to help sustain her through losses she suffered in the coming months. First of these was the death of her brother John, at the age of seventy-eight, in the summer of 1743. During his long life, John had married twice, fathered ten children, and served as a town clerk, selectman, teacher, tavern keeper, surveyor, justice of the peace, military leader, Indian superintendent, representative to the General Court, member of His Majesty's Council, judge, and chief justice. He had also helped organize one of the first library societies in Connecticut (and had amassed an impressive library of his own). In the end, he had come about as far as humanly possible from his youthful indiscretion, when, as a nine-year-old, he had been convicted of "wanton uncivill & unseemly carriages" with his sister Elizabeth. At the time of his death, the *Boston Evening-Post* paid tribute to him as "a Gentleman greatly delighted with Conversation; of a most generous and hospitable Disposition, his Doors being open to all, especially the faithful Ministers of Christ of all Denominations, whom he treated with great Civility and Respect."[57]

According to the *Evening-Post,* a "vast Concourse of People" from Woodstock and neighboring towns turned out to pay their respects at John Chandler's funeral, held two days after his death.[58] He was laid to rest in the Woodstock burying ground near their father (their mother's grave being in New London), his first wife, and some of his children. Although John died a very wealthy man, in his will he requested a simple burial; his grave, which can still be seen today, is marked by a large, flat stone with no inscription.

Several months later, Mehetabel lost her niece Sarah Gardiner Treat, the daughter of her late sister Sarah. Like her mother, Sarah Treat died at the age of thirty-four, leaving behind several young children. Mehetabel's niece Hannah Draper Gore, the daughter of her late sister Hannah, had predeceased Sarah in 1741, at the age of fifty-five. Both women, her sisters' only surviving daughters, died of unknown causes.

Finally, in the autumn of 1744, Mehetabel's husband John, who was just shy of seventy-four, fell seriously ill. Although John had aged so that Joshua Hempstead had begun referring to him as "old Mr Coit" by the late 1730s, he had remained energetic. In fact, Hempstead writes of John's having "bravely" worked at a project that involved digging up large rocks just a few months earlier. This illness, however, proved too much for John, and within a few days he was dead. Hempstead seems to have been deeply moved by the passing of his "near Neighbor" and "good old friend," whom he had gone to visit early in the morning on the day of his passing and had left "grapling with Death." Hempstead, along with Eliphalet Adams, Dr. Jeremiah Miller, the printer and deacon Timothy Green, and neighbors Joseph Truman and William Holt served as pallbearers at John's funeral, which was held two days later.[59]

Mehetabel did not write about John's death in her diary, but it must have affected her profoundly. No evidence survives relating to the nature of their marriage, but it had lasted an almost unheard of fifty years and had likely been a relationship grounded in shared ideals and goals. It may also have been a deeply affectionate and loving partnership. Like many other colonial couples, Mehetabel and John may have found in each other, in the words of early Massachusetts governor John Winthrop to his wife Margaret, a "sweet spouse," who "delight[ed] in the love of eache other as the chiefe of all earthly comforts."[60]

CHAPTER NINE
Endings, 1745–1758

JOHN LEFT behind a detailed will, which he had drawn up in 1741. Since it was customary for a couple to discuss the terms that would be established for a wife's maintenance in the event her husband predeceased her, it is likely that Mehetabel and John did as well. John's will contained provisions that were similar to most other men's wills of the time: he reserved for Mehetabel the traditional dower right, or a third of his personal property, as well as use of a third of his real estate during her lifetime. He also specified that Mehetabel should be given forty pounds annually for her maintenance. John expected that his sons John and Joseph, whom he had named as co-executors of the estate, would oversee their mother's care; among other duties, they were to maintain the two cows left for Mehetabel's use and provide her with "Ten Cord of wood p^r annum Cut fit for the fire."[1]

Like other widows with grown children, Mehetabel was assigned just a portion of the family home to reside in. John specified that she was to have "one half of my now Dwelling House in New London and Celler under the Same," along "with her Necessary Use of the Well and the one half of my Gardens all at her Election"—John's use of the pronoun "my" reflecting the legal realities of the time. John left the other half of the house to his and Mehetabel's nineteen-year-old grandson Thomas, son of their late son of the same name, to be claimed when he reached the age of twenty-one. Thomas also inherited the land to the south of the home on which stood the barn and "other Buildings," including the blacksmith's shop that had belonged to his father, as well as John Coit's wharf. The land to the north of the home, which included an orchard and rope house, went to Mehetabel and John's son Joseph along with an extra fifty pounds "in Consideration of and in full satisfaction for the Great help and assistance" he had given his father "since he arrived to the age of Twenty One Years." John junior received several acres that had belonged to John Coit's parents, while Martha and Lize were each given half of John Coit's land in the common field. (It is notable that John's bequests to Martha and Lize were in land, rather than the conventional personal property.) Since John had owned twenty-seven acres in the "Comon pasture" and fifty acres of additional "Comon Rights," it is not clear how much land Martha and Lize ended up with, but it would have been equal in value to one-sixth of the estate. Thomas and Joseph were also given a sixth of the estate; John junior received two-sixths, the traditional double portion for the eldest son. (John Coit did not make a provision in his will for Lize's brother Samuel, because a clause in Samuel's father's will requested that anything John had intended to give to his daughter Elizabeth, had she lived, go to Lize, Samuel senior "haveing made other Provision in his S^d Will for his S^d Son.")

According to his will, John had already made significant gifts to his children over the years: advancing approximately 400 pounds to John junior, 256 pounds to Martha, 125 pounds to Joseph, 112 pounds to Elizabeth, and 103 pounds to Thomas. The total distributed, almost 1,000 pounds, was a considerable sum by the standards of the time, particularly since the total value of most Connecticut estates throughout the colonial period was less than 500 pounds. The probate inventory taken shortly following John's death clearly substantiates that he and Mehetabel were people of means. In addition to approximately 135 acres of land valued at 3,005 pounds, the inventory lists more than 400 pounds' worth of silver; bonds and notes; 145 sheep (which produced income through their lease to other farmers), six cows, four horses, and seven pigs; elaborate bedding; fine linens; assorted furniture; and high-quality dishware. John Coit's entire estate was valued at more than 5,700 pounds, which would have placed him in the highest economic bracket in New London.[2]

The probate inventory was taken by five appraisers who included John and Mehetabel's nephew Daniel Coit, who was also the town clerk, and Joshua Hempstead (who wrote that he worked so late "apprizing at Ms Coits" one evening that he was invited to stay for dinner). The inventory provides a wealth of information about Mehetabel and John's home and lifestyle and is worth detailed review. Although the appraisers grouped like items together rather than separately listing the contents of each room, it is possible to reconstruct the layout of the house to some extent. For example, at least three rooms were used for sleeping, as the inventory mentions a west chamber, a west bedroom, and a lean-to chamber containing bedding. Mehetabel and John would have had their own bedroom; their children, when young, likely shared sleeping space. (The young apprentices Mehetabel mentions having stayed with the family, along with Mingo, Peter, Nanny, and Nell, may have been assigned space in the attic, in one of the outbuildings, or even on the kitchen floor.) At the time the inventory was taken, Mehetabel and John still owned at least five beds, one of which was a trundle, and various sets of bed curtains, which would have afforded privacy. They also had several feather-beds, which were highly valued and often passed down in families because of the time it took to acquire the necessary amount of feathers. Mehetabel and John's bedding also included bolsters, pillows, mattresses (or "Sacking bottom[s]"), blankets, quilts, coverlets, a white "Counterpin," and expensive bedsheets made of cotton and a fine linen known as "holland." Some of the bedding was described by the appraisers as being "old" or "course"; these pieces may have been remnants from Mehetabel and John's early married life relegated to storage, or they could have been used by Nell, Nanny, Mingo, and Peter.[3]

In addition to the beds, the appraisers took account of pieces of furniture of varying value, including three large tables, two of them oval-shaped; two smaller "old" tables, perhaps one of which served as Mehetabel's writing desk; three chests of drawers; a "couch and furniture"; some trunks; a joint stool; nine "old" chairs; twenty-two black chairs; and six "Turkey work," or embroidered, chairs, which may very well have been the same "Turkey wrought" chairs referred to in Mehetabel's father's estate inventory. The substantial number of chairs they owned suggests that Mehetabel and John did a fair amount of entertaining, as do the large punch bowl, the syllabub pot, the china tea service, and the set of forty-seven pewter plates included in the inventory. Visitors to the couple's home would have perceived signs of their status and refinement in their silver plate; large looking glasses; forks (which many people did not own until the late eighteenth century and beyond); fine "diaper," or patterned linen, tablecloths and napkins; and books, which, regrettably, apart from the Bible were not catalogued by the appraisers. Unlike many elite families, they owned no clocks, although they did have an hourglass.[4]

In addition to Mehetabel and John's finer possessions, the inventory also included their more utilitarian belongings, such as John's carpentry tools (axes, an adze, a hatchet, a handsaw, hammers, files, chisels, a shave, an auger, spike gimlets, tap bores) and farming implements (a plow, hoes, pitchforks, rakes, shovels, a sickle, and scythes). Ordinary household items included brass and other candlesticks, fireplace tools, milk pans, a grindstone, scales, sugar tubs and boxes, trays, pails, small barrels, a candle box, a meal chest, bags and boxes, and a cider press. Earthenware plates, cups, and serving pieces (platters, bowls, jugs); drinking glasses; pots for sugar and mustard; vinegar cruets; a pint pot; a bread tray; and a butter tub were listed, as were Mehetabel's cooking utensils. These included pots, pans, skillets, kettles, a pudding pan, a mortar and pestle, and a "choping knife." The twelve glass beakers included on the inventory may have contained Mehetabel's medical remedies.

Although John's clothing appears on the inventory, Mehetabel's does not, as it was considered hers alone and not part of the estate. Her personal belongings, such as any jewelry she may have owned or small family pieces she inherited, also would have been disregarded by the appraisers.

Conspicuous among John's property listed on the inventory are the names of Nell, Mingo, and Peter. Nell and Mingo were valued at eighty-five pounds, while Peter, who was younger, was valued at one hundred pounds. John specified in his will that Mehetabel was to be given "[his] Negro Woman Called Nell," but in case he "Should Sell S^d Negro woman," Mehetabel would inherit "[his] Negro man called Mingo." Mehetabel did, in fact, retain Nell as her servant, while Mingo, who had served the household for almost forty years, apparently went to live with John junior. (Later entries in Joshua Hempstead's diary indicate that Peter became the property of Mehetabel's son Joseph.) It is strange that John singled out Nell for a possible sale, particularly since, at the time he made his will, she had been with the family for more than two decades. The family clearly did not need the proceeds from selling Nell, so it is possible only to speculate about the circumstances: perhaps John and Nell did not get along or he judged her work to be unsatisfactory, or it is possible that Nell was married to a slave belonging to another master and John was considering selling her so the couple could be together. In any case, the sale never took place, and Nell continued to provide Mehetabel with assistance—and also, perhaps, companionship—for the rest of her life.

For a widow to share her home with other adult family members was a common arrangement, but for many women the situation was not an easy one. Mehetabel was fortunate to have some time to adjust to the prospect, since under the terms of John's will her grandson Thomas would not be able to claim his inheritance for another two years, when he turned twenty-one. By the time Thomas did move in he appears to have been studying medicine, perhaps under the tutelage of his stepfather, Dr. Ebenezer Gray, or locally with Dr. Jeremiah Miller. He began a practice in New London about 1750, and for the next forty years he served, according to Frances Caulkins, as the town's "principal physician."[5]

Thomas likely conducted his practice from Mehetabel's home, and it is possible that she occasionally assisted him in preparing medicines or tending to his patients. Mehetabel's extensive knowledge of botanical remedies and her long experience caring for the sick would have served her grandson well. Medicine became specialized and a male-dominated field by the late eighteenth century, but in the 1740s and 1750s, before the advent of medical schools, there were still opportunities for women to practice alongside men. For his part, Thomas's apparent lack of a formal college education may have made him more open to the ways of folk medicine, at least early in his career. Later in life he himself advocated for the professionalization of the field, becoming one of the founders of the Connecticut State Medical Society and an early member of the New London County Medical Association.[6]

Since Thomas did not marry until 1756, Mehetabel undoubtedly continued as mistress of the household for several years after she was widowed, cooking and doing the laundry, maintaining the gardens, milking the cows, and performing numberless other duties—all, of course, with the assistance of Nell. Perhaps the familiar routine of performing these daily chores, as well as the encouragement of family, friends, and neighbors, helped sustain Mehetabel during those first months following John's death, when she may have felt quite adrift. She may also have taken heart from the examples of her mother and grandmother Annis, both of whom had been widowed and had managed to make new lives for themselves. Above all, her faith likely offered great comfort.

As Mehetabel was adjusting to life as a widow, she also had to come to terms with her daughter Martha's move from New London. The month before John Coit's death, Martha had married Thomas Greene, a wealthy Boston merchant. Martha and Thomas remained in New London for several weeks after their September 6 wedding, but, according to Joshua Hempstead's diary, they along with Martha's five children, then aged four through twelve, left for Boston on October 29, just days after John Coit's death.

As so many others in the Coit-Chandler sphere, Thomas Greene had a

John Singleton Copley, portrait of Thomas Greene, 1758.
Courtesy Cincinnati Art Museum;
gift of Mrs. Carlos A. Hepp / Bridgeman Art Library.

Gardiner connection: his late first wife, Elizabeth, had been a daughter of Lord John Gardiner's by his first wife. Moreover, Elizabeth Gardiner Greene's brother Samuel had been married to Mehetabel's daughter Elizabeth, and her sister Hannah had been married to Mehetabel's nephew John Chandler. Elizabeth Greene had died the previous February, leaving Thomas with five sons and a daughter ranging in age from four to fifteen. (The daughter, Mary, would eventually marry Martha's son Daniel.)[7]

Thomas Greene had a thriving business in overseas trade, a wharf at the end of Boston's Sea Street dock, and a "mansion-house" in a fashionable part of town. He and Martha enjoyed a very high standard of living over the years. According to Martha's descendants, she was charitable with her new-found wealth, and the poor of Boston were known to run after her carriage because of her reputation for distributing alms.[8]

John Singleton Copley,
portrait of Martha Coit Hubbard Greene, ca. 1758.
Courtesy Dietrich American Foundation.

Like many other prosperous Bostonians, Martha and Thomas eventually sat for portraits by the promising young painter John Singleton Copley. Thomas is depicted in his office, reviewing correspondence—the ship in the background symbolizing his position as a merchant; Martha is shown in a moment of leisure, posed against a pastoral scene. Although the color of Martha's clothing is subdued, she wears an elegant dress with lace sleeves. Perhaps the most interesting aspect of the portrait is the directness of Martha's gaze, which almost confronts the viewer.

Mehetabel's pleasure over Martha's finding a new mate—and no longer having to support herself and her children by working as a shopkeeper—may have been tempered by her new son-in-law's religion: Thomas Greene was an Anglican, a member of the Church of England. Established by Henry VIII following his renunciation of Catholicism, the Church of England's "corruption" had been a driving force behind the Puritans' exodus to the New World in the 1600s. Even more than a century after the Great Migration, Congregationalists remained troubled by Anglicanism's focus on ritual, its doctrine that salvation could be earned through good works rather than being preordained, and its lack of emphasis on sustained self-scrutiny.

Perhaps in part because of Thomas's ties to the local Anglican community—he was one of the founders and original trustees of Boston's Trinity Church—Martha herself adopted Anglicanism. At some point after her marriage to Thomas, she began attending services at Trinity, and all of the children they had together were baptized there. In turning from Congregationalism to Anglicanism, not only was Martha abandoning many of the religious beliefs that had been instilled in her from childhood, but she was also breaking with family tradition. It is quite possible that Mehetabel may never have completely accepted Martha's decision.

Martha's affiliation with Anglicanism may have provided her with an opportunity to experience a less daunting, more rewarding relationship with God. It is possible, too, that her relationship with Thomas was also satisfying. According to the eulogy given on the occasion of his death years later, Thomas treated Martha "with the most affectionate regard; and they lived together in the delightful enjoyment of conjugal felicity." Thomas was also said to have been a devoted father, regarding both Martha's children and their own as "the constant objects of his paternal tenderness and concern."[9]

Mehetabel did not make another dated entry in her diary until 1748, although there is no way of knowing how many of the poems and other literary extracts she may have transcribed during these years. That she did not remarry meant that she was able to enjoy more freedom and autonomy in her daily life—additional time to read, write, and reflect. It is clear that she remained "of sound disposing mind and memory" until at least late 1752, when she wrote her will, and it is perhaps a sign of her continued good health that she waited until she was seventy-nine to do so.[10]

The seven years following 1741 comprised the longest period Mehetabel had ever gone without recording a dated entry. When she resumed her diary keeping, she apparently tried to make up for lost time, logging what was, for her, the considerable number of five entries in one year. Four of these had to do with visitors she entertained. On "febr 21," she notes, "Daniel Hubbard came here with his brother thomas Greene and march the 8 day thay away." At the time, Daniel was eleven and his stepbrother Thomas was about nineteen. Daniel evidently returned a few months later, as Mehetabel writes that on "may 1" Martha's fourteen-year-old daughter "Lucretia Hubbard came hear to give us a visit[.] June 7 She went hom and Daniel Hubbard went with her." (Mehetabel did not record the year after "may 1," but it is very likely 1748, since the entry appears near others she recorded that year.)[11]

That fall Mehetabel received two additional sets of visitors. First, on "Sep^tbr 19: 1748," she writes, "my brother Joseph Chandler & his Daughter Susanah Came here[.] the 22 Day thay went home." Joseph's daughter Susannah had previously spent some time with Mehetabel in July 1726, when, Mehetabel wrote, Susannah "came to live with" her.[12] Now the thirty-seven-year-old Susannah, who like her father lived in Pomfret, was married and the mother of several children, including a daughter named Mehitable; in fact, she was well along into a pregnancy at the time of her visit.

The day Joseph and Susannah departed, Mehetabel received what was surely a welcome visit from Martha and Thomas. The couple—and, quite possibly, some of their children—stayed for several weeks; Mehetabel writes that on "September 22 1748 my Son and Daughter Greene Came here," and it was not until "Octo^br 17" that "thay went home."[13] It is surprising that Thomas Greene was able to remain away from his business for so long, but Martha must have been delighted by the opportunity to spend time with her mother.

The last diary entry Mehetabel recorded in 1748 represents one of the few times she mentioned the title of a book she was reading. On "June 13: 1748," she writes, "I began to Read M^r burkitts work upon the new te[s]tement and finished it the 29 of august."[14] Mehetabel was referring to William Burkitt's *Expository Notes with Practical Observations on the New Testament of Our Lord and Saviour Jesus Christ,* subtitled "wherein the sacred text is at large recited, the sense explained, and the instructive example of the blessed Jesus, and his holy Apostles, to our imitation recommended." First published in two volumes in England in the early 1700s, the *Expository Notes* were reprinted many times. (Since an American edition was not printed until 1794, Mehetabel was evidently reading a British copy.)

It is not surprising that it took Mehetabel most of the summer to finish the *Expository Notes,* which in some editions ran to almost a thousand pages. What is remarkable is that, at the age of seventy-five, she was still tackling works that required such intellectual stamina. Evidently not content merely to reread the scriptures, Mehetabel continued to delve into their meaning well into her later years.

In 1749 Mehetabel entered the final dated entries into her diary. She notes that on "may 3: 1749 Russel Hubbard Came here, the 9 day he went to Hartford." Russell, the oldest child of Martha and Daniel Hubbard, was almost seventeen and a student at Yale. After graduating in 1751 and spending some time at sea, he embarked on a successful career as a merchant on New London's waterfront, where he and his uncle Joseph Coit, according to Frances Caulkins, operated two of the "most conspicuous stands for merchandise."[15]

Mehetabel writes that the day before Russell left for Hartford, on "may 8: 1749: Elezebeth Gardiner went to boston," and that "june 8 she Came home."[16] Mehetabel was evidently still deeply invested in the activities of her granddaughter Lize, who was now a mother with young children of her own.

One final entry appears on the last page of Mehetabel's diary. Although it is undated, it may have been written at about this time: "September 27 Mr Gardiner & his wife, & his 2 Sons Came from Boston, the 29 thay went home[.] Mrs Green, & Mrs Sewall & her Son, & Daughter, & M^r wainright, went with them." The identity of these individuals is unclear. "Mr Gardiner & his wife" are not Lize and her husband David, as they lived in New London, not Boston. And "Mrs Green" is probably not Martha, since Mehetabel likely would have referred to her as "Daughter Green," as she had in her 1748 entry. (Perhaps she was Mary Chandler Greene, the granddaughter of Mehetabel's brother John, who was married to Thomas Greene's brother Benjamin.) There were many Sewalls living in Boston at the time, so it is difficult to pinpoint who "Mrs Sewall" was; the full name of "M^r wainright" is likewise uncertain.[17]

Mehetabel's diary entries indicate that she still enjoyed spending time in the company of her family and friends; however, many of her contemporaries predeceased her. Mehetabel outlived not only her brother Joseph, but also John Coit's surviving brothers, Joseph and Solomon. In September 1749 Mehetabel's friend Lydia Adams suffered a fatal stroke. Her funeral, heralded by the respectful sign of the tolling of both church bells throughout the service, was, according to Joshua Hempstead, attended by "a Great number of people." Eliphalet Adams seems to have been deeply affected by the loss of his wife, whom he referred to as "the Desire of my Eyes and the Delight of my Heart" in the sermon he gave at her funeral and later published.[18]

In a strange turn of events, the widower Adams married Mehetabel's friend Elisabeth Slaughter of Boston. (Elisabeth, who had been widowed twice since she sent Mehetabel the picture of Cotton Mather in 1728, had apparently been previously acquainted with the Adamses, since Martha had mentioned in a 1726 letter to Mehetabel that "Mrs Slaughter Desires to know if Mrs Adams Likes her Calico.") The union of Elisabeth Slaughter and Eliphalet Adams lasted just two years; in 1753 the seventy-six-year-old Adams fell victim to an epidemic of dysentery, or "Bloody flux," then visiting the New London area.[19]

Adams's pulpit remained vacant until 1757, when the church invited Mather Byles, a twenty-two-year-old Harvard graduate (and grandnephew of Cotton Mather) to assume the ministry. Although Byles's tenure was marked by repeated provocations by the Rogerenes, he proved to be a highly popular minister. In 1768, however, he delivered a great shock to his congregation when he announced he was leaving to become a clergyman in the Church of England.

The four years during which New London did not have a Congregational minister must have been unsettling for Mehetabel, who for the greater part of her life had been connected with churches headed by charismatic leaders. Unfortunately, her final years were also marked by other sources of discomfort. When she wrote her will in 1752, for example, she included several customary provisions—appointing her sons John and Joseph as co-executors, leaving all her clothing to her daughter Martha and granddaughter Lize, and dividing her estate equally among her heirs (one-fifth each to her three children, one-fifth to her grandson Thomas, and one-tenth each to Lize and her brother Samuel)—but she also established conditions that evidence discord in the family. Noting that she was "desirous that Peace and Love may be kept and maintained in my family after I am gone," she mandated that Thomas and Samuel could receive their portions only if they first disclaimed any further interest in John Coit's estate and if Thomas repaid John, Joseph, Martha, and Lize for the surplus over his appointed share he had received. If Thomas and Samuel refused to comply, Mehetabel wrote, they would not receive their inheritance from her estate and would be given only "five Shillings old tenor Bills." (Five shillings was equivalent to sixty pence or one-quarter of one pound; "old tenor" bills were depreciated currency notes.)

It is not known whether Mehetabel informed her grandsons of the contents of her will or whether her feelings about the division of her husband's estate had affected her relationship with Thomas. What is clear is that, by creating particular conditions in her will, Mehetabel was asserting what relatively little economic power she had as a widow. The terms of John Coit's will had been established to ensure that she remain comfortable, not financially independent. By writing her own will, Mehetabel was not only affirming that she had a stake in the financial future and continued harmony of her family, but she was also utilizing one of the only means available to her by which she might give public expression to her private wishes.[20]

Mehetabel lived for six years after making her will. The year that she died also saw the deaths of Peter and Nell. According to Joshua Hempstead, Peter died in early 1758 at the age of "50 or more," having been "a very faithfull Laborious Servt."[21] Hempstead attended Peter's burial in the New London cemetery, and if Mehetabel were well enough, she certainly would have as well. It is not known whether Peter was survived by his wife, whom Hempstead had mentioned but not named in a 1745 entry, or whether he left behind any children.

Nell died that summer. Hempstead writes that on August 25, "old Nell a faithfull Servt of old Ms Coits ye Widow of old mr Jno Coit Died with a Cancer in her Breast." Given that the sixty-one-year-old Nell had served Mehetabel and her family for her entire adult life, it is to be hoped that Mehetabel ministered to her with particular kindness during her final days, which certainly must have been difficult ones given her diagnosis. As with Peter, it is not clear whether Nell left behind a family.

Mehetabel survived Nell by just a little over two months. Hempstead recorded in his diary on November 3 that "old Ms Mehitable Coit the widow of Mr Jno Coit decd Died ys morning." Remarkably, this was the eighty-year-old Hempstead's final entry in the diary he had kept for forty-seven years; he too died a few weeks later. The cause of his death is unknown, but Hempstead had mentioned in his November 3 entry that he had been feeling "Exceeding Sore in [his] Bowels where the pain was last week" and that his daughter had spent the night with him.

According to Hempstead's diary, Martha and Thomas were in New London a few weeks prior to Mehetabel's death. Although it is almost too much to hope that Martha was able to be with her mother during her final hours, Mehetabel was almost certainly not alone at the end, unless death came suddenly in her sleep. Once she started to show signs of illness or decline, her family would have ensured that someone was with her at all times, as Hempstead's family had, and in her final days neighbors would have stopped in to pay their respects. Death, like birth, in early America was a community event.

Mehetabel's gravestone, Ye Antientist Burial Ground, New London.

Having been taught from childhood the need to face her own mortality, and having believed all her life in the necessity to "seek first the kingdom of heaven," as she had encouraged her daughters to do, Mehetabel would have been spiritually prepared to accept death when the time came. Given her deep faith, she may even have looked forward to the "Joyfull meeting at ye resurrection," when she and the many loved ones who had predeceased her would "never part more but enjoy eternall fellowship & society," as her mother had written many years before.[22]

Mehetabel was laid to rest in the family plot in the New London burial ground, where her gravestone can still be seen today. The stone's simple inscription—"Here lies Buried the Body of Mrs Mehetabel Coit who Departed this Life November ye 3rd 1758 Aged 85 Years"—and its winged death's head carving, meant to emphasize the brevity of life, mark it as being in the traditional Puritan style. Within a few decades, this symbol was largely replaced by cherubs and other less-threatening images that reflected the more hopeful visions of the afterlife that developed following the Great Awakening.[23]

The inventory taken after Mehetabel's death discloses the limited range of personal possessions she retained in her later years: three tables; a couch; a chest and two "old" chests of drawers; a small gilt trunk; two beds; large and small looking glasses; a white chamber pot; table and bed linens; pots, pans, and kettles; fireplace tools; a warming pan; glass bottles; earthenware plates, platters, cups, and porringers; butterpots; a syllabub pot; "old" knives and forks; brass candlesticks; and "good" and "not so good" pewter. She also had nineteen chairs, indicating that she was always able to provide seating for her visitors, and a "Great Bible" and "Sundry Bound Books & Pamphlets," which, unfortunately, were not identified. As a single person living in one-half of a house, she had no need for all of the things she had earlier used when taking care of a family, but it also appears that she may have reduced her belongings further by giving many away.[24]

The most poignant article listed in Mehetabel's inventory is an ear trumpet, revealing that she suffered from hearing loss; the most valuable is her silver plate, which was worth almost fifty pounds. She also owned more than thirty-nine pounds' worth of "new tenor" paper currency, or bills of credit, and over eight pounds' worth of notes, suggesting that she had loaned money and thus remained active in the local economy.

Overall, Mehetabel's estate was worth 144 pounds, a small fraction of the value of her husband's. Her legacy to her children was certainly not material wealth. Although she had brought assets to her marriage in the form of her dowry and inheritance and she had contributed to her family's income through the trade networks indicated by the accounts in her diary, these resources were, by and large, not hers to control. Her true gifts to her children were her teachings, her love and support, her example of how to live a resilient and productive life, and her writings. Indeed, Mehetabel's writings are a gift to all of us who seek a more nuanced and comprehensive understanding of the American past.

EPILOGUE

Mehetabel's children, like their mother before them, lived long, eventful lives. John, perhaps, experienced the most personal misfortune, but he also displayed an ability to try to move beyond his troubles. In the single year after his father's death, he lost his twenty-five-year-old son John, who drowned after being knocked into the sea by his ship's boom, as well as his twenty-three-year-old son Richard and his wife Grace, both of whom appear to have been taken by the "Longfever." (His twenty-eight-year-old son Joseph would fall victim to the same ailment in 1756.)[1]

John's trials must have precipitated some soul-searching, as he joined the New London church a little over a month after Grace's death. He remarried in 1748, and he and his second wife, Hannah, had three children together, one of whom they named Mehetabel. Although John served as New London's town clerk in 1758 and seems to have continued to run the family shipyard for several years, by about 1760 he had decided to start a new life in Newport. Some time after his move, his niece Lydia Coit Hubbard (Joseph's daughter, who was married to Martha's son William) expressed in a letter to her parents her wish that John might "spend the remainder of his days with that ease and Comfort which I believe he has bin A stranger to for some time."[2]

The date of John's death is unclear, although a 1774 letter written by his brother Joseph noting that John and Hannah were visiting from Newport indicates that he lived at least into his late seventies. The fate of Mingo, whom John had inherited after his father's death, is also unknown.[3]

Mehetabel's son Joseph remained active well into his later years, fathering the last of the nine children he had with his wife Lydia when he was nearly sixty. Joseph became a patriot in the years leading up to the American Revolution, joining New London's nonimportation committee opposing the Townshend Acts, which taxed paper, paint, glass, and tea. Although by 1775 business interests and family connections brought Joseph to Norwich, Connecticut, he continued to maintain residential and retail property in New London until much of it was destroyed in General Benedict Arnold's 1781 burning of the town. Joseph lived to an even older age than his mother had, dying in 1787 at the age of eighty-eight.

Martha's life seems to have been a comfortable one. She remained financially secure even after Thomas Greene's death in 1763, and, according to her descendants, she was "beloved and honored" by her extended family. Around the time of the Revolution, Martha also apparently moved to Norwich, where some of her children as well as her brother Joseph lived. In 1782, at the age of seventy-six, she bought a home there that she then deeded to her son Russell, who, like Joseph, had lost property in Arnold's New London assault. Unfortunately, Martha did not leave behind any personal papers, and a comment made in 1765 by her son William that "it is really got to be a great task for Mother to write a letter" suggests that, as she grew older, Martha no longer took the same pleasure in writing she once had.[4]

Martha specified in her will that her considerable estate of almost eight thousand pounds be equally divided among her six living children—to "share & share alike"—and requested that "handsome" silver tankards be purchased from the estate for seven of her grandchildren. At the time of her death in 1784, she was buried in the Greene family vault in the Trinity Church crypt. After Trinity was destroyed in the Great Boston Fire of 1872, the church moved from Summer Street to its current landmark location in Copley Square, and its graves were transferred to a single plot in Cambridge's Mount Auburn Cemetery. Martha's remains, and those of all the other relocated Trinity parishioners, are marked there by a simple memorial stone.[5]

Little is known about the fate of Mehetabel's beloved granddaughter Lize, other than that she remained in New London for the rest of her life. She died in October 1772, just shy of her fifty-first birthday.

Mehetabel's heirs continued to live in the family home, located near the present corner of New London's Coit and Washington Streets, until the late 1800s, when it was sold to the state of Connecticut as the site of an armory. A surviving photograph taken between 1865 and 1880 of what may be Mehetabel's house shows nineteenth-century refinements and includes the figures of a child, a horse, and an unidentified African American man.[6]

Mehetabel's diary and the family letters descended through her son Joseph's family. Joseph's son Daniel left the manuscripts to his daughter Eliza Coit Gilman, whose children published the extracts from Mehetabel's diary,

Coit family home, New London, ca. 1865–1880. © *Mystic Seaport, Photography Collection, Mystic, Conn., #1994.18.35.*

as *Mehetabel Chandler Coit: Her Book, 1714,* and Martha's letters, as *Martha, Daughter of Mehetabel Chandler Coit, 1706–1784,* in 1895. Although the family editors made it clear that they were proud of Mehetabel, whom they understood to be a "good woman, devout, affectionate, [and] housewifely," they were apparently not convinced of her diary's value as a historical resource, dismissing Mehetabel's writings as merely "a brief record of many family events, the birth of her children, the visits of friends, &c., with sundry epitaphs, religious verses, and domestic recipes." Mehetabel's descendants may have believed that her diary contained little of significance because of the domestic and familial nature of much of its content. As Laurel Thatcher Ulrich has illustrated in her discussion of the history of Martha Ballard's diary, women's personal writings have frequently been overlooked or ignored because their concerns have been judged "trivial."[7]

The writings of Mehetabel and her female family members provide a framework for understanding the religious, economic, and social developments that began transforming New England during Mehetabel's lifetime into a more secular, commercial, and socially sophisticated cultural center. The poem and letters of Mehetabel's mother and mother-in-law, for example, display the centrality of faith in people's lives early in this period, while Martha's letters, with their focus on society and fashion, demonstrate the increased emphasis being placed on worldly matters and consumer goods decades later. In the middle ground are Mehetabel's writings, which address both deeply felt spiritual concerns and a variety of earthly interests. Because the pace of transformation quickened during the mid-eighteenth century, the outward contours of Mehetabel's life ultimately were far more similar to her mother's than to her daughter's. By the time of Martha's marriage to Thomas Greene, changes in the marketplace had made the luxury goods filling their "mansion house" more readily available, and new ideas about gentility and refinement made them more desirable. (Martha, of course, went a step further by attending the Anglican church, the place of worship of many of the elite.) While Mehetabel could be said to represent the colonial goodwife known for her industry, sobriety, and piety, Martha led the more leisurely life of a gentlewoman, a role that upper-class women increasingly adopted in the years before the Revolution.[8]

The writings of Mehetabel and her family offer invaluable information about numerous aspects of life in early America: about writing and reading, work and recreation, illness and healing, politics and war, commerce and consumption, cuisine and travel, childhood, parenthood, and old age—and the bonds of "Dear Love" and affection that existed across generations. That this abundance of insights can be gleaned from such neglected—and, perhaps at first glance, unpromising—sources suggests that a potential wealth of material remains to be mined by those interested in early American women's lives.

APPENDIX

Full Text of Mehetabel Chandler Coit's Diary, 1688–1749

Note: Occasional blank pages appear between the following pages of text.

p. 1 (inside front cover)

mdm Adams mony for [milk?]
mr hollom mony for [mulases?]
… weight of … 3 oo
[Sould?] … of the barell
4 3 5 beside what Chamberlin had.

Mehetabel Coit
Her Book 1714

[The following ten lines are crossed
   out:]
September the [?] 4 1712 [?]
M[r] Waters his

an account of y[e]
M[r] Runalds
to Sam Watters
to Jams Rogers
to Thomas W...
to M[r] Sha[pley?]
to m[rs] Holom
Capt …

p. 2

June 4 - 1697
our house was Raised
ye 23 of Septem^{br} following
we cam to live in itt

july 22: 1726
Mr Winthrope wentt
to England

A[p]rill 6: 1728 Martha Coit
went to glasonbury
with Mr Treat
and his wife

June 13: 1748
I began to Read M^r
burkitts work upon
the new te[s]tement
and finished it the
29 of august

p. 3

December ye 14. 1704
the Love & Ann was lancht

November ye 26 the Grac[e]
and Hannah was lancht

September ye 13 Mr Alfords
& vrylands brig. new london
was lancht.

novem^{br} 26, Mr Christophers
Sloop was lancht. 1705
twas Rays'd ye 1 of august,

july 3 1705 Thomas Avery
Came in from barbados the
love & Ann the first voyage

August ye love & Ann sett
sale for barbados ye second
voyage, october she Came
in from Antego. this
a Seacond voyage

july ye 7. 1707 the
Grace & Hannah
sett for barbados,

p. 4

August 2 1707 ye love and
Ann sett saill for barbados
on a satturday

Octo^br the Grace & Hannah
came in from barbados

July 22. 1708 the Grace &
Hannah set saill for barbados
G[e]orge Plumb master

Novem^br 13 he came home again

Novem^br [10?] Mr Richard Christo
phers, set saill for barbados
in the brig Richard & Joseph
the first voyage in 1708
and came home again the
22 of march & Charls
Hill came with him.

August [12?] 1708
M^r vrylands vessell
was burn't upon the
stocks, on a thurdsday, &
John coits foot burnt

p. 5

june 14. 1706
billy Coit fell into the
cove, & was allmost
drowned,

nell Cam to live
here in the year 1717
[smudged word] in September
she [then?] being twenty years
of age
nell ___ __

p. 6

july 3: 1705
Mingo Came here
with Thomas Avery in
the love & ann the
first voiage

[The following four lines are writ-
    ten in another hand:]
July 3 1705   1809   1913

This book was written by [great]
greatgrandmother Coit
1810. Maria Coit

p. 7

feb 1694/5 thomas Avery
came to live with my
husband

may 2 1696 Wait Mayhew
came to live here

October 21. 1699 Joseph Shaply
came to live here

Septem^r 1701 Samuell Loomes
came to live here

April 2: 1705 John Christophs
came to live here,

p. 8

Septem^{br} 1707 My Husbend
and I went to Middletown

October ye 3 we come Home and
mother Coit came with us

Aprill 28 1708 John Coit
went to Middletown with
Mr Arnold by water, and
come home may ye 17

june ye 18 my Husband and
Sister Sarah [and ?] I went
to Stoningtown & brother
Joseph Coite was maried to
Experience Wheler 1707
21 day we came home.

june y^e 15 1705 I came from
Woodstock, my mother
Chandler Came with me

may 24: 1707 my Husband
went to Roadisland.

june 25 Joseph Chandler
went to portryall in 1707
September he came home
Decem^{br} 19 he come to n=london
ye 25 he went home my Husband
& Sarah Coit went with him,

p. 9

Decem^{br} 7 my Husband went
to y^e Ile of wight, Joseph Harris
John Mayhew, Robert James
went with him y^e 12 day
thay came home in 1708

January y^e 3 my Husband
& Robert James went to
Woodstock, y^e 10 they came
home

march 10 1708 Martha Coit's
foot burntt with a
warming-pan

Aprell y^e 29 a plank fell
of the stage upon Thomas
Coit & struck him down
but gott no grate mater
of hurt,

June. 1710 John Coit went
to Nyork with M^r
Arnold

August 10: 17[year missing] the ile
  of wite
taken by the french

p. 10

October 20. 1722
Thomas Coit went to
Rhod=Iland, y^e 26 day he
came hom again, the 29
my husband went to the
ile of wight and East hampton
and Came home the first
of novem^br: on a fryday
the 2 day Thomas Coit was
taken sick very bad all that
weak, the next weak went
a brod again

july 1 my brother john
Chandler Came here
the 2 day my brother Joseph
Came
the 8 day thay went
home fryday

p. 11

Septem^br 2: 1708
my Sister Sarah Coit
was maried to Mr John
Gardiner

feb^r 8 1708/9 Sister gardiner
Came here to Mr Adams's
ordination the 28 she went
home again,

p. 12

Aprill. 15 father Chandler
dyed 1703. in his 69ᵗ year

March. 27. 1704 father Coit
dyed

may 7. 1703 William Coit
dyed

Sepᵗᵗ 23 Mother Chandler
dyed 1705 in her 64 year

feb 3. 1698/9 Daniell Coit
dyed att longiland

march 24 1741
my son Mʳ Daniell Hubbard
Died in the 3

p. 13

june 25. 1695
we ware maried

may 25 1696 John Coit
was born

november. 15 Joseph Coit
was born. 1698

feb 18. 1700 Samuell Coit
was born

june. 1 1702. Thomas Coite
was born.

may. 9. 1703 Samuell Coit
dyed in his 4ᵗʰ year

march 22. 1704 Elizᵗʰ Coit
was born.

Aprill 1. 1706. Martha Coit
was born

July 2. 1719 John Coit was
Marryed to Grace Christophers

April 7ᵗʰ: 1720 John Coit
was born

july 8. 1722 Richard Coit
born

p. 14

Nov: 30th Elizabeth Coit
Born in 1724:
Aprill 25: 1725: Elizabeth Coit
dyed: march 10:
my son Thomas Coit died
October the 1 day
my Daughter Elizabeth
Gardiner Died att
East hamton

p. 15

may 31 1688 my father
with his family went to
live att New Roxbury afterwd
called Wodstock

feb^{br} 6 1688/9 Hannah Gary
born the first Child that
was born in Woodstock

April 18 1689 the Revolution
att Boston

novem^{br} 2: 1694 I came to
new london with my brother
John Chandler & his wife

august 1690 I was taken very
sick att Cambridg

p. 16

feb^r 20: 1724 on a thursdday
my Husband and I went
to gardiners Iland, the next
day to East-Hampton. we
went up from the fire place
a foott to the towne
the 25 day Samuell
gardiner was born,

march 28 I came ["Home"crossed
    out]
from East hampton and stayd
4 days att the Iland, Sarah
Gardiner & Lize Came
Home with me

p. 17

September 1 1735
a Dreadfull storm of thunder
and Lightning which struck
the meetinghouse and killed
ned birch Sabath Day

feb^r 1734/5 Richard Dowglass
Died very Suddingly

p. 18

may 19: 1726
I sett out for Woodstock
stayed att norwich that
night, gott to Woodstock the
02 day on a fryday allmost
tyred to Death
the 25 day Sister Chandler
fell Down and broke her
arm, Election Day

june 1 I Came Home again
itt was butt a malloncholy
visitt, I being not very
well all the time that
I was thair

p. 19

feb^r 21: 1748 Daniel
Hubbard came here
with his brother thomas
Greene and
march the 8 day thay
away

p. 20

Sep^{tbr} 19: 1748
my brother Joseph
Chandler & his Daughter
Susanah came here
the 22 Day thay went
home

p. 21

may 1
Lucretia Hubbard came
hear to give us a visit

June 7 She went hom
and Daniel Hubbard went
with her

September 22 1748 my Son
and Daughter Greene
Came here

Octo^{br} 17 thay went
home

may 3: 1749
Russel Hubbard Came
here, the 9 day he went
to Hartford

p. 22

may 8: 1749
Elezebeth Gardiner went
to boston

june 8 she Came home

p. 23

Wintworth—Sure
twas som stranger—
yes, his stay,—
in helth among us
was but one short day,
then he fell sick,
and langusht but ten more,
Before he payed
Corupted nature's score,
Scorsh't by a fevor
he Refind his breath,
and payed that stated
hommag unto Death.

p. 24

Child of the sumer
Ch[a]rming Rose
no longer in confinment Lie
arise to light thy form disclose
Rival the spangles of the sky

the Rains are gon
the storms are ore.
winter retires,
to make the way
com then thou swea[t]ly
blushing flower.
com lovely stranger come away
the son [sun] is Drest
in beaming smiles
to give thy beauty
to the day
yong zephyrs wait
with gentlest gales
to fan [thy] bosom as thay play
Casimire

p. 25

the ten plagues of Egypt
1 All waters turnd to blood
2 frogs numberless do sworm
3 lice loathsom thick as Dust
4 flys numberless do sworm
5 a murrin bests Disstroys
6 blains vex boath man & beast
7 Hail & fire spoil somthings
8 strang locust spoil the Rest
9 thick Darkness palpable
10 the Egytians first born Die
these ten plagues [of] Egypt felt
Rewards of Cruelty

the sick man fasts
because he cannot eat
the poor man fasts
because he hath no meat
the myser fasteth
to augment his store
the glutton fasts
cause he can eate no more
the just man fasts
because he hath offended

p. 26

the Hypocrite
because hed be Commended

[line crossed out]
for the few Hours of Life
Alotted me
Grant me great god
but bread and liberty
I'll ask no more
if more thou'rt plees to give
I'll thankfully
that overplus Receive
if beyond this
no more be frely sent
I'll thank for this
and go away content

the patience of god to
towards sinners is the
greatest miracle in
the world

p. 27

the Difference betwen
to day, & to morrow

to day man's Drest,
in gold and silver bright,
warpt [wrapped] in a shrowd
before to morrow night,
to day he's feeding
on delicious food
to morrow Dead
unable to do good,
today he's nice
and scorns to fee[d] on crumbs
to morrow
he's a dish himself for worms,
to day he's grand
majestick, all Delight,
gastful and pale,
before to morrow night.
true as the scriptures say,
mans life a span
the present moment
is the life of man.

p. 28

Deliverd in a Dull
and lifeles strain,
the best Discorses, no
attention gain,
for if the orater be
half a sleep,
he[']ll scarce his auditors
from snoring keep.

Darts foresee are
Dintles [?]

a wicked wretch Drag'd
his father along the
House. the father
beg'd of him not to
[drag] him beyond such a
place for (said he)
I Drag'd my father
no ferther.

p. 29

a phylosopher seeing two
vicious persons together
cryed out see how the
viper is borrowing
p[o]ison from the asp.

twas the wish of one
that there was a law
for hanging tale barers
by the toung, and tale
hearers by the ears

Herod might have kept
his oath, and not have
cut of the baptist
head, he only promist to
grant what she ask't
to the half of his
kingdom, wheras the
prophets head was worth
more then the whole

p. 30

the cradle and the tomb
alass so nigh
to live is scarce distinguished
from to Dye

from earth all come
to earth must all Return
frail as the cord
and brittle as the urn.

take but the Humblest
Lily of the field,
and if our prid[e]
will to our Reason yeald,
it must by sure
comparison be known.
that on the Regal seat
grate David's son,
arayed in all his Robes
and tipes of power
shines with [less] glory
then that simple flower
prior

p. 31

to make a fine Drink
take 4 pounds of whitte
Suger, one quartt of lime
Guice; four Gallons of watter
and one Gallon of Rum,
putt 2 Cloves into each
bottle cork them well &
tye them down keep them
Cool in sand & in two or
three weeks itt will bee
fitt for your use.

to make Currant wine
to 1 gall of marshed [mashed?]
    Currants,
putt 1 gall of Cold watter
and work itt well together
by squeezing & then lett itt
settle one night Draw itt
off from the dreggs and
putt to itt 3 pound and a ¼
of good muscovado suger
and stir itt weell together
and in 24 hours turn itt up &
lett itt work (not to much)
stop itt Close and itt will
be fitt to drink in the
next spring

p. 32

yarrow, jillgoBy the ground
and mullin boyld
good for a purging.

to make an oyntment
good for a scold [scalded?] head
    [hand?]
take milelet, sorril, johnwort
English sorril, wood sorril,
cullumbine leaves, and
houslek, bruse them
altogether and put them [in?]
Creem in an earthen pot
bury in the ground
nine days then boyle
it into an oyntment

p. 33

to make basom [balsam] wine
take a gallon of water
make it boyl pour it
into a pound of fresh
balm [balsam] lett it stand
24 hours infusing, then
strain it out, put
three pound of suger
[go over 4?] gallon wine me-
=sure boyl itt 2 hours
Fast, scim itt turn it
up, stop it close 1 month
then bottle it up and
in 2 weeks you may
Drink it

for a cough
take ¼ [?] of figs an ounce
of sugercandy ½ a pint
of brandy, put it into
a cup let it stand a
while & it will be a
thick surrup

p. 34

to keep quinces a year
take your quinces and put
them in to a little vessel
of small beer when it
hath Done working

to keep Iron from Rusting
take Lead filed very
small and put so much
oyl olive upon it as will
cover it in a pot, then
make your Iron very
clean first, and anoint
the Iaron with the oyl
after it hath stood
nine days

p. 35

for all sorts of f[l]uxes
take 2 quarts of
new milk, 2 nutmegs,
eighteen pepper-corns,
eighteen Cloves,
[?] peneworth of sinemon
twise as much of the
outward bark of an old
oak, give it at 4 times
the first time as hot as you
can Drink it. the next
time not so hot
[line crossed out: "give it all at
    4 times"]
give it att 4 a clock in
the morning
at 4 in the afternoon
and at night

p. 36

oyl of camomile made
with thick Creem good
for a sore scurf* in
the face
[*A "scurf" refers to a scaly piece of
    skin.]

to keep your teeth from
Rotting or akeing, wash your
mouth every morning with
the juce of lemmons, and
Rub rub your teeth with
a sage leef, and wash
your teeth after meals with
fair water

powder of earthworms will
make an Akeing tooth fall
fall out of itt selfe

bawm [balm] water distoled
    [distilled?] in may
Restores the memory when
lost, quickens the sences,
strengthens the brain, heart,
and stomake, Causeth a merry
mind and a sweet breath

plantain water good for
the head Ake and Dropt
in to the ear helps the
tooth Ake

fannill [fennel] water good for the
    eyes

p. 37

the marrow of a Deers
foot goo[d] for sore nipples

to procure sle[e]p
bruse Annisseed, and steep
itt in Read Rose water
make itt up in little bags put
them to each nostrill

to heal pimples in the face
take liverwort that grose
in a well stamp it and
streen [strain?] itt and put the juce
into Creem and anoint
the face.   probatum East
["Probatum est" is Latin for "It has
    been proved."]

to Cure the tooth-Ake
take mastick and chew itt
in your mouth till it is as
soft as wax then stope
your tooth with it if
[be?] Hollow and itt will
Certainly Cure you

the tooth of a dead man
Carried about you presently
easeth pain.

p. 38

When you Rost eals parboil
then [them] in salt & water first
and spitt them crosways
on the spit, and put between
each peace a sage leafe
you may Doe the same
when you fry them.

When you boil fish put
in som beer viniger, salt,
fennill, Sweet Herbs, and
lett it boile very well
before you putt in the fish
and then lett it boile
lesurly. serve itt up with
butter & parrsly mingled to=
=gether dont lett the parsly
boile too much

to boile Trouts
wash them very Clean &
Dry them with a Cloath
then take out his guts
and wipe itt very well
within but wash itt not,
and give it 3 gashes with
a knife on one side only
to ye bone. boile it in beer
viniger & water & Sweet Herbs
and

p. 39

and Horse-Radish Roots and the
Rind of a lemmon, garnish
your dish with slices of
lemmon, and with your
butter putt shaved horse
=Radish & genger.

p. 40

[In much smaller handwriting, possibly written by someone else?]

Without a name, forever senceless, dumb.

Dust, ashes, nought Elce Lies within this Tomb.

When T'was I Live'd, or dy'd, it matters not.

To whome Related, or of whom begot.

I was, but am not, ask no more of me.

Tis all I am, and all that you must bee.

to make a Plumb Cake
8 pound flower, 3 pound of butter,
3 pound of suger, 3 pound of
Currants, one ouns of spice,
8 eggs, a[?] pint of wine, and
a little emptins*
3 qu^tt of white suger
[*"Emptins" refers to a type of leavening made from hops or potatoes.]

to make Suger Cakes
take half a pound of flower,
and as much suger, and six
eggs work itt all together into
a past[e] Role itt out in littel
Cakes and put them in a
slow oven.

the Child is the father
in the second Edition

p. 41

french Bread
4 qu^tt of wheatt flower
a pint of yeast, the
whites of 6 new-laid eggs
and a spoo[n]full of Salt.
mix itt with milk and
water, make it plenty [?] stif
and lett itt rise by the
fire.

to make suger Cake
take 1 pound of flower
1 pound of suger
3 qu^r of a pound of butter
6 eggs ½ a pint of Rose
Water, Rub the butter
and suger together
then put in the flower
and eggs & Rosewater
and then beat it a
little while

p. 42

malases [?]
novem^br 17 1738
Lize Gardiner Came home
from Boston with Joseph
printis

Take physack early
medicians come to late
when the doseag
is groan inveterals [intervals?].

p. 43

To make gingerbread
3 pound of flower
1 ½ of suger ¾ of butter
two ounces of ginger
and 6 Eggs a Little
Rose water

to kill a felon* quickly
take Rue and sage stamp
them small put to it the
oyl of the white of an
egg and a Little Honey
and lay it to the sore
[A "felon" is an inflammation
    occurring in the tissues of a
    finger or toe.]

p. 44

[In a different type of handwriting,
    possibly written by someone
    else?]
To Make an Excellent
Swe[e]tt Dram
Sweet Flag, Snake Root
Rosemery Sweet marj[or]am
Sage Cat-nip Balm
fetherfew angileco
hysop ["Some"crossed out] Summer
Savory Tansie merry
Gold New England
Saffaron shill'd [chilled?] all to=
gether.

p. 45

an Excelent Remedy worth
gold for the head Ake
Take the juce of ground=
=seve [groundsel?], snuff itt up into
your nose with a quill.

for a fellon, tak Hony
and the yolke of an Egge
and mix itt together,
with the juce of Rew.

the juce of wormwood
good for vomiting and
loosness

to kill a Corn
tak Ale-yeast that is hard
and sticks to the tub-side,
and a Little fine Salt
work itt well together
and bind it to ye Corn

for an old sore leg
take the whitest hard sope
you can git melt itt with
Deers-suet and boyl itt on the
fire & make a plaster, lay it on
the sore mornig & Evening

p. 46

to make Elder wine
Take 1 quatt of the juice
of elder-berrys to a gallon
of water, & 3 pound of
suger, 2 whits of Eggs
boyl itt well, & take of all
the skim work itt with
yeast, stop itt up close &
in the spring of the year
bottle itt of and keep itt for
your serviz

How to dye purple
to make a good purple you must
first Dye itt blue and then
boile itt in bran & Allom-water
& itt will be a speciall purple.

for a canker in the mouth
take 2 spoonful of
clarrifide Honey, and put
a peice of Allum betwe[e]n
Read hot tongs and lett
itt Drop into the Honey
and Dress [?] the mouth

p. 47

September 30 1712 I went
to Woodstock, & Mr Waters, &
Mr John Gardiner & Joseph Coit
& come hom y^e

July the 1 1714 my husbend &
I went to Wodstock and Come
home the 8 day

Thomas Coit went to Woodstock
Decemb^r the 28th 1720 and
Came home the 4th day of
January following.

july 20 1727
John Coit Martha and
Joseph went to norwich
the same day Lydia Star
married to John Bowles
the 25 day Joseph and
Martha came hom again

july 1718 Mr Waters
went a way

july 2 1726
Susannah Chandler
Came to live
with me

p. 48

how to make Rusk
take 10 pound of fine flower,
& 18 eggs; 1 pound of suger,
1 pound of butter, & a quart of
milk & a little [y]East

[The following lines are crossed out:]
Hannah mannorwing [Manwaring?]
to [1?] yd of Scotch Cloath
att 0 – 5 – 0 [?]
to a quart of Rum 0 –1 – 2 [?]
to half a quarter Scotch Cloat[h]s
    – 0 – 4 [?]
to cotton w[oo?]ll 0 – 4 – 2 [?]

to mak biskitts
2 pound of flower 2
ounces[?] of butter 2 eggs
2 spoonfull of [y]east mix
them together with
good milk
[next two lines blotted and illegible;
    can see "Mrs Ply"]

to 9 pound butt[?] 0-4-[?]

nine million and three
hundred & four
Eggs in one fish

p. 49 (inside back cover)

September 27 Mr Gardiner &
his wife, & his 2 sons Came from
Boston, the 29 thay went home
Mrs Green, & Mrs Sewall &
her Son, & Daughter, & M^r
wainright, went with them

[The following lines are crossed out:]
Daniell Coit 1 – 5 – 0
to [Daktor?] – 1 – 0 – 0
m^{rs} Hallam – … – 2 – 6
John to Woodstock - … - 3 - 00
Darrow – 3 – 10 – 00

Hannah mannorwing
to what was Due – 0 – 1 – [6?]
to a pare stockings – 0 – 5 – 00
[Below this a couple of lines have
    been completely blotted out.]

[The following lines are crossed out:]
margit fox Due[?]
to 2 yd of garlik – 0 – 6 -- 0
to 1 yd garlik att 4s – 0 – 4 – 0
to ½ yd Dito – 0 – 2 – 0
[An illegible fragment ends this
    section.]

NOTES

Introduction

1. Laurel Thatcher Ulrich, *Good Wives: Image and Reality in the Lives of Women in Northern New England, 1650–1750* (New York: Vintage, 1991), 5; Carole Berkin, *First Generations: Women in Colonial America* (New York: Hill and Wang, 1996), 28; Mary Beth Norton, "Getting to the Source: Hetty Shepard, Dorothy Dudley, and Other Fictional Colonial Women I Have Come to Know Altogether Too Well," *Journal of Women's History* 10, no. 3 (Autumn 1998): 149.

2. Peter Benes, "Another Look at Madam Knight," in *In Our Own Words: New England Diaries, 1600 to the Present, Dublin Seminar for New England Folklife Annual Proceedings, 2006/2007,* 2 vols., ed. Peter Benes (Boston University, 2009). Mary Beth Norton has written about other inauthentic colonial women's diaries in "Getting to the Source."

3. Lyle Koehler, *A Search for Power: The "Weaker Sex" in Seventeenth-Century New England* (Urbana: University of Illinois Press, 1980), 69; Estelle Jelinek, *The Tradition of Women's Autobiography: From Antiquity to the Present* (Boston: Twayne, 1986), 59; Kirsten E. Phimister, " 'A Loving Mother and Obedient Wife': White Women in Colonial America," in *British Colonial America: People and Perspectives* (Perspectives in Social History), ed. John A. Grigg (Santa Barbara, Calif.: ABC-CLIO, 2008).

A Note about the Diary

1. Steven Kagle, *American Diary Literature, 1620–1799* (Boston: Twayne, 1979), 29; Steven Kagle, *Early Nineteenth-Century American Diary Literature* (Boston: Twayne, 1986), 2.

2. David D. Hall, *Worlds of Wonder, Days of Judgment: Popular Religious Belief in Early New England* (Cambridge: Harvard University Press, 1990), 114, 82; Kagle, *American Diary Literature,* 147.

3. Kagle, *American Diary Literature,* 28; John Demos, *A Little Commonwealth: Family Life in Plymouth Colony* (New York: Oxford University Press, 1970), 13; John Marshall diary, Massachusetts Historical Society.

4. Kagle, *American Diary Literature,* 16, 28, 185.

5. Hall, *Worlds of Wonder,* 32; E. Jennifer Monaghan, *Learning to Read and Write in Early America* (Amherst: University of Massachusetts Press, 2005), 42; Mary Beth Norton, "Getting to the Source: Hetty Shepard, Dorothy Dudley, and Other Fictional Colonial Women I Have Come to Know Altogether Too Well," *Journal of Women's History* 10, no. 3 (Autumn 1998): 149.

6. Elizabeth Chandler to Mehetabel Chandler Coit, June 1, 1698, Gilman Family Papers, Manuscripts and Archives, Yale University Library (hereafter cited as GFP).

7. Janet Theophano, *Eat My Words: Reading Women's Lives through the Cookbooks They Wrote* (New York: Palgrave, 2002), 163; Tamara Plakins Thornton, *Handwriting in America: A Cultural History* (New Haven: Yale University Press, 1996), 23, 38.

8. Margo Culley, *A Day at a Time: The Diary Literature of American Women from 1764 to the Present* (New York: Feminist Press of the City University of New York, 1985), 13, 4.

9. Judy Nolte Temple, "Fragments as Diary: Theoretical Implications of the *Dreams and Visions* of "Baby Doe" Tabor," in *Inscribing the Daily: Critical Essays on Women's Diaries,* ed. Suzanne Bunkers and Cynthia Ann Huff (Amherst: University of Massachusetts Press, 1996), 76.

1. The Years before the Diary, 1673–1688

1. William Wood, *New England's Prospect,* ed. Alden T. Vaughan (Amherst: University of Massachusetts Press, 1994), 58; Ellen D. Larned, *History of Windham County, Connecticut, 1600–1760,* 2 vols., ed. Leigh Grossman (Pomfret, Conn.: Swordsmith Productions, 2000), 1:13.

2. G. Andrews Moriarty, "Genealogical Research in England: Ancestry of William Chandler of Roxbury, Massachusetts," *New England Historical and Genealogical Register* 85 (1931): 143; Gloria L. Main, *Peoples of a Spacious Land: Families and Cultures in Colonial New England* (Cambridge: Harvard University Press, 2001), 46.

3. Records of the First Church of Roxbury, *The Records of the Churches of Boston,* comp. Robert J. Dunkle and Ann S. Lainhart, CD-ROM (Boston: New England Historic Genealogical Society, 2002).

4. Marylynn Salmon, *Women and the Law of Property in Early America* (Chapel Hill: University of North Carolina Press, 1986), 143.

5. Dane was a very pious man, according to his son John by his first marriage. In his autobiographical narrative, "A Declaration of Remarkabell Provedenses in the Corse of My Lyfe," the younger Dane recounts how his father and mother based their decision to come to New England on a sign from God. John junior writes that he was the first in the family with the desire to emigrate, but that his parents originally opposed the idea. With the hope of settling the matter, he picked up a Bible that happened to be lying nearby, blindly pointed to a passage, and told his parents that if there were anything there to either encourage or deter his inclination, he would abide by it. "The first [line] I cast my eys on," he reports, "was: Cum out from among them, touch no unclene thing, and I will be your god and you shall be my pepell." In consequence, his "fatther and motther ne[v]er more aposd me, but furdered me in the thing; and hasted after me as sone as thay could." John Dane, "A Declaration of Remarkabell Provedenses in the Corse of My Lyfe," 1682, reprinted in *New England Historical and Genealogical Register* 8 (1854): 154.

6. Quoted in George Chandler, *The Chandler Family: The Descendants of William and Annis Chandler Who Settled in Roxbury, Mass., 1637* (Worcester, Mass.: Press of Charles Hamilton, 1883), 1.

7. Leslie Mahler, "The English Origin of Anne Motley/Matley/Mattle, Wife of William Douglas of New London, Connecticut," *American Genealogist* 74 (October 1999): 275–80.

8. Quoted in Walter Eliot Thwing, *History of the First Church in Roxbury, Massachusetts, 1630–1904* (Boston: W. A. Butterfield, 1908), 12. While the extent of John Chandler's property holdings is unknown because some of his land transactions apparently went unrecorded, he seems to have acquired between fifty and seventy acres over the years.

9. Sumner Chilton Powell, *Puritan Village: The Formation of a New England Town* (Middletown, Conn.: Wesleyan University Press, 1963), 59, 105; Chandler, *The Chandler Family,* 2.

10. David Hackett Fischer: *Albion's Seed: Four British Folkways in America* (New York: Oxford University Press, 1989), 69, 96.

11. Quoted in James Axtell, *The School upon a Hill: Education and Society in Colonial New England* (New Haven: Yale University Press, 1974), 10.

12. Quoted in F. Washington Jarvis, *Schola Illustris: The Roxbury Latin School, 1645–1995* (Boston: David R. Godine, 1995), 31, 29; Ola Winslow, *John Eliot: Apostle to the Indians* (Boston: Houghton Mifflin, 1968), 135.

13. Court session of October 31, 1671, *Records of the Suffolk County Court, 1671–1680,* ed. Samuel Eliot Morison (Boston: Colonial Society, 1933), 22; Bruce Daniels, *Puritans at Play: Leisure and Recreation in Colonial New England* (New York: St. Martin's Griffin, 1996), 98–99; court session of January 28, 1672/3, *Records of the Suffolk County Court,* 232.

14. Increase Mather, *Wo to Drunkards: Two Sermons Testifying against the Sin of Drunkenness; wherein the Wofulness of that Evil, and the Misery of All That Are Addicted to It, Is Discovered from the Word of God,* quoted in Edwin Powers, *Crime and Punishment in Early Massachusetts, 1620–1692* (Boston: Beacon Press, 1966), 368, 386.

15. *Massachusetts Laws of 1672,* 235, quoted in Edmund S. Morgan, *The Puritan Family: Religion and Domestic Relations in Seventeenth-Century New England* (New York: Harper & Row, 1966), 149.

16. Court session of July 28, 1674, *Records of the Suffolk County Court,* 478–79.

17. Morgan, *The Puritan Family,* 63; Fischer, *Albion's Seed,* 91.

18. Cotton Mather, *Magnalia Christi Americana; or, The Ecclesiastical History of New-England* (Hartford, Conn.: Silas Andrus and Son, 1855), 1:548. The reaction of the Roxbury church to John and Elizabeth's situation must also be considered in light of the fact that, just a few months earlier, a seventeen-year-old Roxbury youth named Benjamin Gourd had been executed for "committing Bestiality with a Mare." (In New England, fornication with an animal was a capital crime.) What added to the outrageousness of Gourd's offense, as the Boston judge and diarist Samuel Sewall noted, was that he had not only "committed that filthines at noon day in an open yard," but he "had lived in that sin a year." Samuel Sewall, *The Diary of Samuel Sewall,* 2 vols., ed. M. Halsey Thomas (New York: Farrar, Straus and Giroux, 1973), April 2, 1674.

19. Judith S. Graham, *Puritan Family Life: The Diary of Samuel Sewall* (Boston: Northeastern University Press, 2000), 77.

20. Roger Thompson, *Sex in Middlesex: Popular Mores in a Massachusetts County, 1649–1699* (Amherst: University of Massachusetts Press, 1986), 104, 198–99; Emil Oberholzer, *Delinquent Saints: Disciplinary Action in the Early Congregational Churches of Massachusetts* (New York: Columbia University Press, 1956), 30.

21. Records of the First Church of Roxbury.

22. Ibid.

23. William Hubbard, *A Narrative of the Indian Wars in New-England* (1775; Early American Imprints, ser. 1, no. 14120), 152; Thomas Cobbet, "Narrative of New England's Deliverances," 1677, reprinted in *New England Historical and Genealogical Register* 7 (1853): 218.

24. Richard Slotkin and James K. Folsom, eds., Introduction to *So Dreadfull a Judgment: Puritan Responses to King Philip's War, 1676–1677* (Middletown, Conn.: Wesleyan University Press, 1999), 4; Increase Mather, *An Earnest Exhortation to the Inhabitants of New-England,* quoted ibid., 180; Increase Mather, "At a Council Held at Boston, Sept. 17, 1675," quoted ibid., 105; Douglas Edward Leach, *Flintlock and Tomahawk: New England in King Philip's War* (New York: Norton, 1966), 192.

25. Daniels, *Puritans at Play,* 28; E. Jennifer Monaghan, "Literacy Instruction and Gender in Colonial New England," in *Reading in America: Literature and Social History,* ed. Cathy N. Davidson (Baltimore: Johns Hopkins University Press, 1989), 58.

26. Jarvis, *Schola Illustris,* 116; Monaghan, "Literacy Instruction," 60–61.

27. Walter Small, *Early New England Schools* (Boston: Ginn, 1914), 277; Monaghan, "Literacy Instruction," 71.

28. Daniels, *Puritans at Play,* 27–29, 30–31; Kevin J. Hayes, *A Colonial Woman's Bookshelf* (Knoxville: University of Tennessee Press, 1996), 30.

29. Jill Lepore, *The Name of War: King Philip's War and the Origins of American Identity* (New York: Knopf, 1998), 149. The sharing of personal writings among early American women was common; in fact, evidence has been found of a "lively manuscript culture" through which works as varied as spiritual autobiographies and household manuals were circulated among female relatives and friends (Hayes, *A Colonial Woman's Bookshelf,* 4).

30. Elizabeth Chandler, "A Meditation, or Poem, being an Ep[ic?] of the Experiences and Conflicts of a Poor Trembling Soul in yᵉ First Fourty Years of Her Life," GFP, 1, 11, 33, 12, 33, 15.

31. Rev. Benjamin Wadsworth, quoted in Morgan, *The Puritan Family,* 66–67; Judith Graham, *Puritan Family Life,* 97.

32. Records of the First Church of Roxbury, October 4, 1681.

33. Although few eyewitness accounts of Maria's execution have survived, leading some to claim that such a horrific sentence may never have been carried out, the Reverend Peter Thacher of Milton recorded in his diary on September 22 that "Chaney was hanged for a rape, two negroes burnt, one of them was first hanged." And while Cotton Mather's diary entries for this period have not survived, he wrote in his *Magnalia Christi Americana* with regard to the September 22 execution of the convicted rapist, "When he came to the Gallows, and saw Death (and a Picture of *Hell* too in a Negro then burnt to Death at the Stake, for burning her *Master's House,* with some that were in it,) before his Face, never was a Cry for *Time! Time! A World for a little Time! The Inexpressible worth of Time!* utter'd with a more unutterable Anguish." Robert C. Twombly and Robert H. Moore, "Black Puritan: The Negro in Seventeenth-Century Massachusetts," *William and Mary Quarterly,* 3d ser., 24, no. 3 (July 1967): 234; Suffolk Court Files, ccxii.26.559:4, quoted in John Noble, "The Case of Maria in the Court of Assistants in 1681," *Publications of the Colonial Society of Massachusetts,* 6 (January 1900): 326–27; Records of the Court of Assistants, ii.138, quoted in Noble, "The Case of Maria," 328.

34. Twombly and Moore, "Black Puritan," 238.

35. Records of the First Church of Roxbury, August 31, 1670; March 1679; April 18, 1675.

36. Ibid., January 16, 1684; *Sandwich Friends Men's Monthly Meeting Minutes* 40 (1672–1754), 39, 41–43, quoted in Helen Schatvet Ullmann, "Sarah (Chandler) (Cleaves) (Stevens) (Parker) Allen of Roxbury and Sandwich, Massachusetts," *American Genealogist* 80, no. 1 (January 2005): 34.

37. Records of the First Church of Roxbury, March 17, 1682/3; John Parmenter will, March 29, 1671, Suffolk County Probate Records, 146.

38. Annis Parmenter will, November 1, 1672, Suffolk County Probate Records, 430–31.

39. Thomas L. Doughton, "Unseen Neighbors: Native Americans of Central Massachusetts, a People Who Had 'Vanished,'" in *After King Philip's War: Presence and Persistence in Indian New England,* ed. Colin Calloway (Hanover, N.H.: University Press of New England, 1997), 221n2; quote attributed to James Printer in Lepore, *The Name of War,* 94; Larned, *History of Windham County,* 1:10.

40. Quoted in Harral Ayres, *The Great Trail of New England* (Boston: Meador, 1940), 257–58, 188.

41. David Lovejoy, *The Glorious Revolution in America* (Middletown, Conn.: Wesleyan University Press, 1987), 158, 180–81; letter of August 31, 1698, quoted ibid., 181.

42. Francis S. Drake, *The Town of Roxbury: Its Memorable Persons and Places* (Roxbury, Mass.: Published by the author, 1878), 40–41.

43. Quoted in Chandler, *The Chandler Family,* 18; James Fitch deed, May 6, 1686, *Suffolk Deeds, Liber XIII,* ed. William Blake Trask (Boston: Rockwell and Churchill Press, 1903), 485.

2. Coming of Age, 1688–1693

1. Margo Culley, *A Day at a Time: The Diary Literature of American Women from 1764 to the Present* (New York: Feminist Press of the City University of New York, 1985), 8.

2. MCC diary, 15. In writing "my father with his family"—as opposed to simply "my family"—Mehetabel was using a common construction of the time that emphasized the leadership position of the head of a household.

3. Letter dated August, 29, 1694, quoted in Clarence Bowen, *The History of Woodstock, Connecticut* (1926; reprint, Salem, Mass.: Higginson Book Co., n.d.), 39.

4. Quoted in George Chandler, *The Chandler Family: The Descendants of William and Annis Chandler Who Settled in Roxbury, Mass., 1637* (Worcester, Mass.: Press of Charles Hamilton, 1883), 22, 19.

5. Quoted in Walter Eliot Thwing, *The History of the First Church of Roxbury, Massachusetts, 1630–1904* (Boston: W. A. Butterfield, 1908), 90.

6. Mehetabel, like her English and American contemporaries, followed the Roman Julian calendar, in which each new year was perceived as starting on Lady Day, March 25. Under the Julian calendar, March was considered the first month of the year, April the second, and so forth. The Gregorian calendar, introduced by Pope Gregory XIII in 1582, which proposed January 1 as the beginning of the new year, was not adopted by Great Britain or the American colonies until 1752, although it was in use in many European countries prior to that date. For that reason, many English and Americans used the double-year date ("1688/9," for example) from January 1 through March 24.

7. MCC diary, 15.

8. David Lovejoy, *The Glorious Revolution in America* (Middletown, Conn.: Wesleyan University Press, 1987), 239–45; Cotton Mather quoted in Emerson W. Baker and John G. Reid, *The New England Knight: Sir William Phips, 1651–1695* (Toronto: University of Toronto Press, 1998), 65; MCC diary, 15.

9. MCC diary, 26.

10. Abraham Cowley, *Essays of Abraham Cowley* (London, 1869), 1; Mary Beth Norton, *Separated by Their Sex: Women in Public and Private in the Colonial Atlantic World* (Ithaca, N.Y.: Cornell University Press, 2011), 137.

11. Quoted in Bowen, *History of Woodstock,* 31.

12. MCC diary, 15. The Denisons were related to Mehetabel through her grandfather William Chandler. William Chandler's cousin Margaret and her husband, William Denison, had emigrated to Roxbury a few years before the Chandlers. William Denison became a prominent citizen of Roxbury, but he ended up losing his position as a representative to the General Court and was "disarmed" after he became a follower of Anne Hutchinson.

13. John Duffy, *Epidemics in Colonial America* (Baton Rouge: Louisiana State University Press, 1953), 48, 16; George J. Lankevich, *Boston: A Chronological and Documentary History, 1602–1970* (Dobbs Ferry, N.Y.: Oceana Publications, 1974), 12.

14. Duffy, *Epidemics in Colonial America,* 16.

15. Quoted in Kenneth Silverman, *The Life and Times of Cotton Mather* (New York: Welcome Rain Publishers, 2002), 337–38.

16. It is unclear how having smallpox may have personally affected Mehetabel, but her mother's experience of "being Surprized by a Sickness Great" had brought about her spiritual conversion as a young woman (Elizabeth Chandler, "A Meditation, or Poem, being an Ep[ic?] of the Experiences and Conflicts of a Poor Trembling Soul in ye First Fourty Years of Her Life," GFP, 7).

17. Richard D. Brown, "The Healing Arts in Colonial and Revolutionary Massachusetts: The Context for Scientific Medicine," in *Medicine in Colonial Massachusetts, 1620–1820: A Conference Held 25 and 26 May 1978 by the Colonial Society of Massachusetts* (Boston: Colonial Society of Massachusetts, 1980), 40.

18. Quoted in Ethel Farrington Smith, *Colonial American Doctresses: A Genealogical and Biographical Account of Women Who Practiced Medicine and Chirurgery in Colonial America* (Boston: Newbury Street Press, 2003), 43, 4; Patricia A. Watson, "'The Hidden Ones': Women

and Healing in Colonial New England," in *Medicine and Healing: The Dublin Seminar for New England Folklife Annual Proceedings, 1990,* ed. Peter Benes (Boston: Boston University, 1992), 33.

19. Rebecca Tannenbaum, *The Healer's Calling: Women and Medicine in Early New England* (Ithaca, N.Y.: Cornell University Press, 2002), 22, 33–34.

20. George E. Gifford, "Botanic Remedies in Colonial Massachusetts, 1620–1820," in *Medicine in Colonial Massachusetts, 1620–1820,* 265; Tannenbaum, *Healer's Calling,* 5, 6.

21. Ibid., 33–34.

22. Gifford, "Botanic Remedies," 269.

23. MCC diary, 37, 36; Tannenbaum, *Healer's Calling,* 41; David D. Hall, *Worlds of Wonder, Days of Judgment: Popular Religious Belief in Early New England* (Cambridge: Harvard University Press, 1990), 19, 197.

24. MCC diary, 36; Nicholas Culpeper, *Culpeper's English Physician and Complete Herbal* (reprint, London, 1794), 72; MCC diary, 36; quoted in Ann Leighton, *Early American Gardens, for Meate or Medicine* (Boston: Houghton Mifflin, 1970), 132, 136.

25. MCC diary, 42.

26. Mary Beth Norton, *In the Devil's Snare: The Salem Witchcraft Crisis of 1692* (New York: Vintage, 2003), 94.

27. Quoted in Jill Lepore, *The Name of War: King Philip's War and the Origins of American Identity* (New York: Knopf, 1998), 183–84; Colin Calloway, ed., *After King Philip's War: Presence and Persistence in Indian New England* (Hanover, N.H.: University Press of New England, 1997), 6.

28. Ellen D. Larned, *History of Windham County, Connecticut, 1600–1760,* ed. Leigh Grossman, 2 vols. (Pomfret, Conn.: Swordsmith Productions, 2000), 1:2; Richard M. Bayles, *The History of Windham County, Connecticut,* 2 vols. (1889; reprint, Salem, Mass.: Higginson Book Co., n.d.), 847; Bowen, *History of Woodstock,* 37–38.

29. Sarah Chandler to Mehetabel Chandler Coit, October 19, 1696, GFP; Norton, *In the Devil's Snare,* 59.

30. Ibid., 263.

31. Edmund S. Morgan, *The Puritan Family: Religion and Domestic Relations in Seventeenth-Century New England* (New York: Harper & Row, 1966), 150; Baker and Reid, *New England Knight,* 11.

32. Quoted in Sarah Loring Bailey, *Historical Sketches of Andover (Comprising the Present Towns of North Andover and Andover)* (Boston: Houghton Mifflin, 1880), 68–69.

33. Like Francis Dane, Hannah's first husband George also apparently thought very highly of her, as he left her his entire estate, with the exception of the inheritance he had already bestowed upon his eldest son. His rationale for such an unconventional bequest, he wrote, was based on his "great love & affection" for her, the "tender love and respect" she had shown him, and "her care and diligence in helping to gett and save what God hath blessed [them] withall, and also her prudence in management of the same" (will of George Abbot, quoted in Bailey, *Historical Sketches of Andover,* 84–85); Rev. Francis Dane commonplace book, 1648–1697, 48, R. Stanton Avery Special Collections, New England Historic Genealogical Society, Boston.

34. It has been suggested that Phoebe may have overheard rumors about Martha Carrier's supernatural powers at her father's tavern, and that she already held a grudge against her for having reportedly carried into town the smallpox that in 1690 had killed the husband of her half-sister, Elizabeth.

35. The witchcraft hysteria caused many people to act in ways counter to the general regard for family ties: children accused parents, brothers accused sisters, husbands accused wives. Elizabeth and Betty Johnson, in fact, each accused members of their own family, and along with Abigail, made statements that could have implicated their stepsister, Mehetabel's aunt Hannah's daughter Hannah.

36. "Petition of 26 Andover Men Concerning Townspeople Accused of Witchcraft, October 18, 1692," "Petition for Mary Osgood, Eunice Frye, Deliverance Dane, Sarah Wilson, Sr., and Abigail Barker, January 3, 1693," and "Deposition of Thomas Chandler v. Samuel Wardwell," in Rosenthal, *Records of the Salem Witch-Hunt,* 690–91, 739–40, 644.

37. In Andover things were not wrapped up quite so neatly. In some cases it took years for the accused witches to have their convictions reversed, thus forcing them to live under a "perpetuall brand of Infam[y]," as Abigail Faulkner noted in a 1703 petition to the General Court. Many people had suffered greatly during the crisis—emotionally, spiritually, physically, and financially—and the rifts in the community would take generations to heal. As Francis Dane had written to the court in January, the "Conceit of Spectre Evidence as an infallible mark did too far prevail with us[;] Hence we So easily parted with our neighbours, of honest, & good report, . . . hence we So easily parted with our Children . . . hence Such strange breaches in families." Had "Charity been put on," he observed, "the Divel would not haue had Such an advantage against us." "Petition of Abigail Faulkner, June 13, 1700" and "Statement of Francis Dane, Sr., Regarding Some of the Andover Accused, January 2, 1693," ibid., 848, 734; *Andover Historical Society Newsletter* 17 (Autumn 1992): 3, 2.

38. Records of the Second Church of Boston, *The Records of the Churches of Boston,* comp. Robert J. Dunkle and Ann S. Lainhart, CD-ROM (Boston: New England Historic Genealogical Society, 2002); Cotton Mather record book of members, 1650–1741, Second Church (Boston, Mass.) Records, Massachusetts Historical Society. The first reference I came across to Mehetabel's having joined the Second Church was in the notes of the New London historian Frances Caulkins, housed at the New London County Historical Society.

39. John Nicholls Booth, *The Story of the Second Church in Boston* (Boston, 1959), 9; Kenneth Silverman, *Cotton Mather,* 406, 410, 423; Martha Coit to Mehetabel Chandler Coit, June 28, 1726, GFP. The Roxbury church was also prestigious, but the Reverend John Eliot, its charismatic leader, had passed away in 1690.

40. Moses Draper himself died in the summer of 1693 (Boston judge Samuel Sewall remarked in his diary that he had been "a very hopefull young man"), and young Hannah subsequently came under the guardianship of her uncle James Draper of Roxbury. Hannah spent the remainder of her childhood in Roxbury and married and began a family there, but she and her husband eventually moved to a town near Woodstock. Samuel Sewall, *The Diary of Samuel Sewall,* ed. M. Halsey Thomas, 2 vols. (New York: Farrar, Straus and Giroux, 1973), August 14, 1693.

3. Marriage and Motherhood, 1694–1696

1. MCC diary, 15; Richard M. Bayles, *The History of Windham County, Connecticut,* 2 vols. (1889; reprint, Salem, Mass.: Higginson Book Co., n.d.), 848.

2. Upon William Douglas's death in 1682, New London's Rev. Simon Bradstreet, son of the poet Anne Bradstreet and Massachusetts governor Simon Bradstreet, had lamented that he had been "an able christian & this poor ch[urc]h will much want him" ("Bradstreet's Journal," *New England Historical and Genealogical Register* 8 [1854]: 332); quoted in Frances M. Caulkins, *History of New London, Connecticut: From the First Survey of the Coast in 1612 to 1860,* 2 vols. (1895; reprint, Bowie, Md.: Heritage Books, 2000), 1:198 (hereafter cited as Caulkins, *History of New London*).

3. Caulkins, *History of New London,* 1:39, 42; Walter W. Woodward, *Prospero's America: John Winthrop, Jr., Alchemy, and the Creation of New England Culture, 1606–1676* (Chapel Hill: University of North Carolina Press, published for the Omohundro Institute of Early American Culture, 2010), 188, 198–99.

4. Robert Owen Decker, *The New London Merchants: The Rise and Decline of a Connecticut Port* (New York: Garland Publishing, 1986), 29–31; Chester M. Destler, *Connecticut: The*

Provisions State (Chester, Conn.: Pequot, 1973), 11–13; James W. Miller, exec. ed., and Priscilla W. Dundon, assoc. ed., *As We Were on the Valley Shore: An Informal Pictorial History of Sixteen Connecticut Towns* (Guilford, Conn.: Shoreline Times Company, 1976), 117–18.

5. Miller and Dundon, *As We Were,* 117; Lorenzo J. Greene, *The Negro in Colonial New England* (New York: Atheneum, 1968), 345.

6. Barbara W. Brown and James M. Rose, *Tapestry: A Living History of the Black Family in Southeastern Connecticut* (New London: New London County Historical Society, 1976), 65.

7. Caulkins, *History of New London,* 1:359; Joshua Hempstead, *The Diary of Joshua Hempstead: A Daily Record of Life in Colonial New London, Connecticut, 1711–1758* (New London: New London County Historical Society, 1999), May 11, 1716, October 6, 1732, June 15, 1742, April 27, 1718, July 10, 1735, and March 13, 1731 (hereafter cited as Hempstead, *Diary*).

8. Caulkins, *History of New London,* 2:469, 1:200, 1:253; Charles Burr Todd, *In Olde Connecticut* (New York: Grafton Press, 1906), 78.

9. Josiah Cotton quoted in Lisa Wilson, *Ye Heart of a Man: The Domestic Life of Men in Colonial New England* (New Haven: Yale University Press, 1999), 33.

10. Quoted in Thomas Franklin Waters, *Ipswich in the Massachusetts Bay Colony* (Ipswich Historical Society, 1905), 520.

11. Daniel was Martha's fifth child; prior to his birth she had had three healthy babies and one stillborn.

12. Since Martha, like most of her contemporaries, probably followed the Julian calendar, under which the first day of the new year was considered to be March 25, it is likely that her narrative was actually written on March 15, 1689. Martha Coit testimonial, March 15, 1688/9, GFP.

13. Mary Rowlandson, *The Sovereignty and Goodness of God,* ed. Neal Salisbury (Boston: Bedford Books, 1997), 65, 5–6, 46. It must be noted that, although Martha was clearly well acquainted with her Bible, not all of the chapter and verse numbers she cites correspond with the quotations she provides.

14. Decker, *New London Merchants,* 17, 27.

15. MCC diary, 7; Joseph A. Goldenberg, *Shipbuilding in Colonial America* (Published for the Mariners Museum, Newport News, by University of Virginia Press, 1976), 58, 59.

16. MCC diary, 13; David Hackett Fischer: *Albion's Seed: Four British Folkways in America* (Oxford: Oxford University Press, 1989), 79; Edmund S. Morgan, *The Puritan Family: Religion and Domestic Relations in Seventeenth-Century New England* (New York: Harper & Row, 1966), 47; Peter Thacher diary, Massachusetts Historical Society.

17. Morgan, *Puritan Family,* 55; Fischer, *Albion's Seed,* 78; Daniel Scott Smith, "Parental Power and Marriage Patterns: An Analysis of Historical Trends in Hingham, Massachusetts," *Journal of Marriage and Family* 35, no. 3 (August 1973): 426.

18. Morgan, *Puritan Family,* 82, 81.

19. Bruce Daniels, *Puritans at Play: Leisure and Recreation in Colonial New England* (New York: St. Martin's/Griffin, 1996), 117–18; Morgan, *Puritan Family,* 33.

20. Daniel Scott Smith, "The Demographic History of Colonial New England," *Journal of Economic History* 132, no. 1 (March 1972): 177; Marylynn Salmon, *Women and the Law of Property in Early America* (Chapel Hill: University of North Carolina Press, 1986), 187.

21. Carol Berkin, *First Generations: Women in Colonial America* (New York: Hill & Wang, 1996), 28–30.

22. Laurel Thatcher Ulrich, "Big Dig, Little Dig, Hidden Worlds: Boston," *Common-Place: The Interactive Journal of Early American Life* 3, no. 4 (July 2003); James W. Baker, "Yeoman Foodways at Plimoth Plantation," in *Foodways in the Northeast: The Dublin Seminar for New England Folklife Annual Proceedings, 1982,* ed. Peter Benes (Boston University, 1984), 109–10.

23. Sally Smith Booth, *Hung, Strung, and Potted: A History of Eating Habits in Colonial America* (New York: Clarkson N. Potter, 1971), 108.

24. John Hull Brown, *Early American Beverages* (Rutland, Vt.: C. E. Tuttle, 1966), 14.

25. David W. Conroy, *In Public Houses: Drink and the Revolution of Authority in Colonial Massachusetts* (Published for the Institute of Early American History and Culture, Williamsburg, Virginia, by the University of North Carolina Press, 1995), 68, 74, 144; MCC diary, 31.

26. Ann Leighton, *Early American Gardens, for Meate or Medicine* (Boston: Houghton Mifflin, 1970), 245–46; MCC diary, 33, 40.

27. Waverly Root and Richard de Rochemont, *Eating in America: A History* (New York: William Morrow, 1976), 75–76; Booth, *Hung, Strung, and Potted,* 22; Anne Gibbons Gardiner, *Mrs. Gardiner's Family Receipts from 1763, Boston,* ed. Gail Weesner (Boston: Rowan Tree Press, 1988), 65.

28. Weesner in *Mrs. Gardiner's Family Receipts,* 66; Kevin J. Hayes, *A Colonial Woman's Bookshelf* (Knoxville: University of Tennessee Press, 1996), 82; Janet Theophano, *Eat My Words: Reading Women's Lives through the Cookbooks They Wrote* (New York: Palgrave, 2002), 8; MCC diary, 44.

29. Theophano, *Eat My Words,* 108; Hayes, *Colonial Woman's Bookshelf,* 87; MCC diary, 38; Walton quoted in *Mrs. Gardiner's Family Receipts,* 21.

30. MCC diary, 46, 34.

31. Laurel Thatcher Ulrich, *Good Wives: Image and Reality in the Lives of Women in Northern New England, 1650–1750* (New York: Vintage, 1991), 51–52.

32. MCC diary, 7; Laurel Thatcher Ulrich, "It 'Went Away Shee Knew Not How': Food Theft and Domestic Conflict in Seventeenth-Century Essex County," *Foodways in the Northeast,* 98–99.

33. MCC diary, 13; Hempstead, *Diary,* November 28, 1750; Rebecca Tannenbaum, *The Healer's Calling: Women and Medicine in Early New England* (Ithaca, N.Y.: Cornell University Press, 2002), 47.

34. Berkin, *First Generations,* 33; Tannenbaum, *Healer's Calling,* 35, xi; Richard W. Wertz and Dorothy C. Wertz, *Lying In: A History of Childbirth in America* (New York: Free Press, 1977), 5.

35. Berkin, *First Generations,* 150; Steven Mintz and Susan Kellogg, *Domestic Revolutions: A Social History of American Family Life* (New York: Free Press, 1988), 13, 14; Laurel Thatcher Ulrich, *A Midwife's Tale: The Life of Martha Ballard, Based on Her Diary, 1785–1812* (New York: Vintage, 1991), 192.

36. Ulrich, *Midwife's Tale,* 196; MCC diary, 37; Ulrich, *Good Wives,* 141–42. Mehetabel's choice of treatment, although peculiar, is not as strange as another contemporary prescription that called for the ingestion of "Millepedes" with the "Heads off, stampt in white wine or bear" (Patricia A. Watson, "'The Hidden Ones': Women and Healing in Colonial New England," in *Medicine and Healing: The Dublin Seminar for New England Folklife Annual Proceedings, 1990,* ed. Peter Benes [Boston University, 1992], 29).

37. Ellen D. Larned, *History of Windham County, Connecticut, 1600–1760,* ed. Leigh Grossman, 2 vols. (Pomfret, Conn.: Swordsmith Productions, 2000), 1:30–32.

38. "Bowels" is another term for "heart."

39. Sarah was likely referring to Mehetabel's husband rather than their brother.

40. Sarah Chandler to Mehetabel Chandler Coit, October 19, 1696, GFP.

41. Intermarriage between siblings of two families was not uncommon during the period; in fact, it was often considered beneficial, as it served to consolidate family holdings.

4. Establishing Roots, 1697–1706

1. Caulkins, *History of New London,* 1:199–200.

2. Ibid., 215; Barbara W. Brown and James M. Rose, *Tapestry: A Living History of the Black Family in Southeastern Connecticut* (New London: New London County Historical Society, 1976), 2–3.

3. John Rogers, *A Brief Account of Some of the Late Sufferings of Several Baptists in New-London County in Connecticut Colony in New England* (1726; Early American Imprints, ser.1, no. 39855), 25; Sarah Kemble Knight, "The Journal of Madam Knight," in *Colonial American Travel Narratives,* ed. Wendy Martin (New York: Penguin Books, 1994), 62.

4. MCC diary, 25.

5. Quoted in Eve LaPlante, *American Jezebel: The Uncommon Life of Anne Hutchinson, the Woman Who Defied the Puritans* (San Francisco: Harper, 2005), 42.

6. MCC diary, 29.

7. Bruce Daniels, *Puritans at Play: Leisure and Recreation in Colonial New England* (New York: St. Martin's Griffin, 1996), 30–31.

8. MCC diary, 26.

9. Elizabeth Chandler, "A Meditation, or Poem, being an Ep[ic?] of the Experiences and Conflicts of a Poor Trembling Soul in ye First Fourty Years of Her Life," GFP, 63.

10. MCC diary, 25.

11. Ibid., 29.

12. Ibid., 28.

13. Ibid., 2; Daniels, *Puritans at Play,* 94.

14. James Deetz, *In Small Things Forgotten: The Archaeology of Early American Life* (New York: Doubleday, 1977), 111–12.

15. William H. Pierson, *American Buildings and Their Architects,* vol. 1: *The Colonial and Neoclassical Styles* (New York: Oxford University Press, 1986), 58.

16. Caulkins, *History of New London,* 2:621; Ann Leighton: *Early American Gardens, for Meate or Medicine* (Boston: Houghton Mifflin, 1970), 103.

17. Ellen D. Larned, *History of Windham County, Connecticut, 1600–1760,* ed. Leigh Grossman, 2 vols. (Pomfret, Conn.: Swordsmith Productions, 2000), 1:32; Clarence Bowen, *The History of Woodstock, Connecticut* (1926; reprint, Salem, Mass.: Higginson Book Co., n.d.), 52.

18. Gurdon Saltonstall to Nathaniel Saltonstall, August 10, 1697, *The Saltonstall Papers, 1607–1815,* ed. Robert E. Moodey, 2 vols. (Boston: Massachusetts Historical Society, 1972–74), 253; Manasseh Minor, *Diary of Manasseh Minor, Stonington, Connecticut, 1696–1720,* ed. Frank Denison Miner and Hannah Miner (New London: New London County Historical Society, 1915), August 7, 1697.

19. Elizabeth Douglas Chandler to Mehetabel Chandler Coit, June 1, 1698, GFP.

20. Heb. 2:9 reads, "But we see Jesus, who was made a little lower than the angels for the suffering of death, crowned with glory and honour; that he by the grace of God should taste death for every man" (Authorized Version).

21. MCC diary, 13; Laurel Thatcher Ulrich, *Good Wives: Image and Reality in the Lives of Women in Northern New England, 1650–1750* (New York: Vintage, 1991), 139, 135.

22. MCC diary, 12.

23. Elizabeth Douglas Chandler to Mehetabel Chandler Coit, October 7, 1699, GFP.

24. MCC diary, 7; Caulkins, *History of New London,* 1:238; Robert Owen Decker, *The New London Merchants: The Rise and Decline of a Connecticut Port* (New York: Garland, 1986), 22.

25. MCC diary, 13.

26. Ibid., 7, 13, 12.

27. George Chandler, *The Chandler Family: The Descendants of William and Annis Chandler Who Settled in Roxbury, Mass., 1637* (Worcester, Mass.: Press of Charles Hamilton, 1883), 20–21. Not long after John Chandler's death, seventeen-year-old Hannah Draper married Samuel Gore of Roxbury, and Robert Mason moved to Woodstock and settled on the land his grandfather had left him.

28. MCC diary, 12, 13.

29. Steven Mintz and Susan Kellogg, *Domestic Revolutions: A Social History of American Family Life* (New York: Free Press, 1988), 14; MCC diary, 5.

30. Eccles. 3:11: "He hath made every *thing* beautiful in his time: also he hath set the world in their heart, so that no man can find out the work that God maketh from the beginning to the end" (AV).

31. Ps. 68:5: "A father of the fatherless, and a judge of the widows, *is* God in his holy habitation" (AV).

32. Elizabeth Douglas Chandler to Mehetabel Chandler Coit and Sarah Chandler Coit, June 12, 1703, GFP. The paper on which this letter is written is torn, and several words are illegible or missing.

33. Kevin J. Hayes, *A Colonial Woman's Bookshelf* (Knoxville: University of Tennessee Press, 1996), 56–57.

34. MCC diary, 23, 27. I have been unable to ascertain the author of "Wintworth." The author of "The Difference Between Today and Tomorrow" is likewise unclear, although over the colonial period the poem appeared in various publications, including Nathaniel Ames's almanac for 1748 (Boston, 1747, p. 1).

35. Matthew Prior, "Solomon on the Vanity of the World, a Poem in Three Books," bk. 3, lines 844–46.

36. Ibid., lines 528–29; these lines also appear in Prior's poem "Seneca, Troas, Act 2d. the Chorus Translated," lines 26–27.

37. MCC diary, 30; Prior, "Solomon," bk. 3, lines 183–84.

38. MCC diary, 40. Like "The Difference Between Today and Tomorrow," this piece was included in various eighteenth-century publications. An issue of *London Magazine or Gentleman's Monthly Intelligencer* from September 1752, for example, describes the lines as an epitaph taken from a gravestone dated 1721 (429).

39. Janet Theophano, *Eat My Words: Reading Women's Lives through the Cookbooks They Wrote* (New York: Palgrave, 2002), 23.

40. William Coit inventory, June 17, 1703, New London Probate Records, no. 1350.

41. MCC diary, 13, 12.

42. Joseph Coit inventory and settlement, April 27, 1704, June 16, 1704, New London Probate Records, no. 1332.

43. Lorenzo J. Greene, *The Negro in Colonial New England* (New York: Atheneum, 1968), 44.

44. MCC diary, 3; Robert G. Albion, William A. Baker, and Benjamin W. Labaree, *New England and the Sea* (Published for Mystic Seaport by Wesleyan University Press, 1972), 23; Decker, *New London Merchants,* 28–29.

45. Carl Bridenbaugh, *The Colonial Craftsman* (New York: Dover, 1990), 92–94.

46. Joseph A. Goldenberg, *Shipbuilding in Colonial America* (Published for the Mariners Museum, Newport News, by the University of Virginia Press, 1976), 91.

47. MCC diary, 7, 3.

48. Ibid., 8. The Massachusetts governor had been so concerned about Woodstock's vulnerability that he had sent a request to the Connecticut governor to provide special protection for the town. A few months later, when Major James Fitch stopped at Woodstock during the course of his patrols, he "found the people poorly provided and much exposed; the women and children all gathered into garrisons, with but one man to guard them. . . . [while the] other inhabitants were out scouting or in their fields at labor" (Bowen, *History of Woodstock,* 51; Larned, *History of Windham County,* 1:33). David Hackett Fischer, *Albion's Seed: Four British Folkways in America* (New York: Oxford University Press, 1991), 104.

49. MCC diary, 6, 3. After Mehetabel's entry about Mingo is written "July 3 1705 1809 1913." The significance of the dates "1809" and "1913" and the 104-year separation is not explained. Below this line, the commentator continued: "This book was written by [great] great-grandmother Coit." It is signed "1810. Maria Coit." Maria Coit (b. 1793) was a granddaughter of Mehetabel's son Joseph, whose descendants inherited Mehetabel's diary.

50. Caulkins, *History of New London,* 1:240; Greene, *Negro in Colonial New England,* 218.

51. Goldenberg, *Shipbuilding in Colonial America,* 63.

52. William D. Piersen, *Black Yankees: The Development of an Afro-American Subculture in Eighteenth-Century New England* (Amherst: University of Massachusetts Press, 1988), 77, 135, 117, 15, 160.

53. MCC diary, 3, 12.

54. Joseph Chandler, "Upon the Death of my Dear Mother M[rs] Elizabeth Chandler Who Went to Rest on Sabbath day about Sunsett Sep[t]: 23th: 1705," GFP.

55. MCC diary, 13.

56. Ulrich, *Good Wives,* 9.

5. Comings and Goings, 1707–1711

1. The gaps in the diary cover the years 1691–1693, 1697, 1711, 1713, 1715–1716, 1721, 1723, 1729–1734, 1736–1737, 1739–1740, and 1742–1747.

2. Laurel Thatcher Ulrich, *A Midwife's Tale: The Life of Martha Ballard, Based on Her Diary, 1785–1812* (New York: Vintage, 1991), 85–86.

3. MCC diary, 8; Marya C. Myers, "New Information on William James of Newport, Rhode Island, Mariner," *New England Historical and Genealogical Register* 159 (2005): 133; Russell Leigh Jackson, *Physicians in Essex County* (published by the Essex Institute, 1948), 39, quoted in Ethel Farrington Smith, *Colonial American Doctresses: A Genealogical and Biographical Account of Women Who Practiced Medicine and Chirurgery in Colonial America* (Boston: Newbury Street Press, 2003), 46.

4. MCC diary, 8; Manasseh Minor, *The Diary of Manasseh Minor, Stonington, Connecticut, 1696–1720,* ed. Frank Miner and Hannah Miner (New London: New London County Historical Society, 1915), September 18, 1705.

5. MCC diary, 8; R. C. Simmons, *The American Colonies: From Settlement to Independence* (New York: Norton, 1981), 160.

6. Douglas Leach, *Arms for Empire: A Military History of the British North American Colonies, 1607–1763* (New York: Macmillan, 1973), 134; Howard Peckham, *The Colonial Wars, 1689–1762* (Chicago: University of Chicago Press, 1964), 67.

7. Kenneth Silverman, *The Life and Times of Cotton Mather* (New York: Welcome Rain, 2002), 280; Bernard Bailyn, *The New England Merchants in the Seventeenth Century* (Cambridge: Harvard University Press, 1955), 139; Cotton Mather, *Magnalia Christi Americana; or, The Ecclesiastical History of New-England,* 2 vols. (Hartford, Conn.: Silas Andrus and Son, 1855), 1:100.

8. MCC diary, 8; Bruce Daniels, *Puritans at Play: Leisure and Recreation in Colonial New England* (New York: St. Martin's Griffin, 1996), 89.

9. MCC diary, 3, 4; *Boston News-Letter,* September 29–October 6, 1707, no. 181, 2; ibid., November 15–November 22, 1708, no. 240, 4.

10. This work was referred to in the same fashion in the inventory taken after the death of the poet Anne Bradstreet's father, Thomas Dudley, in Roxbury; Bradstreet herself also read the book (Elizabeth Wade White, *Anne Bradstreet: The Tenth Muse* [New York: Oxford University Press, 1971], 386; Charlotte Gordon: *Mistress Bradstreet: The Untold Life of America's First Poet* [Boston: Little Brown, 2005], 35). Mukhtar Ali Isani, "Cotton Mather and the Orient," *New England Quarterly* 43, no. 1 (1970): 57.

11. MCC diary, 48; quoted in Silverman, *Cotton Mather,* 168; Kevin J. Hayes, *A Colonial Woman's Bookshelf* (Knoxville: University of Tennessee Press, 1996), 124, 125, 127.

12. MCC diary, 8.

13. Caulkins, *History of New London,* 2:381.

14. Ibid., 1:239.

15. MCC diary, 9, 4; Joseph A. Goldenberg, *Shipbuilding in Colonial America* (Published for the Mariners Museum, Newport News, Virginia, by the University Press of Virginia, 1976), 60; Hempstead, *Diary,* August 12, 1725, October 26, 1725, and December 26, 1725.

16. Laurel Thatcher Ulrich, *Good Wives: Image and Reality in the Lives of Women in Northern New England, 1650–1750* (New York: Vintage, 1991), 157; MCC diary, 9.

17. MCC diary, 8; Hempstead, *Diary,* June 12, 1722.

18. Edmund S. Morgan, *The Puritan Family: Religion and Domestic Relations in Seventeenth-Century New England* (New York: Harper & Row, 1966), 96–97; Daniels, *Puritans at Play,* 186; Helena Wall, *Fierce Communion: Family and Community in Early America* (Cambridge: Harvard University Press, 1995), 131; Samuel Sewall, *The Diary of Samuel Sewall,* ed. M. Halsey Thomas, 2 vols. (New York: Farrar, Straus and Giroux, 1973), 1:January 13 and February 22, 1696.

19. MCC diary, 28.

20. John Flavel, *The Whole Works of the Reverend Mr. John Flavel,* 6 vols. (London, 1820), 4:375.

21. MCC diary, 40; Thomas Watson, *A Body of Practical Divinity* (London, 1692), 358.

22. Morgan, *The Puritan Family,* 104; Daniels, *Puritans at Play,* 187; Mather, Bradstreet, and Winthrop quoted in Lisa Wilson, *Ye Heart of a Man: The Domestic Life of Men in Colonial New England* (New Haven: Yale University Press, 1999), 115, 133, 139.

23. Quoted in Caulkins, *History of New London,* 2:397–98.

24. Ibid., 2:395, 398; Hempstead, *Diary,* March 1, 1752.

25. Caulkins, *History of New London,* 2:378; Clifford Shipton, *Biographical Sketches of the Graduates of Harvard University,* vol. 4 (Cambridge, Mass., 1933), 187–88, 192–93.

26. MCC diary, 11.

27. John Demos, *Entertaining Satan: Witchcraft and the Culture of Early New England* (New York: Oxford University Press, 1983), 222; T. H. Breen, *Imagining the Past: East Hampton Histories* (Reading, Mass.: Addison-Wesley, 1989), 82.

28. Thomas, *Diary of Samuel Sewall,* 1:423n5; Breen, *Imagining the Past,* 83.

29. Gardiner's access to Native women may have been facilitated by his employment of large numbers of them in growing corn, considered a female specialty, and his ability to speak the local dialect. John Gardiner, *The Gardiners of Gardiner's Island* (East Hampton, N.Y.: Star Press, 1927), 81.

30. MCC diary, 9; Breen, *Imagining the Past,* 241; Hempstead, *Diary,* October 3, 1719; Morgan, *Puritan Family,* 154.

31. Ulrich, *A Midwife's Tale,* 84, 85; Carol Berkin, *First Generations: Women in Colonial America* (New York: Hill & Wang, 1996), 154; Hempstead, *Diary,* July 10, 1712, August 1, 1733, August 7, 1722, June 23, 1733, January 14, 1712, May 11, 1712, September 26, 1712, October 6, 1712, July 14, 1712, July 17, 1720, April 11, 1726, May 29, 1723, June 8, 1723, September 25, 1729, and October 14, 1717.

32. Quoted in Caulkins, *History of New London,* 1:359; Hempstead, *Diary,* February 11, 1717, May 3, 1717; Caulkins, *History of New London,* 1:326.

33. Mary Beth Norton, *Separated by Their Sex: Women in Public and Private in the Colonial Atlantic World* (Ithaca, N.Y.: Cornell University Press, 2011), 106; Caulkins, *History of New London,* 1:372–73. Knight's gravestone is still visible in the New London burial ground.

34. Hempstead, *Diary,* April 22, 1724, April 2, 1723.

35. Ulrich, *Good Wives,* 44; Rebecca J. Tannenbaum, *The Healer's Calling: Women and Medicine in Early New England* (Ithaca, N.Y.: Cornell University Press, 2002), 54–55; Caulkins, *History of New London,* 1:202.

36. Ulrich, *Good Wives,* 44.

37. MCC diary, 9; Daniels, *Puritans at Play,* 82–83; Alice Morse Earle, *The Sabbath in Puritan New England* (Williamstown, Mass.: Corner House Publishers, 1974), 270; Eliphalet

Adams, "The Work of Ministers" (1725), quoted in J. William T. Youngs: "Congregational Clericalism: New England Ordinations before the Great Awakening," *William and Mary Quarterly* 31, no. 3 (July 1974): 481–90.

38. MCC diary, 11.

39. Hazel A. Johnson, *A Checklist of New London, Connecticut, Imprints, 1709–1800* (Charlottesville: Published for the Biographical Society of America by the University Press of Virginia, 1978), 443; Richard L. Bushman, *From Puritan to Yankee: Character and Social Order in Connecticut, 1690–1765* (Cambridge: Harvard University Press, 1967), 150–51.

40. Hayes, *Colonial Woman's Bookshelf*, 88–89; Daniels, *Puritans at Play*, 44; Eliphalet Adams 1717 diary, Massachusetts Historical Society.

41. Paul L. Ford, ed., *The New England Primer: A Reprint of the Earliest Known Edition* (New York: Dodd, Mead, 1899), 44.

42. Joshua Hempstead occasionally writes of borrowing or lending books, and at one point he notes that he "lent ye seven wonders of the world to Eliza Chapman Gedions Datr" (September 6, 1756). Johnson, *Checklist of New London Imprints*, 444; Caulkins, *History of New London,* 1:351.

43. David D. Hall, *Worlds of Wonder, Days of Judgment: Popular Religious Belief in Early New England* (Cambridge: Harvard University Press, 1990), 249.

44. Caulkins, *History of New London,* 2:375; Chester McArthur Destler, *Joshua Coit: American Federalist, 1758–1798* (Middletown, Conn.: Wesleyan University Press, 1962), 5.

45. Leach, *Arms for Empire,* 142.

46. MCC diary, 9; Caulkins, *History of New London,* 2:381.

47. MCC diary, 9.

48. Silverman, *Cotton Mather,* 279; Increase Mather, *Burnings Bewailed in a Sermon Occasioned by the Lamentable Fire Which Was in Boston Octob. 2, 1711* (Boston, 1711; Early American Imprints, ser. 1, no. 1512), 30, ii.

49. Henry Parsons Hedges, ed., *Records of the Town of East Hampton, Long Island, Suffolk Co., N.Y.* (Sag Harbor, N.Y.: John H. Hunt, 1905), 5:588.

6. Mistress and Matriarch, 1712–1725

1. In 1723 Daniel Coit, then in his early twenties, requested a full accounting of John Coit's guardianship. Joshua Hempstead, who perhaps was working on behalf of the court, writes on April 2 of that year that he "Reckned with John Coit" and "ballanced all accots." The accounting apparently showed that John owed money to Daniel, as the next day Hempstead notes that he paid Daniel the balance and interest due on some funds he had previously borrowed from John. The matter does not appear to have ever gone to court (Hempstead, *Diary,* April 2–3, 1723).

2. William C. Gilman, *A Memoir of Daniel Lathrop Coit of Norwich, Connecticut, 1754–1833* (Norwich, Conn.: Bulletin Press, 1907), 4.

3. MCC diary, 1, 47.

4. Hempstead, *Diary,* October 30, 1712; *Boston News-Letter,* August 27, 1713.

5. Hempstead, *Diary,* July 7, 1713.

6. Barbara McLean Ward and Gerald Ward, "Sterling Memories: Family and Silver in Early New England," in *The Art of Family: Genealogical Artifacts in New England,* ed. Brenton D. Simons (Boston: New England Historic Genealogical Society, 2002), 181, 177, 185.

7. Barbara McLean Ward, "Women's Property and Family Continuity in Eighteenth-Century Connecticut," in *Early American Probate Inventories: The Dublin Seminar for New England Folklife Annual Proceedings, 1987,* ed. Peter Benes (Boston: Boston University, 1989), 85. Unfortunately, I have been unable to locate the silver porringer.

8. Hempstead, *Diary,* July 30, 1713, August 31, 1713. Although the Coits and Hempsteads probably saw each other frequently given the proximity of their homes, Joshua Hempstead

documented no further social outings with Mehetabel and John. Their relationship may have changed following the death of Hempstead's wife a few days after she gave birth in 1716.

9. Bruce Daniels, *Puritans at Play: Leisure and Recreation in Colonial New England* (New York: St. Martin's Griffin, 1996), 7.

10. Hempstead, *Diary*, March 30, 1725, April 18, 1729, July 18, 1723, November 17, 1731, February 21, 1754. Then, as now, excessive merriment could sometimes mar an event, as when at a husking party in the fall of 1713 Richard Mitchell decided to "Danc[e] naked wth Wm Harris" and was subsequently arrested (Hempstead, *Diary*, October 3, 1713).

11. Daniels, *Puritans at Play*, 100–101.

12. Hempstead, *Diary*, September 25, 1713, March 30, 1727, December 2, 1719.

13. MCC diary, 47.

14. Kenneth Silverman, *The Life and Times of Cotton Mather* (New York: Welcome Rain, 2002), 269; John Duffy, *Epidemics in Colonial America* (Baton Rouge: Louisiana State University Press, 1953), 179.

15. Silverman, *Cotton Mather*, 246.

16. Charles Hoadley, ed., *The Public Records of the Colony of Connecticut, 1636–1776*, vol. 5 (Hartford: Case, Lockwood, and Brainard, 1870), 436, 531.

17. Eliphalet Adams, *A Discourse Occasioned by the Late Distressing Storm which began Feb. 6th, 1716/17, as It Was Deliver'd March 3d. 1716/17* (New London, 1717; Early American Imprints, ser. 1, no. 1864), 26, 31–32.

18. Richard L. Bushman, *From Puritan to Yankee: Character and Social Order in Connecticut, 1690–1765* (Cambridge: Harvard University Press, 1967), 286–87.

19. MCC diary, 5.

20. Catherine Adams and Elizabeth H. Pleck, *Love of Freedom: Black Women in Colonial and Revolutionary New England* (New York: Oxford University Press, 2010), 34.

21. Hempstead, *Diary*, August 25, 1758.

22. Quoted in Caulkins, *History of New London*, 2:382; Lorenzo J. Greene, *The Negro in Colonial New England* (New York: Atheneum, 1968), 312–13; William D. Piersen, *Black Yankees: The Development of an Afro-American Subculture in Eighteenth-Century New England* (Amherst: University of Massachusetts Press, 1988), 47; Barbara W. Brown and James M. Rose, *Tapestry: A Living History of the Black Family in Southeastern Connecticut* (New London: New London County Historical Society, 1976), 71–72. The year following Jacklin's ordeal, an even more disturbing message was sent to local blacks when an African American man found with a white woman on a road outside New London was castrated by a passing traveler for allegedly attempting to "lye" with the woman against her will. Although no official record of the incident appears to have survived, the *Boston News-Letter* carried the story on March 3, with the chilling "caveat for all Negroes medling for the future with any white Women, least they fare with the like Treatment."

Neither Mehetabel nor Joshua Hempstead recorded anything pertaining to this episode in their diaries; however, about a week before the *Boston News-Letter* item, Hempstead noted an apparently unrelated, yet relevant, tragedy. On February 24, an unnamed "Negro Man" belonging to Jonathan Prentis (Mehetabel's son Thomas's future father-in-law) had "Murdered himself with a Pistol Shot under ye Chin in to his head." Although Hempstead did not speculate on what prompted the man to commit suicide, the possibilities are numerous. Both accounts underscore the often desperate circumstances of local blacks.

23. Hempstead, *Diary*, November 23–26, 1717.

24. MCC diary, 5; Hempstead, *Diary*, December 14, 1717.

25. Hempstead, *Diary*, December 24, November 11, 1717; conversation with Alice Sheriff, then director of the New London County Historical Society, May 25, 2002.

26. Hempstead, *Diary*, August 5, 1718; John and Mehetabel Coit to John Coit, New London Land Records, vol. 8, 74.

27. Hempstead, *Diary,* August 2, 1718; Joseph Coit, quoted in Gilman, *Daniel Lathrop Coit,* 4; Hempstead, *Diary,* April 18, 1719. The location of Joseph Coit's memoir is unknown.

28. Joseph Coit, quoted in Gilman, *Daniel Lathrop Coit,* 4–5.

29. Hempstead, *Diary,* March 16, 1718, May 17, 1719; David E. Stannard, *The Puritan Way of Death: A Study in Religion, Culture, and Social Change* (New York: Oxford University Press, 1979), 50.

30. MCC diary, 13.

31. Ibid; Laurel Thatcher Ulrich, *Good Wives: Image and Reality in the Lives of Women in Northern New England, 1650–1750* (New York: Vintage, 1991), 159.

32. MCC diary, 47.

33. Hempstead, *Diary,* April 23, 1721; Caulkins, *History of New London,* 1:220.

34. Thomas Manwaring had married Esther Christophers, a cousin of Martha's sister-in-law, Grace Christophers Coit, on February 14. Clement Minor/Miner and Abigail Turner were married on January 9. (Abigail Turner was likely the granddaughter of Sarah Douglas Keeny, and thus a cousin of both Mehetabel's and Martha's.) Although Samuel Richards may have been courting Molly Hallam, they each married someone else. No information is available in the New London vital records or Joshua Hempstead's diary regarding the death of Hannah Preston's child.

35. Martha Coit to Mehetabel Chandler Coit, February 23, 1722, GFP.

36. MCC diary, 13, 10; Duffy, *Epidemics in Colonial America,* 215; MCC diary, 35.

37. Martha Coit to Mehetabel Chandler Coit, August 13, 1723, GFP.

38. During the Salem witchcraft crisis, Abigail Wilkins Ellery's family members had claimed that a man named John Willard had been responsible for the deaths of Abigail's brother's wife and a teenage cousin; Willard was later executed.

39. *Boston Evening-Post,* December 20, 1742.

40. L. Douglas Good, "Colonials at Play: Leisure in Newport, 1723," *Rhode Island History* 33 (1974): 9; Daniels, *Puritans at Play,* 151.

41. Richard LeBaron Bowen, "Early Rehoboth Families and Events," *New England Historical and Genealogical Register* 96 (October 1942): 356–57.

42. Charles J. F. Binney, *The History and Genealogy of the Prentice or Prentiss Family* (Boston, 1882), 275–76; Caulkins, *History of New London,* 1:326; John and Mehetabel Coit to Thomas Coit, New London Land Records, vol. 8, 248.

43. MCC diary, 16. The "fire place" Mehetabel refers to in her entry was a landing place on East Hampton's coast. Joshua Hempstead mentions it as well: "wee got well over to the fire place by Dark & went to Supper att Jonat Kings & up a foot to Easthampton" (November 16, 1738).

44. Hempstead, *Diary,* March 5, 1724; MCC diary, 16.

45. While Martha was away, Thomas's wife Mary—whom Mehetabel refers to as "Molly"—seems to have provided her with some companionship. The "late indisposition" Molly was recovering from may have been an illness or possibly a miscarriage (at the time, she and Thomas had been married seven months).

46. Mehetabel Chandler Coit to Elizabeth Coit Gardiner and Martha Coit, June 24, 1724, GFP.

47. Cornelia Hughes Dayton, *Women before the Bar: Gender, Law, and Society in Connecticut, 1639–1789* (Chapel Hill: University of North Carolina Press, 1995), 189.

48. Mary Beth Norton, *Founding Mothers and Fathers: Gendered Power and the Forming of American Society* (New York: Vintage, 1996), 63, 67, 69.

49. Daniel Scott Smith and Michael S. Hindus, "Premarital Pregnancy in America, 1640–1971: An Overview and Interpretation," *Journal of Interdisciplinary History* 5, no. 21 (Spring 1975): 538.

50. Hempstead, *Diary,* September 10, 1721, April 3, 1725, July 11, 1725, February 26, 1727.

51. MCC diary, 14; Hempstead, *Diary,* April 16, 1724.

52. *Boston Gazette,* September 21–28, 1724.

53. Caulkins, *History of New London,* 2:430–31.

54. Hempstead, *Diary,* March 5, 1725, January 16, 1725.

55. Liz Dart may have been the daughter of Richard and Elizabeth Strickland Dart, then in her teens or early twenties. If so, she would recover from her "Raving Distract[ion]" and go on to marry Jonathan Whipple in 1727.

56. Molly Butler was probably Mary Harris Butler (b. 1690), who died on March 4 (Hempstead, *Diary,* March 5, 1725). She had just given birth in January and had lost a child earlier in February. Caulkins writes that before marrying Walter Butler in 1712, Mary Harris "was regarded as the richest heiress in the settlement" (*History of New London,* 1:271). She and Walter had six children together prior to her death; he remarried in 1727.

57. Martha Coit to Elizabeth Coit Gardiner, February 19, 1725, GFP.

58. Ibid., March 8, 1725.

59. MCC diary, 14. Thomas was laid to rest in the family plot in the New London burying ground, where his gravestone can still be seen today.

60. Edward D. Harris, "Ancient Burial-Grounds of Long Island, New York," *New England Historical and Genealogical Register* 54 (July 1900): 302.

61. MCC diary, 14.

7. Letters from Martha, 1726–1730

1. Mehetabel was a contemporary of Elizabeth and Hannah Bradstreet's mother, Hannah Dummer Bradstreet, who was born the year after she was. (This family of Bradstreets does not seem to have been directly related to the poet Anne and Governor Simon Bradstreet.)

2. "Liz" is likely Martha's sister Elizabeth's daughter.

3. Martha Coit to Mehetabel Chandler Coit, May 15, 1726, GFP.

4. Mehetabel's brother John.

5. Martha Coit to Mehetabel Chandler Coit, May 28, 1726, GFP.

6. Martha may have been referring to the Brooks and Royall families of Medford. Her comment about "kings & queens" seems to have been a pun on the Royalls.

7. The only place of worship in Boston with an organ at the time was King's Chapel, an Anglican church. Thomas Brattle, who had imported the organ from England in 1708, had deeded it to the Puritan Brattle Street Church after his death in 1713, but the congregation felt that the instrument—historically associated in the Puritan mind with the Roman Catholic Mass—was out of place in a Puritan meetinghouse and so donated it to King's Chapel. Although no Puritan church kept an organ until 1770, by the 1720s more ministers and laypeople alike had begun to appreciate the function of music in a service. Martha may have gone to King's Chapel just to hear the organ. Bruce Daniels, *Puritans at Play: Leisure and Recreation in Colonial New England* (New York: St. Martin's Griffin, 1996), 59.

8. Martha is here referring to Eunice Waite and her daughters Grace Waite Wallis (b. 1681), Lydia Waite Brown (b. 1684), and Elizabeth Waite Starling/Sterling (b. 1688), along with Grace Wallis's daughter Eunice, who was about Martha's age. (Unmarried women of social standing of the time were sometimes referred to as "Mrs.," or "Mistress.") Eunice, whom Martha mentioned in her letter of May 15, appears to have been visiting her aunt Elizabeth, who was married to Captain James Starling/Sterling of Groton, Connecticut.

9. I have not found evidence of Martha's having any relation with the first name of Chandler, but her kinsman Zachariah Chandler (the son of Mehetabel's uncle William) was a resident of Roxbury.

10. Likely a member of the Sweetland/Swetland family who lived in the New London area.

11. Martha's brother John.

12. Martha Coit to Mehetabel Chandler Coit, June 5, 1726, GFP.

13. Elizabeth Burnall Ruby; Martha's next letter discusses the Burnall family at length.

14. Jonathan Ellery, who was married to Jane Bonner, was the brother of Benjamin Ellery of Newport. He was also the son of John Coit's aunt, Mary Coit Ellery. Mary Whittington Clarke Saltonstall was the widow of Connecticut's former governor.

15. Martha's sister Elizabeth's daughter.

16. The sister of Martha's sister-in-law Grace. Lucretia was to be married to John Braddick of New London on June 19.

17. "Stuff" refers to a durable worsted wool material; calico is a printed Indian cotton. The reason twice as much stuff would be needed is that calicos came in wider lengths. Martha's reference may indicate that younger women were starting to wear "round gowns" that closed in the middle rather than opening to show a decorative petticoat beneath.

18. Martha Coit to Mehetabel Chandler Coit, June 6, 1726, GFP.

19. The Slaughters' eleven-year-old daughter Mary.

20. Samuel and Ann Moore Burnall/Burnell, who were married in 1674, were members of the Second Church of Boston (Cotton Mather's church), whose records indicate that Mehetabel may have joined in 1693. It is possible that this is how Mehetabel first became involved with the Burnalls, who were the parents of "Coz Sarah" and "Coz Rubey." "Coz Noris," Mary Burnall Norris, was the granddaughter of Samuel Burnall's brother John. The Burnalls do not seem to have been related to either the Chandlers or the Coits; however, because of the high value New Englanders placed on kinship ties, they commonly addressed as cousins, brothers, and sisters those to whom they may have been only distantly related by marriage. Edmund Morgan, *The Puritan Family: Religion and Domestic Relations in Seventeenth-Century New England* (New York: Harper & Row, 1966), 150–51.

21. Ann and Samuel Burnall's son Samuel, and his wife Elizabeth (Smith), had a daughter Elizabeth, who married Henry Greenleaf of Newbury on June 26. Samuel and Elizabeth Burnall had earlier lost a child, when in 1724 their sixteen-year-old daughter Rebecca had died after a brief illness. The piety and courage Rebecca displayed in her final days were apparently so exemplary that Cotton Mather himself was moved to publish a sermon on the "uncommon triumphs" she exhibited in meeting her end.

22. Sackposset, a combination of ale, white wine, cream, eggs, sugar, and spices such as cinnamon, mace, and nutmeg, was commonly served at weddings. John Hull Brown, *Early American Beverages* (Rutland, Vt.: C. E. Tuttle, 1966), 14.

23. According to the *Boston News-Letter,* John Slaughter sailed for Madeira on June 29; Martha, evidently, looked forward to his departure.

24. Katherine Saltonstall (b. 1704), the daughter of the late governor.

25. As an example of the extraordinary lengths to which families would go to maintain social networks, Martha here is referring to Mary Mears Bulkeley, the granddaughter of a friend of Mehetabel's grandmother Anne Douglas. (When Anne appeared before the court regarding an inheritance she was due back in England, Elizabeth Mears [b. 1605] accompanied her to testify on her behalf.) "Mrs. Mears" was probably Mary Mears Bulkeley's mother.

26. Lydia Pygan Adams, the wife of New London's minister.

27. The meaning of this reference is uncertain, although it seems to imply that Martha may have begun keeping her own diary.

28. Martha here is probably referring to both her experience hearing the organ at King's Chapel and her attendance at the First Church of Boston, where Reverend Thomas Foxcroft served as minister from 1717 to 1769. The First Church was located on what is now Washington Street, near Boston's Town House. The Browns were Lydia Waite Brown and her husband William, a merchant.

29. In 1725 Bethiah Hicks had married Benjamin Demming, who actually may have been

a *pannier* maker—someone who fashioned the side hoops some women had begun wearing under their dresses. (To Martha, this may have seemed an occupation worth commenting on.) Bethiah gave birth to a daughter later that year.

30. The identity of Mrs. Harris is unclear, although she may have been from New London. Mrs. Proctor was Lydia Richards of New London, who had married John Proctor of Boston in 1725.

31. Like the statement about the trunk, the meaning of this reference is unclear.

32. Probably Eunice Wallis, referred to in Martha's earlier letters. Eunice's uncle, Captain James Starling/Sterling, had recently commissioned a 700-ton vessel from shipbuilder John Jeffrey of Groton, Connecticut. The vessel was first launched in October of the previous year and in August would set out for Lisbon.

33. Martha Coit to Mehetabel Chandler Coit, June 1726, GFP.

34. Mather's Old Testament text dealt with the story of two Israelites who were sent by the prophet Joshua to explore enemy territory. After being rescued from pursuers by a prostitute named Rahab, they promised her that she and her family would not be harmed by the Israelites if she bound in her window the scarlet line she had used to save them.

35. The Slaughter house was some distance away from the Second Church, located in Boston's North End.

36. Samuel and Ann Burnall's son Jonathan, a shipwright.

37. This may have been the home of Martha's unknown suitor.

38. Martha Coit to Mehetabel Chandler Coit, June 28, 1726, GFP.

39. Mehetabel was probably referring to the home of John Bolles Jr., a Rogerene who lived near the main road to Norwich, and to an inn or residence owned by the Lothrop/Lathrop family of Norwich, a town located approximately fifteen miles north of New London. Susannah Morris (b. 1698) was the daughter of Edward and Elizabeth Morris of Woodstock.

40. Mehetabel may have stopped to dine at the home of the Cady family of Canterbury, located to the north of Norwich. Her companion on horseback, Samuel Morris, was Susannah's cousin, a trader and landholder in Windham County. The roughly forty-mile trip from Norwich to Woodstock would have been particularly uncomfortable for Mehetabel if she were riding sidesaddle.

41. Joseph Chandler and his wife Susannah, who was then in the early stages of her tenth pregnancy, lived in Pomfret, where Joseph was active in town affairs. Betty, Mehetabel's companion on the approximately four-mile walk to Pomfret, was John Chandler's twenty-four-year-old daughter.

42. A combination training and election day would have been a festive occasion, and John Chandler's again being chosen representative to the General Assembly in Boston would have been cause for the family to celebrate. "Coz" John Chandler was actually Mehetabel's nephew, her brother John's son. John Chandler III, like his father and grandfather before him, was involved in local government and was well on his way to becoming a large landowner, having just purchased two hundred acres in Woodstock's final land division in 1724. "Coz billy," another of Mehetabel's brother John's sons, was married to the former Jemima Bradbury, a descendant of the Massachusetts Winthrop and Dudley families who was known as a cultured woman with a strong interest in science (Ellen Larned, *Historic Gleanings in Windham County* [Providence: Preston and Rounds, 1899], 62). William and Jemima had a son named Winthrop who became a noted folk artist.

43. "Sister" was Mehetabel's brother John's wife Esther; "coz" Hannah was likely their fifteen-year-old daughter Hannah. The Abbots were Mehetabel's cousins, grandchildren of her father's sister Hannah Chandler Abbot of Andover. James Corbin and Jabez Corbin were brothers and prominent traders; Reverend Josiah Dwight was Woodstock's minister; Edward Morris was a church deacon and the father of Susannah; and Eliphalet Carpenter was a local innkeeper. The individual called in to set Esther Chandler's arm may have been Jacob Parker,

a neighbor of Esther and John's in South Woodstock. Clarence Bowen, *The History of Woodstock, Connecticut* (1926; reprint, Salem, Mass.: Higginson Book Co., n.d.), 548.

44. Probably an edition of *The Turkish History from the Original of that Nation, to the . . . Growth of the Ottoman Empire,* begun by English writer Richard Knolles (1550?–1610) and contributed to and reprinted by various authors over the years.

45. Syllabub is a mixture of wine and milk or cream, flavored with sugar and sometimes lemon. It was often served on special occasions.

46. Dyer bread, apparently a type of sponge cake, also seems to have been known as "diet" bread. A recipe for the latter included in the sixth edition of *The Lady's Companion,* published in London in 1753, calls for a pound of loaf sugar, a pound of flour, seven eggs, and two spoonfuls of orange water (212–13).

47. John Chandler was assigned the first pew in the meetinghouse owing to his status, so Mehetabel would have had a front-row seat for Reverend Dwight's sermon, apparently taken from Ps 144:15: "Happy is that people, that is in such a case: yea, happy is that people, whose God is the Lord." Mehetabel's parenthetical remark about not being happy were she in Reverend Dwight's "peoples Case" is an allusion to the congregation's dissatisfaction with their minister. Unlike Dwight, the Woodstock congregation did not support the Saybrook Platform, which sought to extend ministerial authority, nor did they approve of the trend toward "singing by regular tunes." Although Puritan services had featured the singing of psalms from the beginning, emphasis had traditionally been placed on the words rather than the tune (the results, as Bruce Daniels has written, were, by most accounts, dreadful). By the late 1600s some clerics had begun pushing for musical reform, and between 1721 and 1730 more than thirty sermons were published on the benefits of singing by note. Many laypeople—particularly in more conservative, rural areas—did not support these reforms, however: some resented being told how to express themselves in worship, and others perceived the attempt to enforce "regular singing" as an attempt by the clergy to seize more control over services. When Dwight published *An Essay to Silence the Outcry That Has Been Made in Some Places against Regular Singing,* in which he berated congregations' generally slipshod approach toward music in worship, he offended many in Woodstock. A few months after Mehetabel's visit, the congregation voted overwhelmingly to dismiss him. Daniels, *Puritans at Play,* 54–55; Laura Henigman, *Coming into Communion: Pastoral Dialogues in Colonial New England* (Albany: State University of New York Press, 1999), 101; Ellen D. Larned, *History of Windham County, Connecticut, 1600–1760,* ed. Leigh Grossman, 2 vols. (Pomfret, Conn.: Swordsmith Productions, 2000), 1:48–49.

48. Sarah Chandler Wright was Mehetabel's cousin, daughter of first cousins Hannah Abbot—a daughter of Mehetabel's aunt Hannah Chandler Abbot—and Captain John Chandler—a son of Mehetabel's uncle Thomas Chandler. (Hannah and John Chandler's Andover garrison house was alleged to be a meeting place for witches during the 1692 witchcraft crisis.) In 1737, Sarah Chandler Wright, her young son Abiel, and a black servant named John Page were killed in a fire at the home Sarah and her husband Joseph had been renting from Mehetabel's nephew John Chandler III.

49. Mehetabel and her brother Joseph and sister-in-law Abigail Coit (who was married to John Coit's brother Solomon) seem to have dined at the Plainfield home of John Coit's brother, the Reverend Joseph Coit, and his wife Experience.

50. Samuel Chandler was the son of Mehetabel's brother John. Mehetabel's route back to New London apparently followed the course of the Quinebaug River to the Shetucket River, which flows into Norwich. Paddling a canoe over the rough waters of Shetucket Falls would not have been an easy task, and it may have been the most arduous part of what seems to have been a trying journey for Mehetabel.

51. Sarah Shackmaple was the daughter of John Shackmaple, Connecticut's first royal customs collector. On July 10 Sarah became published to John Gidley of Newport, the son of a

former judge of Great Britain's Vice Admiralty Court. "Mrs. Eunice" was likely Eunice Wallis, who would have been visiting her aunt and uncle, Elizabeth and James Starling/Sterling. Captain Starling/Sterling and John Shackmaple were among the parishioners of New London's first Anglican church.

52. Mehetabel evidently still had connections in Roxbury; it is not known whom she would have known in Dorchester or Charlestown.

53. The "cousin" Mehetabel was referring to was likely one of her nephews. Mary Truman of New London married Peter Harris on July 3.

54. Mehetabel Chandler Coit to Martha Coit, July 4, 1726, GFP.

55. MCC diary, 18.

56. Steven Kagle, *American Diary Literature, 1620–1799* (Boston: Twayne, 1979), 99; Sarah Kemble Knight, "The Journal of Madam Knight," in *Colonial American Travel Narratives,* ed. Wendy Martin (New York: Penguin Books, 1994), 55.

57. Mary Beth Norton, *Separated by Their Sex: Women in Public and Private in the Colonial Atlantic World* (Ithaca: Cornell University Press, 2011), 105; Laurel Thatcher Ulrich, *Good Wives: Image and Reality in the Lives of Women in Northern New England, 1650–1750* (New York: Vintage, 1991), 140.

58. MCC diary, 10, 47.

59. Ibid., 2.

60. Hempstead, *Diary,* September 7, 1726, October 5, 1726; Mary Maples Dunn, "Saints and Sisters: Congregational and Quaker Women in the Early Colonial Period," *American Quarterly* 30, no. 5 (1978): 594.

61. Benjamin Trumbull, *A Complete History of Connecticut, Civil and Ecclesiastical,* 2 vols. (New London: H. D. Utley, 1898), 2:540; Hempstead, *Diary,* July 8, 1736.

62. Six months after the death of Mehetabel's daughter Elizabeth, the Ellerys also lost a young married daughter. Twenty-eight-year-old Abigail Ellery Wanton died in May 1726, leaving behind several young children. The distraught George Wanton had the following lament inscribed on his wife's tomb:

If tears alas could speak a husband's wo,
My verse would straight in plentiful numbers flow;
Or if so great a loss deplored in vain
Could solace so my throbbing heart from pain
Then could I O sad consolation chuse
To soothe my careless grief a private muse;
But since thy well known piety demands
A public monument at thy George's hands,
O Abigail, I dedicate this tomb to thee,
Thou dearest half of poor forsaken me.

63. Mr. Parnell's identity is unknown, but he does not seem to have been a resident of New London.

64. Martha's letters illustrate that physical ailments were a constant source of concern in early America. While on her trip to Boston the previous year, Martha had been "Disorderd by the teeth ach"; on this visit she was evidently recovering from some type of eye problem. Concurrently, Mehetabel was having trouble with her hand, and Mrs. Ellery was experiencing an issue with her ears. The lime water Martha refers to was probably an alkaline water solution of calcium hydroxide used as an antacid and may have been of Mrs. Ellery's concoction (see Martha's letter of August 13, 1723, in Chapter 6).

65. Perhaps Benjamin Starr (b. 1702) of New London.

66. The "apperishon" Martha refers to is likely the individual she intended to avoid on her trip to Boston the previous year. The meaning of Martha's comment about local people's "very wrong notions about things" is unclear.

67. Martha Coit to Mehetabel Chandler Coit, July 8, 1727, GFP.

68. Charles Hoadley, ed., *The Public Records of the Colony of Connecticut, 1636–1776*, vol. 6 (Hartford: Case, Lockwood, and Brainard, 1872), 205; Hempstead, *Diary,* September 29, 1720, November 15, 1722.

69. Eliphalet Adams to Joseph Talcott, May 3, 1728, *Collections of the Connecticut Historical Society,* vol. 4 (Hartford: Case, Lockwood, and Brainard, 1892), 107–9. As part of the colony's efforts to christianize the Indians, Connecticut passed a law in 1727 requiring all masters and mistresses of Indian children servants to instruct them to read and to teach them the catechism. That year a school was built for the Mohegans; Captain John Mason, whose family had acted as agents for the Mohegans for generations, took on the role of schoolmaster. In the spring of 1728, Mason arranged for seven of his pupils to demonstrate their progress before Eliphalet Adams, who reported that the children were able to read from their psalters and their primers, and that they seemed "to love their books and to be desirous of learning" (ibid.).

70. MCC diary, 47; *Barbour Collection of Connecticut Town Vital Records, New London, 1646–1854,* comp. Nancy E. Schott (Baltimore: Genealogical Publishing, 2000), 42. It was not a particularly favorable time for Mehetabel's children to be in Norwich, as their visit seems to have coincided with some sort of epidemic. An October 18 article in the *Boston News-Letter* reported that in the summer "hundreds" had lain sick at once and that forty people had died by fall. Since Mehetabel noted nothing to the contrary, it appears her children managed to avoid infection. Martha and Joseph's return to New London ahead of John was probably unrelated to the epidemic, since Mehetabel likely would have indicated if John had fallen ill, as she had done in an earlier entry about her son Thomas.

71. Walter W. Woodward, *Prospero's America: John Winthrop, Jr., Alchemy, and the Creation of New England Culture, 1606–1676* (Chapel Hill: University of North Carolina Press, published for the Omohundro Institute of Early American Culture, 2010), 204–5; Patricia A. Watson: "'The Hidden Ones': Women and Healing in Colonial New England," in *Medicine and Healing: The Dublin Seminar for New England Folklife Annual Proceedings, 1990,* ed. Peter Benes (Boston: Boston University, 1991), 27–28; *Colonial Collegians: Biographies of Those Who Attended American Colleges before the War for Independence,* CD-ROM (Boston: Massachusetts Historical Society, New England Historic Genealogical Society, 2005).

72. Hempstead, *Diary,* October 18, 1727, October 21, 1727.

73. Anne Lombard, *Making Manhood: Growing Up Male in Colonial New England* (Cambridge: Harvard University Press, 2003), 47.

74. Lisa Wilson, *Ye Heart of a Man: The Domestic Life of Men in Colonial New England* (New Haven: Yale University Press, 1999), 15; Hempstead, *Diary,* April 5, 1728. Not long after John Coit's visit to New Haven, New London experienced a violent earthquake that was felt across New England. Joshua Hempstead writes that on Sunday, October 29, "about 10 Clock at night an Earthquake Shook the houses[;] Continued about 1 minute & half. ye Earthquake was Terrible in Boston Colony as here. An Irruption at Newbury [a town north of Boston] but a Rumbling noise & trembling of the earth & all things." The earthquake has since been estimated as having had a Richter magnitude of 5.5; strong aftershocks were felt for months afterward (and have continued to be felt north of Boston as recently as October 2007). Although buildings and property were damaged, miraculously no one was killed (www.thebostonchannel.com/asseenon5/14309733/detail.html; *Boston Weekly News-Letter,* November 3, 1727, 2).

75. MCC diary, 2.

76. Mehetabel was not actually suffering from a plague, but a letter Martha sent her that summer does indicate that she was experiencing some type of physical discomfort.

77. This may be a reference to Martha's persistent suitor, although there does not appear to have been anyone by the name of "Soleits" living in New London at the time.

78. Martha is obviously poking fun at herself in this line, but it is unclear why she calls herself a "mear [mere] witch."

79. Martha here is likely alluding to her needlework.

80. The identity of "Dolley" has not been determined; perhaps Martha was referring to Charles Treat's twenty-four-year-old sister Dorothy. Noag was a part of Glastonbury.

81. Martha sends her love to her brother John (Joseph was probably away at sea); the identity of "D——t" is unknown.

82. Martha Coit to Mehetabel Chandler Coit, April 8, 1728, GFP.

83. Martha is likely referring to the Ellerys' son William and his wife Elizabeth Almy Ellery, who settled in Newport after their marriage in 1723. William was a successful merchant who eventually served as Rhode Island's lieutenant governor. He also actively participated in the transatlantic slave trade. Years later, William and Elizabeth's son William became a member of the Continental Congress and a signer of the Declaration of Independence.

84. The meaning of this reference is unclear.

85. Martha Coit to Mehetabel Chandler Coit, June 14, 1728, GFP.

86. Martha's brother Joseph was evidently in Newport for a time between voyages. The "letter" Martha refers to may have been a letter of marque, an official document authorizing Joseph Coit to become a privateer. The pistoles she mentions were European gold coins, possibly originating from Spain. The identity of Mr. Cotton has not been determined.

87. Martha seems to have taken Lydia Adams into her confidence regarding her unwanted suitor, but her promise to be adamant in refusing him—of "Saying . . . NO, thô tis to the minester himSelf"—is boldly worded.

88. Katherine Winthrop (b. March 1711) was the daughter of John Winthrop (who in 1726 had sailed to England to pursue his claim to his father's estate) and Ann Dudley. Katherine may have been visiting Newport with her older sister Mary, who married Joseph Wanton—a brother of George Wanton, the husband of the Ellerys' daughter Abigail—the following summer. In 1732 Katherine married Samuel Browne, an extremely wealthy merchant of Salem, Massachusetts, and soon afterward the couple had their portraits painted by the well-known artist John Smibert.

89. Martha seems to have been designing the robe she describes for the Ellerys' thirteen-year-old daughter Mary.

90. The identity of Mrs. Burnham is unknown.

91. "Lutestring" was a type of silk.

92. The chaise owned by William Ellery would have been a small two- or three-person carriage and was a symbol of his affluence. Mrs. Almy was William's sister Anstis, who was married to John Almy.

93. Martha seems to be implying that her brother John and his wife Grace were experiencing marital problems in which gossip was a factor. Unfortunately, neither she nor Mehetabel left any details regarding this situation.

94. Martha Coit to Mehetabel Chandler Coit, July 5, 1728, GFP.

95. Martha Coit to Mehetabel Chandler Coit, August 13, 1723, and ibid.; Susan P. Schoelwer, *Connecticut Needlework: Women, Art, and Family, 1740–1840* (Hartford: Connecticut Historical Society, distributed by Wesleyan University Press, 2010), 3; Judith Reiter Weissman and Wendy Lavitt, *Labors of Love: America's Textiles and Needlework, 1650–1930* (New York: Wings Books, 1994), 113.

96. Ellen Hartigan-O'Connor, "Collaborative Consumption and the Politics of Choice in Early American Port Cities," in *Gender, Taste, and Material Culture in Britain and North America, 1700–1830,* eds. John Styles and Amanda Vickery (New Haven: Yale Center for British Art, distributed by Yale University Press, 2006).

97. Martha Coit to Mehetabel Chandler Coit, May 28, 1726, June 6, 1726, April 8, 1728; Kate Haulman, *The Politics of Fashion in Eighteenth-Century America* (Chapel Hill: University of North Carolina Press, 2011), 5–6.

98. Elisabeth Slaughter to Mehetabel Chandler Coit, August 27, 1728, GFP.

99. Kenneth Silverman, *The Life and Times of Cotton Mather* (New York: Welcome Rain, 2002), 410.

100. A flair for literary creation evidently ran in Daniel's family; his older brother John wrote poetry. One of his poems, "A Monumental Gratitude," about the experience of a group of Yale students (including Daniel) who were safely delivered from a shipwreck during a storm off the coast of New London, was published by the New London press in 1727.

101. Daniel Hubbard to John and Mehetabel Coit, December 1730, printed in the *New England Historical and Genealogical Register* 48 (October 1894): 465. The location of the original manuscript is unknown.

8. Transitions, 1731–1744

1. Daniel Hubbard to Martha Coit, January 15, 1731, in Maria Perit Gilman, Emily Serena Gilman, and Louisa Gilman Lane, *Martha, Daughter of Mehetabel Chandler Coit, 1706–1784* (Norwich, Conn.: Bulletin Print, 1895), 25–27. According to the authors, at the time of their book's publication in 1895, the original letter was "in the possession of Mrs. Anson G. P. Dodge of Alexandria, Va."; its current location is unknown.

2. Daniel Hubbard to Martha Coit, April 27, 1731, in Edward Warren Day, *One Thousand Years of Hubbard History, 866 to 1895* (New York: H. P. Hubbard, 1895), 413–14. No information is given regarding the source of this letter.

3. MCC diary, 24.

4. MCC diary, 23.

5. Matthew Prior, "Solomon on the Vanity of the World, a Poem in Three Books," bk. 1, lines 100–105. (Variations from Prior's poem are bracketed.) As mentioned in chapter 4, Mehetabel also copied into her diary two other sets of verses from "Solomon." Both were taken from book 3, and like several other extracts in Mehetabel's diary, focus on the brevity of life.

6. MCC diary, 30.

7. Ellen Rothman, *Hands and Hearts: A History of Courtship in America* (New York: Basic Books, 1980), 175–76, discussed in Laurel Thatcher Ulrich, *A Midwife's Tale: The Life of Martha Ballard, Based on Her Diary, 1785–1812* (New York: Vintage Books, 1991), 142.

8. Arthur Reed Kimball, "The Changing Character of Commencement," *New England Magazine,* new ser., vol. 12 (Boston: Warren Kellogg, 1895): 189.

9. Reverend Eliphalet Adams, a Yale trustee, was evidently present at the commencement.

10. "Aunt" Ruggles, the former Mary Hubbard (1673–1742), was Daniel's father's sister. Originally from Boston, Mary Hubbard Ruggles lived in Guilford, Connecticut, on the coastal road between New Haven and New London.

11. "Sister" Woodbridge was likely the oldest of Daniel's half sisters, Elizabeth, who was born circa 1715.

12. Eunice Talcott was the twenty-two-year-old daughter of Connecticut's governor, Joseph Talcott.

13. John Hubbard and his wife Elizabeth had several young children, including a newborn (the eventual wife of Yale president and Revolutionary War patriot Ezra Stiles), so it is not surprising that their home was noisy and chaotic.

14. It is not clear why Martha addressed Lydia Adams as "Aunt" Adams, who she meant by "L——n," or why she omitted letters from their names.

15. Martha Coit Hubbard to Mehetabel Chandler Coit, September 10, 1731, GFP. Martha evidently began to write "Coit" after signing her first name; interestingly, she did not cross out the "C" that precedes "Hubbard."

16. Samuel Sewall, *The Diary of Samuel Sewall,* ed. M. Halsey Thomas, 2 vols. (New York: Farrar, Straus and Giroux, 1973), September 16, 1718.

17. Martha's brother Joseph apparently accompanied her to Woodstock, where she stayed at

the home of her uncle John Chandler. Still living with John and his wife at the time was their youngest daughter, Mehitable, who was a year younger than Martha.

18. Martha went from her uncle's house to the home of his son John and his wife Hannah, who was the daughter of Lord John Gardiner by his first wife. John and Hannah and their family soon relocated to Worcester, Massachusetts, where John served as register of probate for the newly formed Worcester County; his father served as chief justice of the court of common pleas and judge of the probate court. (Woodstock, still considered part of Massachusetts, was part of the new county.)

At the time of Martha's writing, John and Hannah had seven young children; Hannah died a few years later at the age of thirty-nine while giving birth to her ninth child. Martha was not alone in judging her "hearty, good, and kind," as the obituaries carried by the Boston newspapers deemed her "a Gentlewoman of a sweet and engaging temper" (*Boston Gazette,* January 6, 1738; the obituary was also carried by the *New England Weekly Journal* and the *Boston Evening-Post*).

19. "Old Mr Morris" was likely Samuel Morris, whom Mehetabel had mentioned visiting in her 1726 letter from Woodstock (at his home she had "Eate[n] Trouts").

20. "Cozn Lydia" seems to have been Lydia Christophers Coit, the wife of Martha's cousin Daniel.

21. "Cozn Thos." was probably the twenty-two-year-old son of Mehetabel's brother John, who may have been traveling to New London on business.

22. Martha Coit Hubbard to Mehetabel Chandler Coit, October 4, 1731, in Gilman, Gilman, and Lane, *Martha,* 28–29. The whereabouts of the original letter are unknown.

23. Hempstead, *Diary,* October 22, 1731.

24. Hempstead, *Diary,* May, 13, 1731, May 30, 1739.

25. Chester McArthur Destler, *Joshua Coit: American Federalist, 1758–1798* (Middletown, Conn.: Wesleyan University Press, 1962), 4; Joseph Coit quoted in Mary E. Perkins, *Old Houses of the Antient Town of Norwich, 1660–1800* (Norwich, Conn.: Bulletin, 1895), 160; Hempstead, *Diary,* March 15, 1725, April 10, 1733, January 25, 1750; Perkins, *Old Houses,* 128.

26. Hempstead, *Diary,* July 28, 1735.

27. Ibid., October 13, 1734. In August 1738, when Mary became engaged to Captain John Bulkeley, Joshua Hempstead noted in his diary that, "She is Suposed to be a widow. Jonath Gardiner hath been gone to Sea 3 year Last winter & not heard off therefore suposed to be Dead" (August 6, 1738).

28. MCC diary, 17; Hempstead, *Diary,* February 26, 1735.

29. *New England Weekly Journal,* April 7, 1735. One comfort to Mehetabel at this time may have been the presence in New London of Jonathan's sister, Sarah Gardiner Treat, whose husband Charles seems to have purchased a house there in 1736. The Treats moved back to Glastonbury a few years later.

30. MCC diary, 17; Hempstead, *Diary,* August 31, 1735.

31. Eliphalet Adams, *God Sometimes Answers His People by Terrible Things in Righteousness. A Discourse Occasioned by that Awful Thunder-Clap which Struck the Meeting-House in N. London, Aug. 31st, 1735* (New London, 1735; Early American Imprints, ser. 1, no. 3861), 25, 26, 35; *New England Weekly Journal,* September 9, 1735.

32. Adams, *God Sometimes Answers,* i, iv, iii, 39, title page, 28.

33. Ellen D. Larned, *History of Windham County, Connecticut, 1600–1760,* ed. Leigh Grossman, 2 vols. (Pomfret, Conn.: Swordsmith Productions, 2000), 1:180.

34. Mercy Wheeler, *An address to young people, or Warning to them from one among them yet may be called warning from the dead* (Boston, 1733; Early American Imprints, ser. 1, no. 3732), 1, ii, iv, iii, 1, 5; Elizabeth Chandler to Mehetabel Chandler Coit, June 1, 1698, GFP; Mehetabel Chandler Coit to Elizabeth Coit Gardiner and Martha Coit, June 24, 1724, GFP. Readership figures are not available for Wheeler's pamphlet, but her personal story

ultimately received unprecedented attention when she experienced a seemingly miraculous full recovery a decade later. Wheeler's separated ankle bones had previously prevented her from walking, but during a prayer meeting in her home, she "rose up and walked away among the People, with evident Sprightliness and Vigour, . . . crying out, 'Bless the Lord Jesus, who has healed me!'" Benjamin Lord of Norwich, who was among those in attendance at the prayer meeting, wrote an account of Wheeler's providential delivery that went through several printings, its popularity fueled by the religious revivals then sweeping New England. *God Glorified in His Works, of Providence and Grace* (Boston, 1743; Early American Imprints, ser. 1, no. 5228), 36.

35. Benjamin Colman and Ebenezer Turell, *Reliquiae Turelliae, et Lachrymae Paternae: The Father's Tears over His Daughter's Remains* (Boston, 1735; Early American Imprints, ser. 1, no. 3888), 82.

36. Eliphalet Adams, *A Sermon Preached on the Occasion of the Execution of Katherine Garret, an Indian-Servant, Who Was Condemned for the Murder of Her Spurious Child* (New London, 1738; Early American Imprints, ser. 1, no. 4215), 38. As N. E. H. Hull has shown, infanticide, which in the majority of cases was of an illegitimate child, was the most common serious crime committed by women in colonial New England. *Female Felons: Women and Serious Crime in Colonial Massachusetts* (Chicago: University of Illinois Press, 1987), 46, 47.

37. Katherine Garret, "Confession and Dying Warning," in Adams, *Execution of Katherine Garret* 43; Adams, *Execution of Katherine Garret,* 39; Hempstead, *Diary,* January 29, 1738, March 12, 1738.

38. Adams, *Execution of Katherine Garret,* 42; Hempstead, *Diary,* April 30, 1738. According to Joshua Hempstead's diary, Martha and Daniel's new house had been raised just a few days before Elizabeth's baptism (April 24, 1738).

39. F. W. Chapman, *The Coit Family, or the Descendants of John Coit* (Hartford, Conn.: Case, Lockwood, and Brainard, 1874), 31.

40. Hempstead, *Diary,* February 14, 1741; John Duffy, *Epidemics in Colonial America* (Baton Rouge: Louisiana State University Press, 1953), 225.

41. MCC diary, 42, 12.

42. The story of Martha's having kept a shop is apparently confirmed by a few of Joshua Hempstead's diary entries that mention payments he made to Martha for cloth and to pay down the debt on his son John's "acco[un]t" (June 8, 1741, January 5, 1743). Gilman, Gilman, and Lane, *Martha,* 6; Susan P. Schoelwer, *Connecticut Needlework: Women, Art, and Family, 1740–1840* (Hartford: Connecticut Historical Society, distributed by Wesleyan University Press, 2010), 30.

43. George Whitefield, *A Sermon on Regeneration* (Boston, 1739; Early American Imprints, ser. 1, no. 49787), 5; Hempstead, *Diary,* July 5, 1741; Barbara E. Lacey, ed., *The World of Hannah Heaton: The Diary of an Eighteenth-Century Farm Woman* (DeKalb, Ill.: Northern Illinois University Press, 2003), 12–13.

44. Hempstead, *Diary,* June 5, 1741.

45. Peter S. Onuf, "New Lights in New London: A Group Portrait of the Separatists," *William and Mary Quarterly* 37, no. 4 (October 1980): 632; Henry S. Stout and Peter S. Onuf, "James Davenport and the Great Awakening in New London," *Journal of American History* 71, no. 3 (December 1983): 561, 560. The number of New London Congregational church members was lower than in most Connecticut towns, which in general included an average of 24.7 percent of their populations. In northeastern Connecticut (the Woodstock area), an average of 32.9 percent of the population were church members (Onuf, "New Lights," 632n19).

46. Quoted in Stout and Onuf, "James Davenport," 563. Ironically, Adams himself had been at the forefront of a revival movement decades earlier; in fact, Thomas Kidd has called him the "key early evangelical minister in Connecticut." Along with the Reverends Timothy Edwards and Solomon Stoddard (Jonathan Edwards's father and grandfather), Benjamin

Lord, Samuel Whiting, and Jonathan Marsh, Adams helped promote revivals in the Connecticut River valley in the 1710s and 1720s, believing, as Kidd writes, that this would "spark a larger revival fire, which might ultimately consume the globe." *The Great Awakening: The Roots of Evangelical Christianity in Colonial New England* (New Haven: Yale University Press, 2007), 8–9.

47. Caulkins, *History of New London,* 2:452; Stout and Onuf, "James Davenport," 567, 563; Onuf, "New Lights," 633.

48. Stout and Onuf, "James Davenport," 570–71; Reverend Solomon Williams quoted in Kidd, *Great Awakening,* 112; *Boston Evening-Post,* July 5, 1742.

49. Hempstead, *Diary,* November, 17, 1741; *Acts and Laws Passed by the General Court or Assembly of His Majesty's Colony of Connecticut* (May 1742; Early American Imprints, ser. 1, no. 4920), 510.

50. Hempstead, *Diary,* February 26, 1742, April 2, 1742, April 16, 1742, May 28, 1742, July 2, 1742, July 30, 1742.

51. Richard Warch, "The Shepherd's Tent: Education and Enthusiasm in the Great Awakening," *American Quarterly* 30, no. 2 (Summer 1978): 188; Hempstead, *Diary,* February 7, 1743.

52. Stout and Onuf, "James Davenport," 556; Caulkins, History of *New London,* 2:454; *Boston Evening-Post,* April 11, 1743.

53. Ibid., March 14, 1743; *Boston Post-Boy,* March 28, 1743.

54. *Boston Gazette,* April 12, 1743; *Boston Evening-Post,* April 11, 1743; Hempstead, *Diary,* March 31, 1743.

55. James Davenport, *The Reverend Mr. James Davenport's Confession and Retractions* (Boston, 1744; Early American Imprints, ser. 1, no. 5374), 8, 6; Kidd, *Great Awakening,* 154; Caulkins, *History of New London,* 2:457. Joshua Hempstead ultimately bought the Shepherd's Tent property in 1757.

One lasting legacy of the Great Awakening was the introduction of nontraditional ministers; as Barbara Lacey notes, several years later Jemima Wilkinson, a New London Separatist, began preaching on her own to groups as large as three thousand people. "Gender, Piety, and Secularization in Connecticut Religion, 1720–1775" *Journal of Social History* 24, no. 4 (Summer 1991): 810.

56. Martha Coit Hubbard to Mehetabel Chandler Coit, May 9, 1743, GFP.

57. *Boston Evening-Post,* August 22, 1743.

58. Ibid.

59. Hempstead, *Diary,* March 26, October 22, and October 24, 1744.

60. Quoted in Edmund S. Morgan, *The Puritan Family: Religion and Domestic Relations in Seventeenth-Century New England* (New York: Harper & Row, 1966), 50.

9. Endings, 1745–1758

1. Cornelia Hughes Dayton, *Women before the Bar: Gender, Law, and Society in Connecticut, 1639–1789* (Chapel Hill: University of North Carolina Press for Institute of Early American History and Culture, 1995), 44; will of John Coit, November 2, 1741, New London County Probate Records, no. 1330.

2. Jackson Turner Main, "The Distribution of Property in Colonial Connecticut," in *The Human Dimensions of Nation-Making: Essays on Colonial and Revolutionary America,* ed. James Kirby Martin (Madison: State Historical Society of Wisconsin, 1976), 99.

3. Inventory of the estate of John Coit, November 22, 1744, New London County Probate Records, no. 1330; Hempstead, *Diary,* November 16, 1744; Peter Benes, "Sleeping Arrangements in Early Massachusetts: The Newbury Household of Henry Lunt, Hatter," in *Early American Probate Inventories: The Dublin Seminar for New England Folklife Annual Proceedings, 1987,* ed. Peter Benes (Boston: Boston University, 1989), 143.

4. Laurel Thatcher Ulrich, *The Age of Homespun: Objects and Stories in the Creation of an American Myth* (New York: Knopf, 2001), 291.

5. Caulkins, *History of New London,* 2:476.

6. Laurel Thatcher Ulrich, *A Midwife's Tale: The Life of Martha Ballard, Based on Her Diary, 1785–1812* (New York: Vintage, 1991), 254; Benjamin Marshall, *A Modern History of New London County, Connecticut,* 2 vols. (New York: Lewis Historical Publishing, 1922), 1:389.

7. According to family records, Martha's wedding fan was "cherished by some of her descendants" through the late nineteenth century, but I have been unable to discover its current location. Maria Perit Gilman, Emily Serena Gilman, and Louisa Gilman Lane, *Martha, Daughter of Mehetabel Chandler Coit, 1706–1784* (Norwich, Conn.: Bulletin Print, 1895), 32.

8. Ibid., 4.

9. William Hooper, *A Sermon Preached in Trinity Church at the Funeral of Thomas Greene, Esq., August 5, 1763* (Boston: Richard and Samuel Draper and Thomas and John Fleet, 1763), 22.

10. Will of Mehetabel Chandler Coit, October 20, 1752, New London County Probate Records, no. 1340.

11. MCC diary, 19, 21.

12. Ibid., 20.

13. Ibid., 21.

14. Ibid., 2.

15. Ibid., 21; Caulkins, *History of New London,* 2:476.

16. MCC diary, 22.

17. Ibid., 49.

18. Hempstead, *Diary,* September 7, 1749; Eliphalet Adams, *A Short Discourse Delivered at New-London, Sept. 10th, 1749, after the Funeral of my Wife, Mrs. Lydia Adams, (Who was, the Desire of my Eyes and the Delight of my Heart)* (New London, 1751; Early American Imprints, ser. 1, no. 6625).

19. Martha Coit to Mehetabel Chandler Coit, n.d., June 1726, GFP; Hempstead, *Diary,* October 4, 1753.

20. Vivian Bruce Conger, *The Widows' Might: Widowhood and Gender in Early British America* (New York: New York University Press, 2009), 8.

21. Hempstead, *Diary,* February 19, 1758.

22. Mehetabel Chandler Coit to Martha Coit and Elizabeth Coit Gardiner, June 24, 1724, and Elizabeth Douglas Chandler to Mehetabel Chandler Coit, October 7, 1699, both GFP.

23. James Deetz, *In Small Things Forgotten: The Archaeology of Early American Life* (New York: Doubleday, 1977), 71.

24. Inventory of the estate of Mehetabel Chandler Coit, December 22, 1758, New London County Probate Records, no. 1340.

Epilogue

1. Hempstead, *Diary,* March 28, October 3, and November 11, 1745, October 23, 1756.

2. Lydia Coit Hubbard to Joseph and Lydia Coit, February 21, 176[6?], GFP.

3. Joseph Coit to Daniel Lathrop Coit, May 28, 1774, GFP.

4. Maria Perit Gilman, Emily Serena Gilman, and Louisa Gilman Lane, *Martha, Daughter of Mehetabel Chandler Coit, 1706–1784* (Norwich, Conn.: Bulletin Print, 1895), 3; Mary E. Perkins, *Old Houses of the Antient Town of Norwich, 1660–1800* (Norwich, Conn.: Press of the Bulletin Co., 1895), 252; William Hubbard to Joseph and Lydia Coit, May 2, 1765, GFP. According to Martha's descendants who published the collection of her letters, one instrumental figure in keeping her memory alive was an old family servant and former slave named Bristor—also referred to as "Uncle Boo"—who continued to tell stories about Martha for many years (Gilman, Gilman, and Lane, *Martha,* 3).

5. Will of Martha Coit Hubbard Greene, September 3, 1782, Suffolk County Probate Records, no. 18358.

6. The picture is labeled "Coit House, Coit and Washington Streets, New London," where the seventeenth-century Coit homestead was supposed to have stood.

7. Maria Perit Gilman, Emily Serena Gilman, and Louisa Gilman Lane, *Mehetabel Chandler Coit, Her Book 1714* (Norwich, Conn.: Bulletin Print, 1895), 1, 5; Laurel Thatcher Ulrich, *A Midwife's Tale: The Life of Martha Ballard, Based on Her Diary, 1785–1812* (New York: Vintage, 1991), 8–9.

8. Laurel Thatcher Ulrich, *Good Wives: Image and Reality in the Lives of Women in Northern New England, 1650–1750* (New York: Vintage, 1991).

INDEX

MICHELLE MARCHETTI COUGHLIN is an independent scholar and former editor who holds graduate degrees in history and English and American literature. She lives south of Boston with her husband, Mark.